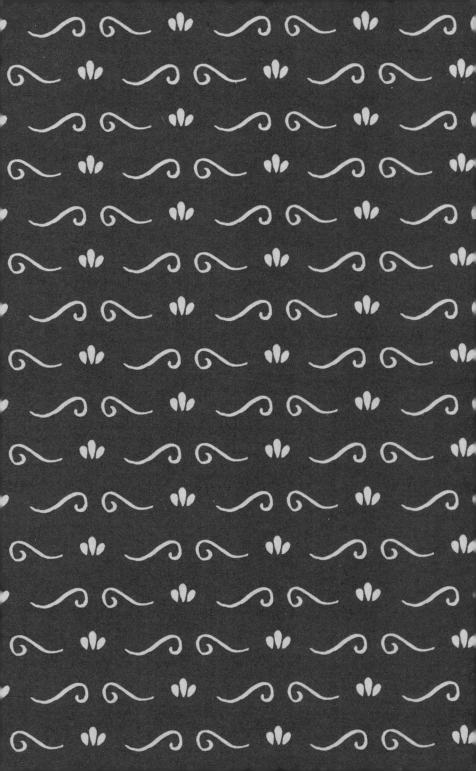

Monster, She Wrote

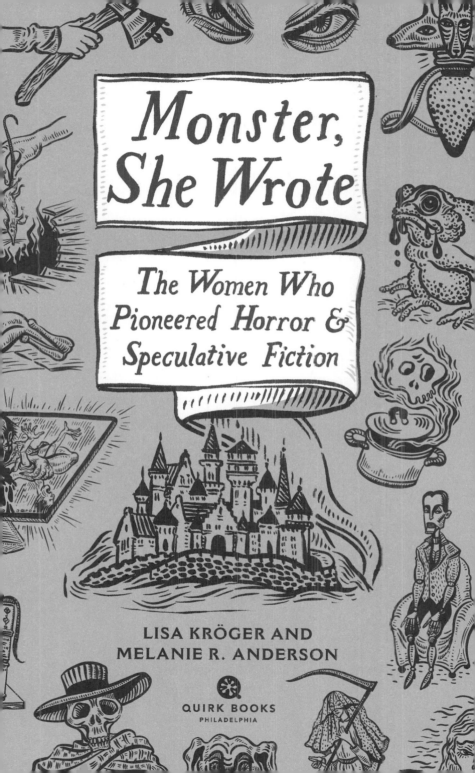

Monster, She Wrote

The Women Who Pioneered Horror & Speculative Fiction

LISA KRÖGER AND
MELANIE R. ANDERSON

QUIRK BOOKS
PHILADELPHIA

Library of Congress Cataloging in Publication Number: 2019930321
ISBN: 978-1-68369-138-9

Printed in China

Typeset in Garamond Premier Pro, Mr. Eaves, Clearface Gothic LH,
Jacob Riley, and Cantoria MT
Designed by Andie Reid
Illustrations by Natalya Balnova
Production management by John J. McGurk

Quirk Books
215 Church Street
Philadelphia, PA 19106
quirkbooks.com

10 9 8 7 6 5 4 3 2

*To all the girls
who still sleep with the lights on,
but read the scary stories anyway*

Contents

Introduction

Why are women great at writing horror fiction? Maybe because horror is a transgressive genre. It pushes readers to uncomfortable places, where we aren't used to treading, and it forces us to confront what we naturally want to avoid.

And women are accused of being transgressive all the time—or, at the very least, they are used to stepping outside of the carefully drawn boundaries that society has set for them. Women are told what to do and who to be. Women are taught to be sweet, to raise children, to stay in their place. Women are pushed to the edges of society, where they are expected to keep their mouths shut and their heads down. The marginalization of women may have been more overt in the past, at times when women couldn't vote or own property or work outside the home, but it still happens today. Women are still instructed to be good girls.

In any era, women become accustomed to entering unfamiliar spaces, including territory that they've been told not to enter. When writing is an off-limits act, writing one's story becomes a form of rebellion and taking back power. Consider, for example, Margaret Cavendish, who in the 1600s brazenly wrote about science and philosophy, two subjects then considered the purview of only male minds. More recently, Jewelle Gomez brought an African American and lesbian perspective to the vampire tale, which had long been the province of European male protagonists. Today, writers like Carmen Maria Machado and Helen Oyeyemi subvert the so-called safe storytelling formats of the fairy tale and the supernatural yarn, adding women's voices to these traditional narrative forms.

For women especially, writing is often a kind of noncompliance, which calls to mind the prisoners in the comic book series *Bitch Planet* by writer Kelly Sue DeConnick and artist Valentine De Landro (Image Comics, 2014–17). The comic is brilliant—it tells a female-driven dystopian story about women sent to a prison planet as punishment for being noncompliant. What a great word to describe the women in this book.

The writers you'll meet in *Monster, She Wrote* are all rule breakers. And here's the funny thing: society doesn't always pay attention to what's happening over there on the edges. So while society was ignoring them, they were taking up their pens. While everyone else has been doing their own thing, women have been doing theirs, crafting tales about scientifically reanimated corpses, ghosts of aborted children, postapocalyptic underground cities.

Horror has been penned by men and women alike, but it's important to acknowledge that women have been contributing to the genre since its inception. As you'll discover in the following pages, the horror genre that readers love today would likely be unrecognizable without the contributions of these women.

These misbehaving women who write horror in all its nasty forms.

PART ONE

The Founding Mothers

orror, strangeness, and fear have always been part of literature. Humans love their monsters; for evidence, look back, oh, four thousand years, give or take, to *The Epic of Gilgamesh*. Or consider that the "Inferno" section of Dante's *Divine Comedy* is by far the most popular among readers, thanks to the descent into Hell. Shakespeare wrote about ghosts and witches, and his *Titus Andronicus* (first performed in 1594) is one of the bloodiest and most violent plays of his career (maybe even the bloodiest play in European history . . . until the Grand Guignol, that is).

Clearly, audiences have always craved horror. But like all fiction, horror and other types of so-called weird fiction have ebbed and flowed in popularity, as well as changed forms, throughout history. So where did it all begin? There's a strong argument that horror as it exists in the twenty-first century evolved from the Gothic novel, a literary style fashionable in England in the late eighteenth and early nineteenth centuries.

Gothic fiction started with Horace Walpole's *The Castle of Otranto*, published in 1765. The novel tells of a royal wedding that goes very, very wrong. Manfred, owner of the titular castle, is obsessed with marrying his son to a beautiful princess, Isabella, in order to continue his family line and secure wealth. The only problem? His son, Conrad, is rather sickly, and not a great prince at all. Before Conrad can marry Isabella, he is crushed to death . . . *by a giant helmet*.

The castle, you see, is cursed by a statue of a knight that has come to life and is causing general chaos. Manfred is so fixated on perpetuating his family name that he decides to marry Isabella himself (not even his pesky wife can get in the way of his plans). But he thinks Isabella is in love with the mysterious Theodore . . . who actually loves Manfred's daughter, Matilda. Confused? So is Manfred, and he kills his own daughter thinking that she is Isabella. Things go downhill from there, with plenty of mistaken identities and lots of knives that are meant for one person but end up in someone else's heart. As nuptial celebrations go, the book makes the Red Wedding in *Game of Thrones* seem not so bad.

Walpole's novel became so popular that it created a genre called the Gothic, named for the architecture found in so many of these books. And in the following decades, the new genre's popularity would shoot through the roof, primarily due to the work of women writers.

Gothic fiction might never have taken off without Ann Radcliffe, the English author who published *The Romance of the Forest* (T. Hookham & Carpenter, 1791), *The Mysteries of Udolpho* (G. G. and J. Robinson, 1794), *The Italian* (Cadell and Davies, 1797), and other novels. Radcliffe's writing popularized the genre, but truth be told, her books seem tame compared to works that came after; they're more like cozy mysteries than eerie horror stories. Her spooky and dark castles played on the imagination without delivering actual ghosts.

An army of women writers followed Radcliffe, using the Gothic formula she'd developed to explore their own bloodier, more violent, and fantastic nightmares. These women, whom you're about to meet in turn inspired generations of authors and filmmakers, including those creating horror stories today. Without Radcliffe and her successors, we wouldn't have the 1977 nightmarish fairy tale film *Suspiria*—or its 2018 remake. Likewise the quiet but brooding domestic horror of Daphne du Maurier or Shirley Jackson. The women who put pen to paper back at the beginning of horror and weird fiction—even before such terms were used—were unafraid to try new things, to take their stories into unexplored territory. And in doing so, they inspired and enabled writers for centuries to come.

SPOTTING THE GOTHIC

Here's a handy checklist of attributes that indicate you're reading a Gothic novel.

- ☐ A virtuous young woman who's prone to quoting poetry and/or singing music while deep in the woods (not unlike Snow White), and equally prone to fainting and/or falling unconscious (also not unlike Snow White).

- ☐ A handsome man with a mysterious background who shares the heroine's love of poetry and/or music and/or the forest.

- ☐ A sinister-looking villain (almost always male, usually foreign, and — *gasp!* — Catholic) who's out for money (especially if the heroine is loaded and an orphan)

- ☐ Some sort of crumbling castle or abbey or convent—really any kind of once-majestic building now in ruins.

- ☐ A supernatural being (a ghost, a talking portrait, a giant statue that kills people by dropping helmets on them) that makes life difficult. Bonus points if the supernatural element is revealed by the end of the book to be not supernatural at all.

Margaret Cavendish

1623–1673

In a time when women had few career options outside the home, and even fewer rights, one lady was writing a breathtakingly prolific body of work that prefigured the genre we now call speculative fiction.

Margaret Cavendish is an outlier, producing her strange fiction a century before Gothic novels came along. That seems appropriate for a woman who so refused definition. She was a poet. She was a philosopher whose intellect was on par with that of Thomas Hobbes—famed English political philosopher—and other thought leaders of the day, and she boldly added her voice to male-only discussions of politics and philosophy. She wrote an autobiography when this literary form was relatively new. More than that, she published plays, essays, and novels. And Cavendish may well have been one of the first literary "celebrities" in English history. Her open pursuit of fame was one of her ways of thumbing her nose at society—she was a Kardashian before there were Kardashians.

She was born in 1623 to the wealthy Lucas family of Essex—but her parents were not part of the titled aristocracy. Tragedy struck early; her father died when she was a young child. Her mother raised Cavendish as other daughters of rich families were raised, which meant no formal education, especially not in the sciences. Instead, she was taught to entertain in polite society, which included learning to read and write (as well as to sing and dance). Some women of her rank were afforded private tutoring, but Cavendish was not. So she read every book she could find, embarking on a self-navigated education in history and philosophy. Her brother John, who was highly educated in these fields, taught his sister what he learned.

In 1643 Cavendish applied to be, and was accepted as, a "maid of honour" to Queen Henrietta Maria, wife of King Charles I. Though her parents had been wealthy, Cavendish inherited no money following the death of her father (and certainly received no dowry for marriage). She knew she'd have to make her own way in the world. When the queen was exiled to France (following the execution of Charles I in the First English Civil War), Cavendish moved to Paris with her. There Cavendish met her husband, William, who would become Duke of Newcastle Upon Tyne. Despite protests from friends (they felt William was on the "wrong side" politically), theirs was a good match. William had been educated by Thomas Hobbes, and he found Cavendish to be his intellectual equal. The couple traveled before settling in England, where they began to restore the Cavendish estates that had been confiscated during the war. And soon Margaret Cavendish became socially infamous, known among the upper-class circles as "Mad Madge" for her wild fashion and her loud, flirtatious behavior.

Calling her the Kardashian of her day is no exaggeration; Cavendish was acutely aware of her notoriety and cultivated her reputation as a celebrity. Once, in London's Hyde Park, she was mobbed by crowds, hoping for a glimpse of the infamous woman. How infamous was she? Cavendish scandalized polite society more than once; on one occasion, she showed up to a theater event wearing a dress that exposed her breasts, including her nipples, which she had thoughtfully painted red. Samuel Pepys, the famous diarist, called her "mad, conceited and ridiculous."

Which is perhaps another way of saying that Cavendish pushed against the societal roles available to women in her day, who were expected to be demure and polite and, most important, silent in social situations. Women certainly were not supposed to speak about what were believed to be "men's subjects" like philosophy or politics. And, should they know how to write, women definitely were not supposed to publish their writings. Not only did Cavendish read the major philosophers of the day, like Hobbes and Descartes, but by 1668 she had published numerous letters and essays on matters of philosophy, all with her name proudly on the front page.

Out of This World

Most relevant to our purposes, Cavendish wrote what could well be considered the first science-fiction novel. Her 1666 book *The Description of the New World, Called the Blazing World* (often shortened to simply *The Blazing World*), was published some 150 years before Mary Shelley's *Frankenstein*. To be clear, scholars debate who holds that title of "first," or if Cavendish's book is even science fiction. Perhaps it's better described as speculative fiction or philosophy. Ultimately, that's not the point. *The Blazing World* is a breathtakingly creative narrative, worthy of study particularly for its treatment of women and its inventive technology. The main character, simply named the Empress, is kidnapped by a lovesick sailor and finds herself on a ship meeting a storm at sea. The crew doesn't survive, but our protagonist is thrust into a magical world—what science-fiction readers would recognize as an alternate universe, entered through a portal.

This "Blazing World" is full of dreamlike inventions. Enormous boats are propelled by air-powered engines and can lock together in an intricate design to make them impermeable to weather. The society the Empress encounters is a feminist utopia where science and philosophy reign supreme. The adventure is part fantasy, part philosophical enquiry, part almost steampunk.

This new world is a vehicle for Cavendish's own philosophies (the author even shows up as a character named the Duchess), which resemble those of Thomas Hobbes. This doesn't mean she wasn't an original; she published several works detailing her personal theories. Like philosophers Hobbes and David Hume, Cavendish was a naturalist, believing that everything in the universe had a purpose and a mind—and every working part collaborated in the machine of the greater universe. She was interested in the intellect of humankind and the motions at work in the universe, much of which helped her build *The Blazing World.*

Cavendish wrote for most of her life, penning poetry, plays, and philosophical essays. She and her husband lived happily and never had children. But as possibly the first woman to publish science fiction, and the female frontrunner in the speculative fiction genre, she left quite a legacy.

Reading List

Not to be missed: *The Blazing World* is in the public domain and not hard to find with some online searching. The breadth of Cavendish's imagination makes for a fun read.

Also try: If Margaret Cavendish's outrageous life sounds like fiction, readers may be interested in Katie Whitaker's book *Mad Madge* (Basic Books, 2003), which explores the paradoxes in the real Duchess's life. For instance, Whitaker speculates that Cavendish was dyslexic, though she pushed herself to read and write.

Related work: The *Black Dossier* graphic novel from Alan Moore's League of Extraordinary Gentlemen series (DC Comics, 2010) takes its characters on a trip to the Blazing World . . . which appears in 3-D when viewed with the glasses included with the book.

"*I had rather die in the adventure of noble achievements, than live in obscure and sluggish security.*"

—The Blazing World

Terror over Horror
Ann Radcliffe
1764–1823

She's not a horror writer, let's get that straight. Ann Radcliffe wanted to terrify her readers, make them feel alive through her words. She wrote about blood and murder and terrifically terrifying villains. But she wasn't a *horror* writer, not in the least.

She didn't have to be. Eighteenth-century English readers couldn't get enough of the macabre, and by the latter half of the century, the Gothic novel was the most popular genre of literature. Enter Ann Radcliffe, who wrote the most popular Gothic romances of the 1790s, making her a best-selling writer in her day and establishing the definitive formula for the genre. She is still considered the most significant Gothic writer in eighteenth-century English literature and, in the last decade of the 1700s, was at the forefront of a uniquely female-driven moment of women writing novels for women.

So who was Ann Radcliffe?

She was born Ann Ward in 1764 in Holborn, England, to a haberdasher and his wife. (Doesn't that sound like the most British thing you've ever heard?) Not much is known about her childhood, though it's said she was curious and clever—and a voracious reader, thanks in part to an aunt who left young Ann a number of books in her will. She also loved theater and the opera and attended both regularly as an adult. In 1787, around age 23, she married a journalist named William Radcliffe, who edited a radical paper called the *Gazette*, notable for its pro–French Revolution stance. The couple lived in London, though they traveled across Europe, including Switzerland, Germany, and Austria—places that would later inspire the long, detailed descriptions of landscapes in her writing.

Just two months after her marriage, Radcliffe began to write, anonymously publishing her first novel *The Castles of Athlin and Dunbayne* with Hookham in 1789. It earned Radcliffe three shillings. The setting is the Scottish Highlands; the plot involves a peasant boy who discovers he is in fact an aristocrat. The book was not widely reviewed, but it set Radcliffe on the path to a career writing the Gothic. Her second novel, *A Sicilian Romance* (Hookham, 1790), was the first to bear her name on the cover; the book drew more reviews, many of them positive. Additional novels followed, including *The Romance of the Forest* (Hookham, 1791) and her most famous novel, *The Mysteries of Udolpho*, published in 1794 by G. G. and J. Robinson. By now, Radcliffe's readership was well established, and the sale of her fourth book brought in £50. She continued to write for enjoyment, and in doing so became one of the era's most successful female writers.

Mrs. Radcliffe's Castle

The Mysteries of Udolpho takes place in the sixteenth century in southern France, where the young and beautiful Emily St. Aubert is living the perfect life, full of poetry and long walks in the woods. Emily and her father leave on a trip through the Pyrenees, where she meets the handsome and equally poetic Valancourt. If *The Mysteries of Udolpho* were a love story, then the tale might end here. However, this is a Gothic novel, so Emily's father dies, leaving her an orphan. She goes to live with a wealthy aunt in the drafty castle Udolpho, only to be held captive there when her aunt marries the villainous Montoni.

Montoni tries to force Emily to marry his friend, the Count Morano, in a ploy for the two men to steal the women's large estate. Also, the castle may or may not be haunted . . . (Spoiler: it's not.) The castle at first *seems* haunted, thanks to various ghostly sights and sounds. But Radcliffe preferred the narrative technique of the "explained supernatural," meaning that the spooky atmosphere turns out to have real-world explanations. For example, Emily is horrified to find, lurking behind an ominous black curtain, what she thinks is a rotting corpse but turns out to be a melted wax figure. That may seem like a letdown to modern horror readers (show us the bloody corpse, please), but Radcliffe's choice was intentional. Ghosts are spooky, but the true threat was one she saw in the real world: men who were willing to abuse women in order to gain wealth.

Patriarchy and greed. They'll get you every time, no supernatural phenomenon required.

Radcliffe's popularity increased with each new book. She published her final Gothic novel, *The Italian*, in 1797. The plot revolves around a pair of star-crossed lovers, the orphan Vivaldi and the lovely Ellena. Vivaldi woos Ellena, but the girl's mother and the villainous monk (seeing a trend here?) Father Schedoni scheme to keep the lovebirds apart. The book garnered rave reviews from, among others, writers Samuel Taylor Coleridge and Frances Burney; Radcliffe did receive some criticism for anti-Catholic sentiment in her narratives. Maybe one less evil monk, Mrs. Radcliffe? Her final work, *Gaston de Blondeville*, was released posthumously in 1826, though Radcliffe may have had reasons for not publishing it when she was alive. Although it is a typical Gothic novel, it is more than a bit rambling (read: looooooooooong). And the plot doesn't always make sense, especially when she plays around with the supernatural (with real ghosts this time).

Today, Radcliffe is considered not only a pioneer of her genre but also a voice for women's rights. Her particular (and incredibly popular) take on the female Gothic focused on the abuses women suffered at the hands of men, especially through traditional institutions like marriage.

Though she might not have written horror per se, Radcliffe knew how to terrify, and her work inspired countless writers who came after her. Sir Walter Scott, the Marquis de Sade, and even Edgar Allan Poe have cited her influence. She was particularly important as an example of a successful female author. In her day, so many women writers took to writing Gothic novels that critics began to call them the "Radcliffean school." It's difficult to imagine the horror genre without the familiar elements of the Gothic, and without Radcliffe's captivating storytelling, we may not have had the Gothic horror novel at all.

HORROR VS. TERROR

In an 1826 essay, Ann Radcliffe wrote:

"Terror and horror are so far opposite, that the first expands the soul, and awakens the faculties to a high degree of life; the other contracts, freezes, and nearly annihilates them."

In other words, terror was high art, meant to shake the reader alive. Terror is standing on the edge of a cliff, feeling both fear and the overwhelming beauty of the scene in front of you. Horror pushes you over that cliff, leaving no appreciation for beauty or the sublime, just sheer and blinding fear followed by blood and guts. For Radcliffe, horror was low art, a bomb that destroys feeling, leaving the reader numb—and something true writers shouldn't aspire to. Fortunately, not all writers of the Gothic agreed!

Reading List

Not to be missed: If you read only one Radcliffe novel, make it *The Mysteries of Udolpho*. Newer editions are widely available. It's a long book, and the first third or so is basically a travelogue, with lengthy descriptions of various landscapes. Expect lots of meaningful stares at mountain scenery—Emily St. Aubert and her family love nature and spontaneously break out into poetry when the views so move them. Don't let this dissuade you; once the orphaned Emily is with her aunt, the action picks up and the book becomes one chill-inducing read. Consider it Terror 101, and enjoy seeing where many of your favorite authors found their inspiration.

Also try: Perhaps more than any of her other books, *The Italian* shows Radcliffe's skills as a writer. It features a scheming monk as the villain, which has led scholars to speculate that Radcliffe wrote the book in response to Matthew Lewis. She famously hated his novel *The Monk* (Joseph Bell, 1796).

Related work: Jane Austen parodied the Gothic novel in her novel *Northanger Abbey* (John Murray, 1817). One of the main characters in Austen's book is presented as rather naïve simply because of her choice of reading material, which includes Radcliffe's *Udolpho* and *The Italian*. In related media, a film about Austen's life, *Becoming Jane* (2007), featured an appearance by Helen McCrory as Ann Radcliffe. That may be as close as we get to a biopic of Radcliffe, given how little is known about her life.

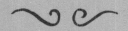

"I tasted too what was called the sweet of revenge—but it was transient, it expired even with the object that provoked it. Remember, sister, that passions are the seeds of vices as well as virtues."

—The Mysteries of Udolpho

The Original Goth Girl
Mary Wollstonecraft Shelley
1797–1851

The creation of Frankenstein is perhaps the most famous origin story about a work of literature. The setting is about as Gothic as it gets: the moody Villa Diodati in the midst of a thunderstorm on a lake in Switzerland. The book's author, Mary Godwin, as she was known then, had traveled with her future husband, the poet Percy Bysshe Shelley, and her stepsister Claire Clairmont to Lake Geneva, where they met up with the poet Lord Byron and his personal physician John Polidori. The trip reeked of teenage angst and clandestine affairs, with a good dose of young rebellion and spring-break hormones mixed in.

It was June 1816; Mary had met Percy two years earlier. She was all of 16 years old then, and he, barely 22, had just left his wife (who committed suicide soon after). In 1814 the happy couple eloped and were expecting a child. Mary's parents were infuriated and disowned her. The pair struggled financially and, during their first year together, suffered the loss of their first child, born prematurely. They hoped the Switzerland trip, with their second child William in tow, would bring some relief from their sorrows.

By the time of the gathering, Byron had slept with Claire. He was, to put it mildly, over their dalliance. She, however, was not. It was Claire who suggested that they all go to visit him in Switzerland.

Fate seemed to conspire in creating the perfect writing environment. This was the so-called year without a summer; a volcanic eruption in Indonesia had caused so much sulfur dioxide pollution that global temperatures dropped. The resulting cold and dreary climate, and seemingly never-ending rain, kept everyone at the villa indoors. And as the lightning sparked and the thunder roared, Lord Byron suggested a little contest: Who could write the scariest story?

It was amid this moody atmosphere charged with sexual tension that *Frankenstein* was born . . .

Her Mother's Daughter

Mary Shelley's story began long before that stormy vacation, of course. She was born in 1797 to the well-known philosopher William Godwin and Mary Wollstonecraft, an accomplished writer known for her feminist principles and advocacy of women's rights. Considered by some to be "Britain's first feminist," Wollstonecraft authored *A Vindication for the Rights of Woman* (J. Johnson, 1792) and was among the first to fight publicly for that cause. She argued that both girls and boys should receive an education and that parental responsibilities should be equally shared.

Wollstonecraft died eleven days after Mary's birth, so the young girl came to know her mother mostly through her writings. Mary's other primary source of information was her father's 1798 biography of her mother, which brought lots of shade to the family because it revealed the Godwins' relaxed attitude toward monogamy.

As proof of the scandal, Mary was raised in a blended family with an older half-sister, Fanny, daughter of Wollstonecraft and her lover, Gilbert Imlay. In 1801 Mary's father married his lover, Mary Jane Clairmont, and became a stepfather to her daughter Claire. Born only a few months apart, Claire and Mary grew up together and were close friends. Mary and her stepmother, however, had a contentious relationship throughout their lives.

As you might expect, Mary received more education than most women of her day. She seemed to share her mother's intellectual prowess as well as her penchant for breaking with social norms—

particularly when it came to her affair with the poet Shelley. Early on, the two arranged for secret liaisons at Mary's mother's grave; it's been said that she lost her virginity there. After declaring their mutual love and eloping, Mary and Percy lived together for more than two years before marrying.

The death of her firstborn in 1815 shattered the young mother, and the loss was one of Mary's primary inspirations for *Frankenstein*. She wrote in her journal about harrowing dreams in which she was able to bring her infant back to life by rubbing her beside a fire. The nightmares continued even after the birth of William the following year, as well as during her travels through Switzerland that summer. In the preface to the 1831 edition of *Frankenstein*, Mary recounts a nightmare she had while at Villa Diodati, in which she saw a "hideous" man waking to a new life: her first imaginings of her famous monster.

There was more behind *Frankenstein*'s provenance than bad dreams and painful memories, though. While the rain pelted the Swiss villa, the friends kept themselves busy by reading; Mary was particularly inspired by Étienne-Gaspard Robert's *Phantasmagoria*, a French book about German ghost stories. She was likely influenced by Percy and Byron's frequent philosophical debates on the nature of life. She was also knowledgeable about scientific experiments of the day; she'd seen demonstrations at the Royal Institute in London showing how electricity could be used to induce movement in dead muscles. In addition, some critics have speculated the Shelleys visited the actual Castle Frankenstein, located along

the Rhine River in Germany, where they would have heard the story of Konrad Dippel, a mad scientist trying to make an oil that would ensure immortal life.

It was under these unique circumstances that an eighteen-year-old girl created the Gothic and horror genres as we know them today. In fact, the contest—which Mary won—produced not one, but two of the most famous modern Gothic stories: Mary Shelley's *Frankenstein; or, The Modern Prometheus* (Lackington, Hughes, Harding, Mavor, & Jones, 1818) and Polidori's *The Vampyre* (*New Monthly Magazine*, 1819), the first modern vampire novel written in English. But it's *Frankenstein* that went on to become an undying, foundational text of horror.

Mary Shelley wrote her book in nine months, while pregnant with her third child. Both Byron's and her now-husband Percy's publishers refused to publish the book. But on January 1, 1818, the novel was published in three volumes by Lackington and Company, with an initial printing of 500 copies. The author remained anonymous, although the book contained a preface by Percy Bysshe Shelley and a dedication to Mary's father.

Some reviewers assumed that Percy Bysshe Shelley had written the novel, but even early on many readers knew that "William Godwin's daughter" was responsible. Negative reviews focused on the story's excessive romanticism, and in September 1818 the *British Critic* wrote, "the horror that abounds . . . is too grotesque and *bizarre*." But many more people loved *Frankenstein*. Walter Scott wrote in *Blackwood's Edinburgh Magazine* (March 1818) that Mary Shelley possessed "original genius and happy power of expression." In 1823, the novel was published in a new edition, this time with a cover bearing Mary Shelley's name.

For the first edition, scholars believe that Shelley's husband helped with both editing the manuscript and finding a publisher; he heavily revised the book, focusing on making the language more poetic (maybe those negative reviewers were on to something). By 1831, Shelley wanted ed to release a revised text. After all, she'd been a teenager when the first version was published; she wanted her most famous novel to reflect her talents as a more experienced author. Most editions published today use this 1831 version.

Mary Shelley had begun writing as a child, and she would keep writing and publishing until the years right before her death. She continued even after the untimely death of her husband in 1822, when his small boat was lost in a storm off the coast of Italy. She became a well-known, best-selling author, though for most of her life she was still considered "the daughter of William Godwin" or "the wife of Percy Bysshe Shelley." Despite it all, she remained a voice for her mother's feminism, both in her writing and in her donations to women shunned by society (usually for some kind of sexual scandal). As for her personal life, there's no denying that it was marked by grief. Only one of her four children outlived her, and she never fully recovered from Percy's death.

THE HEART OF A POET

Legend has it that Mary Shelley kept her late husband Percy's heart wrapped in some paper printed with his poetry, which upon her death was interred in the family burial vault. Keeping a memento from the corpus of a deceased loved one was not unusual in her day, but nonetheless the story appears to be apocryphal. Percy Bysshe Shelley was cremated, so it's unlikely his heart would have survived the flames. Most scholars believe that Mary did keep some part of his body—a bone fragment or part of a calcified organ, perhaps—which may be the source of the legend.

Today, Mary Shelley's two-hundred-year-old reanimated monster is ubiquitous across genres, living on in countless iterations in film, television, books, comic books, cartoons, and video games. But her legacy is deeper than that. Horace Walpole established the Gothic novel, and Ann Radcliffe claimed it for women writers, but it was Mary Shelley who forever linked Gothic with horror as a literary combination, one so effective that it's still in use today. She lived a life that contained remarkable success and intense sorrow; she endured tremendous personal loss and knew passionate love. For Shelley, death and romance were never far apart. It's no wonder that she defined what Gothic literature looked like for those who came after her . . . and it's no surprise that numerous books and films have been written about her macabre-laden life. She was the original Goth girl.

Reading List

Not to be missed: If you've already read *Frankenstein*, try Mary Shelley's *Mathilda*. It's a controversial (yet exceedingly Gothic) novella about a dying young woman who is in love with a devastatingly handsome poet *and* involved in an incestuous relationship with her widower father. It's no wonder this steamy story was first published only in 1959 (by the University of North Carolina Press), a full century after Shelley's death.

Also try: *The Last Man* (Henry Colburn, 1826) is Shelley's postapocalyptic novel, set in a future world that has been decimated by a plague-like disease. Don't worry; the book stays true to Shelley's Romantic roots. The main character is an orphan who spends much of the novel ruminating on large ideas like love. Of course, the world is ending, so the ruminations on humankind and the world become increasingly dark as the main characters realize their desire to live is no match for the emotionless force of nature.

Related work: Mary Shelley's hideous progeny still inspires writers to create their own sewn-corpse monsters. Sarah Maria Griffin's *Spare and Found Parts* (HarperCollins, 2016) imagines a world ravaged by an epidemic that leaves the survivors with missing body parts. The daughter of the scientist who invented biomechanical replacements is lonely in this new world . . . and she sets out to create a companion for herself. Ahmed Saadawi took Shelley's story to modern-day, war-torn Iraq with *Frankenstein in Baghdad* (English translation: Penguin, 2018).

Among the most faithful film adaptations of Shelley's *Frankenstein* are Kenneth Branagh's 1994 film of that name and, perhaps surprisingly, the iconic 1931 motion picture by Universal Pictures (based on a play based on the book) starring Boris Karloff as the monster who set the tone for all future patchwork corpses to come. Completists will enjoy the very first film adaptation, a 15-minute silent film by Edison Studios, widely available on the internet (though without musical accompaniment). More recently, the Showtime television series *Penny Dreadful* offered a rather heartbreaking storyline involving the monster and his horrified creator.

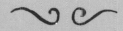

"If I cannot inspire love, I will cause fear."

— Franker stein

Scandalizing Jane Austen
Regina Maria Roche

1764–1845

Regina Maria Roche's Gothic novels were so popular that Jane Austen name-checked one of them in *Northanger Abbey* (John Murray, 1817), a satire of the Gothic novel. Austen's character Isabella Thorpe, a beautiful but conniving woman with a proclivity toward what we today might term trashy novels, describes her reading list: "I will read you their names directly; here they are, in my pocketbook. *Castle of Wolfenbach, Clermont, Mysterious Warnings, Necromancer of the Black Forest, Midnight Bell, Orphan of the Rhine,* and *Horrid Mysteries.* Those will last us some time." Austen's satire suggests the opinion that a woman who read novels like *Clermont* had neither brains nor common sense or gentlewomanly manners.

Though Roche is considered a founding mother of the Gothic genre, little is known about her life. She was born in Waterford, an Irish seaport, in 1764 and grew up in Dublin. After marrying, she moved to London, where she lived with her husband, Ambrose Roche. A voracious reader as a child, by 1789 she had turned her love for words into a career as a novelist, beginning with *The Maid of the Hamlet: A Tale* in 1793 (Newman).

Roche was a minor literary star of her day. Her first two novels were romances, but she found success in darker material. Her third novel, *The Children of the Abbey* (1796), sold better than Ann Radcliffe's *The Mysteries of Udolpho* and was a best-selling hit for Minerva Press. The novel is a love story, but Roche included some sordid details, including stolen inheritances and forged documents—elements that would feel at home in any modern soap opera.

Roche's novel *Clermont*, published by Minerva Press in 1798, was her most Gothic work to date. The heroine, Madeline, is appropriately pale and beautiful and virtuous, but, alas, she faces torment after torment. Her idyllic life in the countryside is interrupted one night when she is attacked in a gloomy castle, prompting her to flee to a criminal-ridden forest. Early in the novel she falls for the hero, de Sevingie, but trouble hits paradise quickly. Madeline is whisked away to live with a family friend, a countess who is fatally stabbed and bleeds out before our innocent heroine's eyes. Now Madeline is caught in a dangerous game of cat-and-mouse, and she doesn't know if she can trust anyone—not even her own father or her new love.

Roche likely wrote as a means to support her family. She penned Gothic novels when Gothic novels were the fashion. When her readers demanded a change, Roche made a sharp left turn and changed her subject matter, focusing on Ireland and its social problems. In doing so, she managed to create and, more important, sustain a long and successful career.

Reading List

Not to be missed: *Clermont* may be the most Gothic of Gothic novels.

Also try: Regina Maria Roche did not deviate from the Gothic script in any of her fiction, to the point of being formulaic. Her novels are full of banditti-riddled forests, haunted and crumbling ruins in the midst of idyllic pastures, perfectly pale heroines of unparalleled virtue, and fainting women. So many fainting women. Her novel *The Children of the*

Abbey (also a Minerva Press title, published in 1796) tells the story of siblings Amanda and Oscar who are cheated out of their rightful inheritance. As in most good Gothic novels, Amanda falls in love with a noble gentleman but is relentlessly pursued by a lecherous villain and corrupt relatives. Valancourt Books revived the text in 2016.

Related works: In addition to Roche's works, Minerva Press published other Gothic novels by women authors. Standouts include *The Castle of Wolfenbach* by Eliza Parsons (1793) and *The Orphan of the Rhine* by Eleanor Sleath (1798). Though these writers received little critical attention at the time (perhaps due to Jane Austen's disdain for them), they are beginning to enjoy popularity today. Valancourt Books in particular has been tracking down out-of-print Gothic novels and restoring them for contemporary readers.

"Here she paused, and looking in, beheld, with equal horror and astonishment, an old woman wretchedly clad, and worn to a skeleton, kneeling in the corner of an ill-furnished room, before a wooden crucifix."

—Clermont

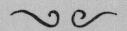

Purveyor of Guts and Gore
Mary Anne Radcliffe

circa 1746–1810

Twenty-first-century filmmakers often portray nineteenth-century British life as a Jane Austen novel, prim and proper etiquette with lace and tea everywhere. But the fiction of the time, especially popular novels, paints a starkly different picture. Readers of the day had a healthy appetite for violence and gore.

Take, for example, *Manfroné; or, The One-Handed Monk*, published in 1809 (J. F. Hughes). The story starts violently: A young woman named Rosalina, alone in her bedroom at night, is assaulted. Her screams attract attention and her would-be rapist is scared off, losing a hand in the process of escaping. Then Rosalina's father is murdered, and things only get bloodier. Rosalina is pursued relentlessly by a man who wants to hold her prisoner so he can control her wealth; at the same time, she meets a hero who wants to save her ... proving his good intentions by kissing her cheek while she's knocked unconscious. The story is so violent that several publishers refused to print it.

The author of this bloody book is credited as Mary Anne Radcliffe, though scholars can't agree on who she was. The name is likely a pseudonym, especially given its resemblance to Ann Radcliffe, the most recognizable name in Gothic fiction. It could have been created by a publisher in order to gain favor with readers seeking a female author, though evidence suggests that a real woman was behind the fake moniker. A Louisa Bellenden Ker claimed authorship decades after the novel's publication, though her writing style doesn't corroborate her claim. Most modern critics accept one of two other possibilities: Either the woman was an obscure writer who never rose to fame (or died before she could assert ownership of the text), or the author was the feminist Mary Ann Radcliffe, who wrote *The Female Advocate* (Vernor and Hood, 1799).

That Mary Ann Radcliffe was born Mary Clayton around 1746 to a wealthy family in Scotland. The death of her father left her with a sizable inheritance. She visited London in 1761, and there she eloped with Joseph Radcliffe, who was by all accounts a useless alcoholic. Radcliffe and her husband had eight children, but gradually the marriage disintegrated. By the age of thirty-three, Radcliffe was essentially living on her own and acting as the sole provider for her family. Unfortunately, her inheritance had disappeared as well. Radcliffe found work as either a housekeeper or a governess before she turned to writing.

Radcliffe wrote several sensational novels, including *Radzivil* and *The Fate of Velina de Guidova*, both published by Minerva Press in 1790. Radcliffe's later writings were feminist manifestos, highly influenced by the work and philosophy of Mary Wollstonecraft (mother of Mary Shelley; see page 28). In *The Female Advocate; or An Attempt to Recover the Rights of Women from Male Usurpation* Radcliffe, like Wollstonecraft, argued that women should be educated and given more opportunities for employment, both of which would provide them with greater freedom.

Radcliffe also wrote personal nonfiction. In her memoirs, she expressed a desire to publish her fiction anonymously, which was common at the time. But her publisher pressed her to use her real name, due to its resemblance to Ann Radcliffe. (Although this Mary Ann Radcliffe most certainly wrote Gothic novels, it is sometimes difficult to tell which were hers and which were published under her name for this reason.)

So little is known about the other contender, Louisa Bellenden Ker, that it's difficult to speculate on the truthfulness of her claim and scholars remain skeptical. Her name appears in court documents (sometimes as Kerr, only adding to the confusion) for fraud charges, and although in her testimony she makes no mention of being a novelist, there is evidence that she attempted a writing career early in her life. She seems to have turned to petty crime when writing didn't pan out.

In any case, we thank Mary Anne Radcliffe—whoever she was—for giving readers such a gloriously over-the-top tale of gore.

Reading List

Not to be missed: A new edition of *Manfroné* was published in 2007 by Valancourt Books, which includes an illuminating essay by Gothic scholar Dale Townshend exploring the possible authorship of the novel. Assuming Mary Anne Radcliffe is the author of *Manfroné*, we recommend *Radzivil, A Romance* (1790) and *The Secret Oath; or, Blood-Stained Dagger* (1802). Both novels were published anonymously (though are widely attributed to the feminist writer); they are difficult to find in modern editions but worth looking for.

Also try: Monks (and nuns and abbeys, too) have long been staples of the Gothic novel. Drawing upon the popularity of Matthew Lewis's violently horrific novel *The Monk* (discussed later in this chapter; see page 45), authors began to write all manner of villainous clerical types into their fiction. One fun read is *Terrific Tales* by Isabella Lewis (first published 1804; reprint 2006, Valancourt Books), which is said to be a collection of stories collected from ancient monastic texts. Lewis may be a false name (perhaps meant to evoke Matthew Lewis), but these short tales are presented as true. They include horrific stories of hobgoblins, angels, and ghosts of all kinds.

Related work: Rosalina is a popular name for Gothic heroines. It sounds just romantic enough (and by romantic, we mean vaguely Italian) to be perfect for a main character about to be pursued by evil men who never learned to keep their hands to themselves. In the case of Catherine Smith's novel *Barozzi; or, The Venetian Sorceress* (A. K. Newman, 1815), the heroine Rosalina witnesses her father being brutally murdered. Luckily, she is rescued by a handsome man, who whisks her away to his Venetian palace. All is well until Rosalina meets a sorceress (Surprise! The villain is a woman!) at a masked ball, and this evil woman just might want to sacrifice Rosalina to the devil. Valancourt Books made this Gothic classic available to modern readers with a new edition published in 2006.

> "She shrieked at seeing the dismembered arm, and, with a dreadful groan, fell senseless on the earth."
>
> — *Manfroné; or, The One-Handed Monk*

Exhibitor of Murder and Harlotry
Charlotte Dacre

circa 1771–1825

Novels of the eighteenth and nineteenth centuries are novels of sensibility, right? They have a refined air. A sense of decorum. Characters displaying the delicate touch of fine manners. Women who faint, or sit around looking pale and sad. There's poetry.

The Gothic novels of the time, though, were more Stephen King than delicate romances. Demons were everywhere. Monks were just as likely to murder as they were to pray. The devil lurked around every corner. As did, in at least one case, a worm-ridden dead baby.

And in this environment Charlotte Dacre thrived.

"Charlotte Dacre" was one of the many pen names for Charlotte Byrne, née King, who was born in London (most likely; even her birthplace is shrouded in mystery, like the plot of one of her stories) sometime in the latter half of the eighteenth century (the exact year is still debated). Her father, John King, was a Jewish money broker who scandalized the family when he divorced Charlotte's mother and began an affair with a widowed countess. A bit of a rogue, he ended up in legal trouble numerous times, facing charges of extorting money from the prime minister *and* the British royal family; his troubles caused him to flee England twice, in 1784 and 1802. Nonetheless, Charlotte dedicated poems to her father and often cited him as the reason that she was educated. (Later in life, he returned to his Jewish roots, publishing a defense of his religion that earned him the nickname "the Jew King.") Some literary scholars argue that the abandonment Charlotte and her mother experienced led her to imagine men who did the same. It's true that her plots often involve women who have been abandoned, in one way or another.

In 1805 Charlotte began an affair with Nicholas Byrne, the owner and editor of the British newspaper *The Morning Post*; the couple had three children together. Like her father—who'd changed his name from Jacob Rey—she chose a pseudonym that she believed lent her an air of aristocracy. Dacre's first book, *The Confessions of the Nun of St. Omer* (Hughes, 1805), was reportedly written when she was only eighteen years old. It was received well by critics, but the same cannot be said about her next one. *Zofloya; or, The Moor* (Longman, Hurst, Rees, and Orme, 1806) scandalized the literary world, and some critics considered it downright pornographic. One reviewer wrote that the book was filled to the brim with "courtesans of the lewdest class, and murderers of the deepest dye . . . an exhibition of wantonness of harlotry, which we would have hoped, that the delicacy of the female mind, would have been shocked to imagine." What a blurb! In fact, Dacre's book that caused so much pearl-clutching was a feminist revision of another popular book at the time: *The Monk*, a highly horrific Gothic novel by Matthew Lewis (J. Saunders, 1796).

The Monk tells the story of the titular monastic, who, driven wild by desire for a young woman in his town, plots to kidnap her with the help of a young woman named Matilda—who is dressed as a young man named Rosario. Confused yet? Lewis can do that. There's enough trickery and debauchery in the book that that it reads like a soap opera written by Clive Barker. Lewis's novel introduced to the Gothic world such tropes as the lecherous monk, the cross-dressing woman with a dangerous obsession, and the aforementioned dead infant. The book also gave Dacre one of her other pseudonyms: Rosa Matilda. In

Lewis's novel, Rosa Matilda is both a victim of the monk's lust and a seducer of the pious. Some have even called Rosa Matilda the "demon lover" of Lewis's monk. Dacre adopted the pen name intentionally, most likely to bolster sales with the connection to Lewis's best seller, but also to slyly suggest women writers could also deal with the themes of violence and sexuality that their male counterparts so freely wrote about.

Reading List

Not to be missed: Like many female authors of her day, Dacre wrote romances, but she is best known for *Zofloya*. This novel follows Victoria, an adulterous woman who is not at all the typical virginal heroine. Of course, her (*ahem*) extracurriculars are rewarded with a date with the literal Devil. The novel's plot hinges on Victoria's obsession with her rival Lilla, whose chastity infuriates Victoria so greatly that she practices poisoning elderly women in preparation for when she has a chance to off Lilla. When Lilla's time finally comes, she is drugged, kidnapped, and chained inside a mountain cavern.

Also try: After *Zofloya* sold well enough to cement Dacre's reputation as a best-selling author and fan favorite, she continued to push boundaries. *The Libertine* (T. Cadell and W. Davies, 1807), written as Rosa Matilda, tells the story of an innocent girl seduced by an Italian libertine who can't settle down. Her last novel was *The Passions* (T. Cadell and W. Davies, 1811).

Related work: Readers interested in Matthew Lewis's Rosa Matilda character can easily find a copy of *The Monk* thanks to the 2013 edition by Valancourt Books, featuring an introduction written by the master of horror, Stephen King.

"She turned of an ashy paleness as cold hatred and desire for revenge took possession of her vindictive soul."

—Zofloya

PART TWO

Haunting Tales

Pale women fainting at the sight of a specter. Dark-haired men brooding on a foggy English moor. Psychics conducting séances. Photographs of the dead and of ectoplasm, the ghostly substance of the spirit world. All standard stock in horror stories of the nineteenth and early twentieth centuries . . . but not always fictional.

In the latter half of the nineteenth century, scientists and seekers of spiritual knowledge alike were exploring the mystery of what happened to a person after death. The Swedish philosopher Emanuel Swedenborg, for example, described in his 1758 book *Heaven and Its Wonders and Hell from Things Heard and Seen* different levels of the afterlife, including a kind of spiritual pit stop for disembodied souls. Academics pooled knowledge and resources to form interest groups, like the Society for Psychical Research in England, with the aim of studying psychic phenomena, including telepathy, astral projection, and clairvoyance.

As shadowy fact and spooky fiction fed into each other, the ghost became a popular character in prominent literature of the day by such writers as Charles Dickens, Wilkie Collins, M. R. James, and Sheridan Le Fanu. Even authors who wrote tales of realism and local color—Mary N. Murfree, Sarah Orne Jewett, Mary E. Wilkins Freeman—dabbled in the supernatural. And it was women who took the genre to the political realm, making their ghostly tales much more than just scary stories to tell in the dark.

In the United States, a spiritual firestorm soon swept the nation, and it was two young women who lit the flame. On the eve of April Fool's Day in 1848, sisters Margaretta "Maggie" and Kate Fox tapped into the growing public interest in spiritual matters quite literally: by "talking" to ghosts via knocks on a wall. They told their parents they could speak to the spirit realm and that the spirits would answer back, rapping once for yes and twice for no. Stunned, the family invited neighbors to see what their daughters could do. It was the beginning of an odyssey that would take the sisters onto the global public stage and, in the process, create what essentially became a new religion: Spiritualism.

Within months, Maggie and Kate were "performing" their conversations with the dead at town halls around the world. People flocked to the events hoping to communicate with loved ones and beloved historical figures. (Benjamin Franklin and Abraham Lincoln seemed to have had particularly active afterlives.) The movement spread like wildfire, and people began holding home séances and developing beliefs about the fate of the soul after death. Sherlock Holmes creator Sir Arthur Conan Doyle was one devotee.

Skeptics believed the Fox sisters were perpetuating a long hoax on the world. And the sisters admitted as much in 1883, though later recanted the confession. Genuine or not, their performances created a platform for women to not only speak publicly but also assume previously unattainable leadership roles in both politics and religion. Because séances were usually conducted by women, these events afforded women a unique, unprecedented opportunity to speak freely outside the home. Their communicants from beyond often preached abolitionist and feminist views to audiences. It was a win-win situation: the women were able to speak their political views while blaming it all on the inhabitant of the Great Beyond. In an interesting historical side note, the Spiritualist Victoria Woodhull was the first woman to run for president, with the abolitionist and former slave Frederick Douglass as her running mate.

With Spiritualism in the ether and feminism in the air, women who wrote Victorian ghost stories did more than conjure specters—so much more. Elizabeth Gaskell and Violet Paget, whom you're about to meet, shaped horror fiction into a genre familiar to twenty-first-century readers. Neither fit the mold of a proper Victorian woman. A friend to the author Charlotte Brontë, Gaskell lived one life as a wife and mother and another as a published writer, working closely with such literary luminaries as Charles Dickens (with whom she often argued over style and editing decisions). While Gaskell downplayed her success as a writer, Paget flaunted it—so long as she could maintain her privacy behind her male pen name of Vernon Lee. She was a feminist, a lesbian, a voracious traveler, and once the subject of a painting by the renowned artist John Singer Sargent.

The Victorian ghost story shared some elements with its Gothic predecessor, in particular the setting of the isolated, old manor home, far from civilization. But the Victorian ghost story was decidedly un-Gothic in many ways. Gothic writers reveled in Romance, in the un-realistic over-the-top expression of emotion. By contrast, the Victorian ghost story blurred the lines between spiritualist science and social realism. The specters in these tales returned for one reason: to exchange knowledge with the living. Some ghosts merely wanted their living relatives to find the hidden fortune they'd left behind. Others warned about impending doom. Either way, these visitations were presented as warranting serious study.

The Spiritualist movement started in 1848 with the incredible Fox sisters. The Victorian ghost story took flight around the 1840s, too, with the publication of popular Christmas ghost stories, such as those Charles Dickens was writing. Both infatuations would pass; by the fin de siècle, cynicism had displaced the Victorian ghost story, and Spiritualism faded as prominent mediums were exposed as relying on stagecraft to achieve their otherworldly communications. Yet many of our modern ideas about ghosts, and ghost stories, originated in this era, when the veil between the living and the dead seemed real enough to touch.

Ghosts Are Real

Elizabeth Gaskell

1810–1865

Women in the nineteenth century were expected to be good home-makers, both as wives and mothers. The household was their domain. The men went out to work in the city while their wives stayed at home, overseeing the daily domestic duties.

Elizabeth Gaskell—Mrs. Gaskell to most who knew her—was so successful at managing her home life that she managed an entire *second* home, without her husband even knowing she owned it.

How did she do it? Mrs. Gaskell wrote ghost stories.

When most people call to mind Victorian writers of ghostly tales, they think immediately of Charles Dickens and Wilkie Collins. Elizabeth Gaskell is another who springs to mind; she contributed spectral tales to Dickens's *Household Words* magazine and was a literary power-house in her own right. She first won Dickens's praise with *Mary Barton* (Chapman and Hall, 1848), a novel that examined the social problems in British society, which was a topic that interested Dickens also.

But though Dickens called her his "dear Scheherazade," the two didn't always see eye-to-eye when it came to the scribblings of his editorial pen, nor did she shy away from disagreeing with her celebrated colleague's criticisms. In addition, Gaskell had trouble keeping up with his deadlines and didn't always understand his edits to her manuscripts. He seemingly became so frustrated with her that in 1855 he wrote in a letter to a friend, "Oh, Mrs. Gaskell, fearful—fearful! If I were Mr. G, Oh Heaven how I would beat her."

The pair's contentious relationship began before they even met. Gaskell's publisher sent him *Mary Barton*, and he didn't personally respond (though he did publish his praise). Gaskell took offense at the slight but nonetheless published several stories with Dickens. They continued to argue, especially when he would make changes to her stories without her authorization. He famously angered her when he deleted a reference to the Pickwick Papers (his own work) in her first *Cranford* story. The two also disagreed over the place of the supernatural in fiction. Despite having written about the most famous Christmas spirits of all time, Dickens thought that ghosts lessened a story's impact. This disagreement came to a head when Dickens was preparing to publish Gaskell's "The Old Nurse's Tale" in the December 1852 issue of *Household Words*. He pointed to Shakespeare as an example, arguing that ghosts only weakened strong stories, and pushed Gaskell to adopt a rationalist point of view. She refused to give in, and the story—one of her most famous—was published as she originally wrote it.

Dickens's frustrations must have subsided, though, because the two continued to work together for most of her career.

Spirits of the Times

Gaskell is best known for her realist novels that criticized the social ills of her day. In the 1830s she and her husband and daughters lived in Man-

chester, England, a hotbed of industry and radical politics and a microcosm of the problems facing the nation. The once-small town was booming thanks to the explosion of industrialization and factory work. Child labor was common, as was unemployment—without a constant need of workers, factories would lay off employees often and without warning. Though the working class was growing in numbers, it remained unable to catch up to the aristocratic upper class in affluence. Gaskell's desire to help alleviate poverty and call attention to the plight of women in particular led to some of her best-known work and, at one point, the destruction of a few copies of one of her books by her Unitarian minister husband's church congregation (against his wishes)—including the aforementioned novel *Mary Barton*, *North and South* (1854–55) and *Cranford* (1851–53), which was adapted for television by the BBC in 2007.

Gaskell explored social issues in her novels, but she used the short story format to delve into more ghostly subjects. These works appeared frequently in Dickens's periodicals, especially his supernatural-themed Christmas issues. She was fascinated by English folklore, and often her stories take the form of a tale handed down through generations, with a kernel of truth at the center. Her belief in the adage that power corrupts, as well as her fascination with the repression of past abuses in family histories, became recurring themes in her short fiction.

In her best-known tale, "The Old Nurse's Story," published in the 1852 Christmas edition of *Household Words*, a ghost haunts a young orphan girl who has come to a relative's manor home, which, of course, is sufficiently spooky. Entire rooms are off-limits, and organ music plays at odd hours. (What is it with ghosts who play the organ? We're waiting for one to pick up the clarinet.) We won't spoil the ending, but the house is doomed to repeat past abuse, and the little orphan is caught in the deadly haunting. Another shorter work, "The Poor Clare" (*Household Words,* 1856), boasts all the typical characteristics of a Gothic tale, along with a little dash of *The Twilight Zone*: a tense mother-daughter relationship, a witch, an abusive husband and father, a haunted house, a Catholic nunnery in a foreign land torn by war and revolt, a curse, and a doppelgänger demon. So many elements in one story could be disastrous in the hands of a less talented writer, but this novella is one of Gaskell's best, demonstrating her mastery of fiction.

Another cautionary tale of terrible men—this time, a mother warning her daughter not to marry an evil man, as the former unknowingly did—is Gaskell's "The Grey Woman," published in the Dickens-owned magazine *All the Year Round* in 1861. The titular character grows pale and gray after witnessing horrors at her husband's castle, followed by an escape fraught with close calls. Like the working women Gaskell described in her realistic novels, often those in her supernatural tales find themselves working against, and sometimes defeated by, larger societal forces. Yet even in defeat, their stories and their traces remain with the reader.

Elizabeth Gaskell pioneered a new kind of Gothic writing. In the earliest Gothic novels, particularly those influenced by Ann Radcliffe, plots revolved around the "explained supernatural" (that is, Radcliffe's heroines thought they were being haunted by ghosts when in fact they were being stalked by predators or gaslighted for their inheritances). By the time women of Gaskell's era were writing, the crumbling castles and ruined abbeys of Radcliffe's settings had been replaced by old English manor homes. But while the Gothic settings became more realistic to the contemporary reader, the ghosts in these stories became less so. Hauntings no longer had rational explanations, as Dickens would have preferred. Rather, Gaskell's ghosts were presented as truly supernatural, which seemed even more eerie contrasted with the realism of her settings.

Gaskell enjoyed literary success in her lifetime. She was well-loved by readers, thanks in large part to her collaboration with Dickens, and her success brought her wealth and a degree of independence not possible for most women of her day. She tired of living in cold, dreary Manchester, in the north of England, and in 1865 bought a house in the southern town of Hampton, more than 200 miles away—and kept her husband in the dark. She knew he was reluctant to leave Manchester, which had been their home for so long, and hoped to convince him that a change in scenery would do them good. While she waited for the right time to break the news, she frequently visited her new home in secret with her daughters.

The Hampshire house was such a well-kept secret, in fact, that Mr. Gaskell learned of its existence only when his wife died of a heart attack there. Elizabeth Gaskell pushed the boundaries of what a woman could do—even in death.

THE GHOST STORY: A CHRISTMAS TRADITION

If a hearth was blazing on a December night in nineteenth-century England, folks were gathered around it telling spooky tales. *A Christmas Carol* is the most famous expression of the tradition of sharing scary stories in the dark, which goes back centuries, but in Dickens's day most writers of the supernatural took a stab or two at a Christmas ghost story. By publishing special Christmas-themed issues of his magazines, Dickens cemented this custom, which may be why his tale of the spirits who visited Ebenezer Scrooge continues to be shared and adapted for modern audiences.

The English yuletide bonfire tradition has not continued in the United States, thanks to the Puritans who snuffed out the fun practice. We say it's time for a revival—throw in a roasted marshmallow or two for a perfect winter's night.

Reading List

Not to be missed: Gaskell's stories are often included in modern horror anthologies, particularly collections that focus on Victorian and Edwardian ghost stories, alongside such writers as M. R. James and Wilkie Collins. In 2004, Penguin published a collection of her ghost stories called *Gothic Tales* that includes some of her best work, including "The Poor Clare" and "The Old Nurse's Tale."

Also try: Gaskell's novella *Lois the Witch*, which looks at the Salem witch trials, is worth reading. The story is about an orphaned English girl who is sent to live with distant relatives in New England. Her Puritan family, however, doesn't fully understand the girl's English ways; the cultural confusion results in Lois, along with a Native American girl, being accused of witchcraft in the midst of the local witch hysteria. It's both a story about cultural misunderstandings and a warning about believing in cultural superiority.

Related work: While not as well known as Gaskell, Eliza Lynn Linton wrote short fiction in the Christmas ghost story vein. Her "Christmas Eve in Beach House" (*Routledge's Christmas Annual*, 1870) is a supernatural drama set against the Cornish coast.

"'I hear voices!' said she. 'I hear terrible screams— I hear my father's voice!'"

—"The Old Nurse's Story"

Charlotte Riddell

1832–1906

Why do ghosts come back to haunt the living? Maybe the afterlife doesn't live up to expectations. How great can the great beyond be given how many ghosts spend eternity hanging around abandoned buildings and scaring teenagers who dare to sneak in? Occasionally, ghost stories center on a spirit whose agenda goes beyond haunting a specific place. As Charlotte Riddell's ghost stories suggest, some come back because they want their murder to be solved.

Charlotte Riddell played with traditional supernatural images in her stories, giving us familiar characters like the devil, the banshee, the poltergeist, and the cursed nun. Often her ghosts return to show the living where bodies are buried (or unburied), or where deeds are hidden, or to provide solutions to cold murder cases. Riddell's hauntings were usually connected to people through places and personal history, but occasionally she incorporated the phenomenon of precognition, rather than the strictly spectral. Like Elizabeth Gaskell (see page 53) she was known for penning social realism novels and was a prolific ghost story writer.

Riddell's ghost stories marked a phantasmal paradigm shift. In early nineteenth-century stories, a ghost was typically a sort of metaphorical mirror for the protagonist, reflecting what was already haunting the character. Consider, for example, Washington Irving's ghost of Henry Hudson, who visits Rip Van Winkle in his long sleep in the Catskills, or the spirits that visit Ebenezer Scrooge in *A Christmas Carol* to teach him an important lesson. In these stories, supernatural beings are meant to help the living—not the other way around. Riddle's ghosts, however, have agency. They have lives (or afterlives, as the case may be) that exist beyond the character arc of the story's protagonist And they won't go away with a sprinkle of salt. Instead, they continue to wreak havoc until the living satisfy their demands.

Riddell's well-known short story "Nut Bush Farm" depicts a ghost who returns to reveal that a murder has occurred. The young man who rents the titular haunted farm initially doesn't believe in ghosts, but learns the truth the hard way. He also learns that they're very persistent, and if you try to stand in a ghost's way, it keeps going. . . which leaves you very cold and very scared. The story is primarily a neat little mystery; the narrator solves a murder by observing the ghost near a footbridge and then (after fainting) investigating on his own. In "A Strange Christmas Game," one of Riddell's holiday ghost stories, a young man and his sister inherit a haunted house from a wealthy family member whom they know next to nothing about. During the course of the tale, the siblings solve the murder of another relative, who mysteriously disappeared on a long-ago Christmas and has been haunting the home ever since. As one does.

Ghostwriter

In her life, Riddell was just as restless as her ghosts. She forged a career in writing and publishing that many women authors of the time only dreamed of. Her mother said that as a young girl Riddell invented stories before she could even hold a pen in her tiny hands, dictating them to her mother. A friend of Riddell's mother worried that encouraging the budding writer was akin to teaching her to lie and told her that writing should be avoided at all costs. It's a good thing Riddell didn't listen.

Called "a born story-teller" by the literary critic S. M. Ellis, the Irish-born Charlotte Eliza Lawson Cowan wrote more than fifty novels and short stories to support herself and her husband (until his death in 1880). She also did editorial work for the magazine *Home* and *St. James Magazine*, which she co-owned briefly with its founder, Anna Maria Hall. In the

nineteenth century, publishing was dominated by men. Women authors often had trouble breaking into the industry and making any kind of livable wage—especially considering they were often paid less than men for their work. To even the playing field somewhat, some established their own magazines and presses.

Early in her career Riddell published under the pseudonym F. G. Trafford, before settling on the Victorian commonplace of using her married name, Mrs. J. H. Riddell. Rumors swirled about her husband being in prison at one point. True or not, his inability to support himself was evident, and the constantly indebted Riddells faced bankruptcy. Nevertheless, Riddell proved just as stubborn as the spirits in her stories, refusing to let go of her passion, no matter what obstacles arose. Her family survived on the payments she earned for her writing, though she lamented that she always felt rushed because of their financial problems. Her personal story did not have a happy ending; she died penniless, still trying to write despite being ill with cancer and accepting financial help from the Society of Authors.

Fortunately, her stories survived, so we will always have a good Riddell ghost tale to keep us up at night.

"He wrung his hands with a despairing gesture, and disappeared. At the same moment, moon, dell, bridge, and stream faded from my sight—and I fainted."

—"Nut Bush Farm"

Reading List

Not to be missed: A collection of Charlotte Riddell's work, titled *Weird Stories*, was published in 1882 by James Hogg. *The Collected Ghost Stories of Mrs. J. H. Riddell* (Dover, 1977) is one of the most complete recent collections, and several newer collections exist, including *The Open Door* (Dodo Press, 2008) and a new edition of *Weird Stories* (Victorian Secrets, 2009), which includes some of her best-loved tales: "The Open Door," "Nut Bush Farm," "Sandy the Tinker," and "Old Mrs. Jones." Most of her stories are still in print, largely due to the efforts of literary critics and academics dedicated to keeping her works in the public arena, though we think a more complete collection of her work is long overdue. You'll often find a Riddell tale or two included in Victorian ghost story anthologies, such as volume three of the excellent compilation *The Valancourt Book of Victorian Ghost Stories* (Valancourt Books, 2018).

Also try: Riddell participated in the Victorian trend of Christmas horror tales with her novellas *Fairy Water*, *An Uninhabited House*, *The Haunted River*, and *The Disappearance of Mr. Jeremiah Redworth*, all of which were published in serial and book form throughout the 1870s and into the 1880s. In 2019 British Library Publishing republished *Fairy Water* and *An Uninhabited House* as *Haunted Houses*, edited by Andrew Smith.

Related work: Victorian ghost stories written by women are becoming increasingly hard to find. For a deeper dive into this storytelling tradition, we recommend Ellen Wood. Her story "The Ghost of the Hollow Field" makes for perfect fireside reading on a wintry night.

The Most Learned Woman
Amelia Edwards
1831–1892

Picture a writer, a world traveler, an expert in ancient Egyptian. An adventurer who traversed dangerous mountains and sailed the Nile to excavate tombs of pharaohs, in search of treasures from antiquity.

Are you imagining Indiana Jones? You're not far off. Amelia Edwards's story sounds like something straight out of a Steven Spielberg summer blockbuster.

She was born Amelia Ann Blanford Edwards in London in 1831. Her father was a banker; her mother educated young Amelia at home. From childhood, Edwards gravitated toward the literary, publishing her first story at age twelve (or perhaps age nine, according to some scholars, though the only known facts are that it may have been a submission to a contest). She proved to be an intelligent and creative child, showing talent in not only writing but also painting and music. By her twenties Edwards was focusing solely on writing, publishing her first novel, *My Brother's Wife*, in 1855 (Harper) and, after her father lost his banking job, supporting her parents as a journalist for the *Saturday Review* and the *Morning Post*.

Edwards loved to travel and published books about her adventures in Italy and France. But her life changed in the winter of 1873–74, when the gloomy, rainy climate of Europe prompted a trip to Egypt, where she found the sunny climate much more appealing. She and Lucy Renshawe, her travel companion, hired a boat and sailed the Nile River, a trip that resulted in one of her most popular travel books, *Thousand Miles Up the Nile* (Longmans, Green & Co., 1877). With the publication of that book, Edwards traded in her ink and pen for a career as a researcher. She taught herself to read hieroglyphs and worked to maintain the integrity of archeological digs, after witnessing the appallingly improper handling and care of artifacts. Following her trips to Egypt, Edwards spent the 1880s and 1890s lecturing in Britain and the United States on a wide variety of subjects relating to archeology and Egyptology, including the role of women explorers in a male-dominated field. In 1882 she founded the Egypt Exploration Fund in order to ensure that future Egyptian studies would be handled with care.

Of all her writing, Edwards was probably proudest of her travel books, in which she detailed her adventures and her work in various archeological digs across Egypt, so much so that, by the end of her career, her writing largely focused on travel. She often wrote about the inspiration and emotion that landscapes stirred in her, as in this description of traveling through the Italian mountains:

"The Dolomites! It was a full fifteen years since I had first seen the sketches of them made by a great artist not long since passed away, and their strange outlines and stranger colouring had haunted me ever since. I thought of them as every summer came round; I regretted them every autumn; I cherished dim hopes about them every spring. Sketching about Venice in a gondola a year before the time of which I write, I used to be ever looking towards the faint blue peaks beyond Murano."

Edwards's prose, which was very accessible to the average reader, made her a popular author. Her beautiful and haunting descriptions of her travels are well worth seeking out.

The Still of the Night

But Edwards's fiction is what most interests us and earns her a spot among the top writers of the Victorian ghost story. She wrote extensively—poetry and novels in addition to travel writing—and though her ghost stories were only a small part of her career, she excelled at this format. Edwards's creepy tales were not always intended to frighten and they included neither gore nor violence. Rather, they were quieter fare, meant to be enjoyed by a fireside, given the gentle chills they induce.

"The Story of Salome" (*Tinsley's Christmas Annual*, 1867) is a perfect example. In this tale, a young man traveling across Europe spies the most beautiful woman he has ever seen. She's breathtaking, but this mysterious woman also possesses a quiet sadness . . . appropriately so, given that she's visiting a grave when the man first sees her. Our hero is so taken with his new love that he returns to said grave to take a rubbing of it. The inscription is in Hebrew, which he cannot read, so he sends it off to a friend to decipher. The romantic hero's obsession grows until he must find out everything he can about this woman—which leads him to discover that he is in love with a ghost. Cue spooky music.

Another classic, quietly ghostly Edwards tale is the short story "The Phantom Coach" (*All the Year Round*, 1864). A lonely and lost man. A snowstorm. A strange and possibly deadly encounter with the unknown. Edwards is at her best when describing a haunting landscape, probably thanks to her skills honed while writing about her travels. Here's how she sets the scene:

"Although the wind had fallen, it was still bitterly cold. Not a star glimmered in the black vault overhead. Not a sound, save the rapid crunching of the snow beneath our feet, disturbed the heavy stillness of the night."

She so excelled at evoking an eerie atmosphere that readers would have shivers even before the ghost showed up.

Edwards was a fierce defender of women's rights, proving through her journeys that a woman could do anything a man could and using her writing talent to further the cause. Her heroines were usually headstrong and fiercely intelligent, like the title character of her novel *Barbara's History* (1864), which tells the story of an awkward but intelligent orphan who falls for a mysterious older man with a secret. It's a bit like *Jane Eyre*, and the novel was successful enough to boost Edwards's literary career. She was among the first writers published in the *English Woman's Journal*, a periodical established in 1858 and run by women's rights activist Emily Faithfull. Later in life, Edwards became an active member and, at one point, vice president of the Society for Promoting Women's Suffrage. Her work in Egyptology earned her the title "the most learned woman in the world," bestowed by the *Boston Globe*.

These days Amelia Edwards has become an important figure among defenders of gay and lesbian rights. Edwards flouted convention by often traveling with female rather than male companions. One such companion was Ellen Braysher, who would become Edwards's longtime travel partner (and possible romantic partner, though Edwards was never outspoken on the subject). Edwards died of influenza at age sixty-one and was buried, fittingly, under an Egyptian obelisk and stone ankh. She was interred beside Ellen, who had passed away only a few months before. A marker commemorates the lives of these adventurous spirits, and the site has become a place of pilgrimage for the LGBTQ community in the United Kingdom and beyond.

Reading List

Not to be missed: *The Collected Supernatural and Weird Fiction of Amelia B. Edwards*, published by Leonaur in 2009, contains twenty spooky tales as well as two adventure novellas.

Also try: Edwards's accounts of traveling up the Nile are still readily available. Norton Creek Press released a fully illustrated edition in 2008. As with Elizabeth Gaskell and Charlotte Riddell, her works are often included in anthologies of Victorian and Edwardian ghost stories. Her story "The Four-Fifteen Express," originally published in 1867, can be found in *The Wimbourne Book of Victorian Ghost Stories* (Wimbourne Books, 2018).

Related work: Like Edwards, the American author Barbara Mertz, who earned a PhD in Egyptology, was interested in studying other cultures in order to write fiction. She used her knowledge to write mystery books. We recommend the Amelia Peabody series (William Morrow, 1975–2010 and 2017), about a plucky and adventurous woman who is inspired partly by Amelia Edwards.

His face was as purple as a corpse and his lips were pulled back as if in the agony of death, showing his bright teeth."

—*"The Phantom Coach"*

The Most Productive Writer
Pauline E. Hopkins
1859–1930

The history of African American speculative writing goes back to the nineteenth and early twentieth centuries, beginning with writers such as Martin Delany and his alternate-history serialized novel *Blake; or, The Huts of America* (1859–1862), Sutton Griggs's 1899 utopian novel *Imperium in Imperio*, Charles Chesnutt's 1899 story collection *The Conjure Woman*, and W. E. B. Du Bois's apocalyptic tale "The Comet" (1920). All are engaging examples of speculative fiction that grappled with the racism of the day. Another writer who worked in this vein during this period is Pauline Elizabeth Hopkins.

Hopkins's name may not be familiar to twenty-first-century readers, but according to the scholar Richard Yarborough, she was "the single most productive black woman writer at the turn of the century." He notes that between 1900 and 1905 Hopkins published four novels, at least seven short stories, a historical booklet about Africa, more than twenty biographical sketches, and numerous essays and feature articles for the magazines *The Colored American* (for which she was literary editor from 1903 to 1904) and *The Voice of the Negro*.

Pauline E. Hopkins was born in Portland, Maine, in 1859 and raised in Boston. She was interested in writing and the arts at a young age; when she was fifteen years old, her essay "Evils of Intemperance and Their Remedy" won a writing contest sponsored by abolitionist writer William Wells Brown. As a young woman, Hopkins wrote plays and acted and sang in a performing group called the Hopkins Colored Troubadours, which included her family members and friends. Although much of her work as a playwright has been lost, Yarborough notes that a record exists of a play she wrote titled *Slaves' Escape; or, The Underground Railroad*, which her troupe performed in 1880. She often gave lectures on important figures in African American history. Like all writers, Hopkins needed a day job in addition to her creative work, so she studied stenography and worked for the Massachusetts Bureau of Statistics and Labor and the Massachusetts Institute of Technology, among other institutions.

Hopkins is best known to literary critics and historians for her novel *Contending Forces: A Romance Illustrative of Negro Life North and South* (Colored Co-operative, 1900). The book, an example of the eighteenth-century literary genre known as sentimentalism, addressed racial issues in society by influencing readers' emotions. This was a common characteristic of abolitionist writing and the work of African American activists and allies during and after Reconstruction. Sentimentalists would offer noble and morally strong protagonists and build readers' compassion for characters who worked to better their financial standing and achieve education. These writers also strove to build sympathy for characters who were victims of abuse, such as young women whose virtue was under siege by unsavory villains. *Contending Forces* challenged damaging and horrific stereotypes of black sexuality, including misconceptions that African American men were a danger to white women and that African American women were responsible for sexual abuse inflicted upon them by slaveholders. The book also contained elements of the supernatural.

Hopkins's fourth novel, *Of One Blood; or, The Hidden Self*, serialized in *The Colored American* from 1902 to 1903, fully embraced the speculative themes of the day, incorporating a "lost race" archeological adventure with romance and aspects of the occult, from mesmerism and spiritualism to ghosts to automatic writing. The protagonist, Reuel Briggs, is a medical student who hides his African American identity and has an interest in mysticism and the occult. He falls in love with a woman whom he sees in dreams and then meets in real life performing at a concert. On Halloween, he and some colleagues are investigating the grounds of a haunted house, and she appears to him again and asks for his help. When she shows up seemingly dead at the hospital where Briggs studies, he employs his mystical knowledge and revives her with a vial of life-giving powder of his own formulation. As the story progresses, Briggs is unlucky in love, and he sets out on an archaeological trip to Africa to look for artifacts and treasures. Instead he discovers a hidden country untouched by colonialism. (Sounds familiar to anyone who has seen the 2018 film *Black Panther*.) This lost civilization is the root of all culture and knowledge on Earth, much older than any Western civilization. Briggs finds more than he bargained for, and if you read the book, so will you.

Reading List

Not to be missed: *Of One Blood* is a reworking of the tropes in Victorian-age "lost race" books like *She* by H. Rider Haggard (serialized in *The Graphic* magazine, 1886–87), upending those novels' Eurocentric views of Africa. Washington Square Press reprinted the novel in 2010 with an introduction by scholar Deborah McDowell.

Related work: Nisi Shawl's book *Everfair* (Tor, 2016) is set in the time of European expansion into Africa and focuses on the town of Everfair, a utopia carved out of the Belgian Congo for native people. It's also a steampunk tale that explores what developing steam-power technology in the late nineteenth century could have meant for communities living in the Congo. Shawl wrote an article for Tor.com about Hopkins's novel, entitled "What Men Have Put Asunder: Pauline Hopkins' *Of One Blood*," in June 2018.

Anyone interested in African American speculative fiction should check out the collection *Dark Matter: A Century of Speculative Fiction from the African Diaspora* (Warner Books, 2000) edited by Sheree R. Thomas. The table of contents includes names well known to readers of speculative fiction and horror, such as Linda Addison, Tananarive Due, Nalo Hopkinson, Octavia Butler, and Samuel R. Delany, as well as Shawl and Hopkins's peers Charles Chesnutt and W. E. B. Du Bois. Sadly, Hopkins is not included.

> # "The supernatural presides over man's formation always."
>
> —*Of One Blood; or, The Hidden Self*

Ghostwriter à la Garçonne
Vernon Lee
1856–1935

Ghosts and hauntings are related, but not exactly the same thing. Ghosts are specters of the past—people who have lived before and cannot quite leave this mortal realm behind. But hauntings are more broadly defined. People can be haunted by ideas, by the past, by an obsession. Inanimate objects can be haunted as well, holding on to some nameless evil or trauma that won't dissipate. Vernon Lee's brand of supernatural fiction fits this latter category: less about ghosts resolving their mortal issues and more about people who can't escape their own psychology. Lee's characters are women obsessed with strange ancestors, or men who are artistically—and sometimes sexually—frustrated. And they're all dangerously preoccupied with, and almost possessed by, the past.

"Vernon Lee" was the pen name of the British writer Violet Paget, who became known for her supernatural tales as well her views on aesthetics. Born in 1856 to expatriate British parents living in France, Lee led a wandering existence. Her mother, Matilda, was an heiress, though her inheritance was locked in legal battles. So they were not exactly poor, but the Pagets frequently had to move to more affordable locales. Violet was a bright child who spoke several languages; she was friends with John Singer Sargent (who would later gain fame as an artist) and his sister Emily. The children reportedly played together frequently; a favorite game was to read about historical executions in books and then act them out. Emily and Violet remained close throughout their adult lives.

Violet enjoyed writing from an early age, publishing her first story (in French no less) called *"Les aventures d'une pièce de monnaie"* in 1870, when she was fourteen years old, in the Swiss magazine *La Famille*. The story is about the adventures of a coin as it travels from person to person, moving through history. As she continued to write, her work showed her range of interests, from history to art to philosophy, and particularly the philosophy of aesthetics, or the study of beauty. In 1873, her mother finally received her full inheritance, and the family settled in Florence, a place that Violet would always consider home.

In 1875, Paget adopted the public name of Vernon Lee, though she would alternate between the two in her personal life. At that time it wasn't imperative for a woman to adopt a male name in order to be published—Lee's female contemporaries were writing under their own names—but Lee felt that she would not be taken seriously as an art critic and philosopher if she used a woman's name. According to Vineta Colby's 2003 biography, Lee said, "No one reads a woman's writings on art, history and aesthetics with anything but unmitigated contempt."

Spectral Psychology

We may think of people who lived during the Victorian era and the decades after as staid, prudish, buttoned up, and intolerant, but Lee wore her feminism—and, during World War I, her pacifism—on her sleeve. In fact, she literally used her wardrobe to show how she felt about Victorian conventions. In an 1881 painting by Sargent, she wears men's clothing (known as *à la garçonne*, or more masculine "gentlewoman," fashion), highlighting her famous androgynous style. Her choice of Vernon as a pen name shows a rebellious attitude toward social constructions of gender (as was Lee, which was her half-brother Eugene's surname).

She also was openly involved in long-term romantic relationships with women, including the writer Mary Robinson, beginning in 1878. At this time, Lee was writing prolifically, sometimes publishing more than one work per year; her highly praised book on art, *Studies of the Eighteenth Century in Italy,* was published during their relationship. Also during this prolific period, Lee began a friendship with the author Henry James, to whom she would dedicate her 1884 novel *Miss Brown* (W. Blackwood). (James hated the book, saying it wasn't representative of Lee's talent.) Unfortunately, the happy streak did not last.

Robinson broke off their relationship in 1887 and married a man soon after. Lee almost immediately began a new relationship with Clementina "Kit" Anstruther-Thomson. Lee, who had always been prone to anxiety, struggled to recover from Robinson's abrupt departure, and her writing changed significantly following the breakup. Roughly from 1889 to 1902, she began to write more supernatural tales, particularly with a psychological haunting at their core. In an essay in her book *Belcaro* (W. Satchell, 1881), she detailed her thoughts on how hauntings and ghosts function in art and literature: "We none of us believe in ghosts as logical possibilities, but we most of us conceive them as imaginative probabilities. . . . By *ghost* we do not mean the vulgar apparition which is seen or heard in told or written in tales; we mean the ghost which slowly rises up in our mind, the haunter not of corridors and staircases, but of our fancies."

Ghosts interested Lee not because they could be real, but because of what they revealed about the people telling (and reading) the stories about them. Her ghost stories were less chilling and more psychological excavations into how humanity sees itself.

Lee's two best known supernatural works were the short novel *A Phantom Lover* (Roberts Brothers, 1886) and the collection *Hauntings* (Heinemann, 1890). In her preface to *Hauntings*, she dismissed the investigations of psychical societies and their attempts to collect evidence of genuine ghosts. In Lee's view, people tell and read such stories because ghosts are mysterious, weird, and strange. Ghosts engage our imaginations.

Her stories often feature women who defy societal expectations in their behavior and dress. One of the female characters in *A Phantom Lover* is a cross-dresser with a penchant for Elizabethan fashion who becomes the object of another woman's obsession. Lee's hauntings often manifest as possessions, allowing her to explore lesbian love and women's relationships as subtext, at a time when society did not accept them.

UGLY ENDING

Vernon Lee's longest love connection was with Clementina "Kit" Anstruther-Thomson. In her 2003 biography of Lee, Vineta Colby described their partnership as a type of marriage. It was brought down by scandal—but not over their same-sex relationship. Lee was struck by Kit's physical responses to beauty and adapted her aesthetic theories accordingly. Together the couple wrote an essay about the physical and emotional experience of art, titled "Beauty and Ugliness." The pair was accused of plagiarism, and though the accusations were later discredited, Kit never recovered from the stress of the controversy, and the relationship did not survive.

Reading List

Not to be missed: Vernon Lee's ghost stories are best when she relies on her education in history and art to help set the stage. Broadview Press published *Hauntings and Other Fantastic Tales* in 2006, a collection of

"'If there are such things as ghosts,' he replied, 'I don't think they should be taken lightly. God would not permit them to be, except as a warning or a punishment.'"

—Oke of Okehurst; or, A Phantom Lover

Lee's best-known ghostly tales. "A Phantom Lover" is set in an English manor house, but many of her other supernatural stories take place in Germany, Spain, or Italy. "Amour Dure" is about a historian who falls in love with a woman he sees in a medieval painting. Another selection worth seeking out is "Prince Alberic and the Snake Lady," which involves a tapestry that features a snake-tailed woman whose image haunts the protagonist.

Also try: For those interested in Lee's life, the scholar Vineta Colby wrote *Vernon Lee: A Literary Biography* (University of Virginia Press, 2003), a meticulously researched biography that takes readers through Lee's bohemian childhood and into her remarkable life as an intellectual and writer.

Related work: Readers who like a bit of psychology and art with their spirits may enjoy Charlotte Perkins Gilman's "The Yellow Wall-Paper" (first published in the *New England Magazine*, January 1892). The ghosts in this story dwell not in the walls but in the mind of the main character, whose psychosis only worsens when her access to art and society is taken away from her. The story is widely anthologized and should be read by anyone interested in psychological horror.

— *Voice for the Dead* —
Margaret Oliphant

1828–1897

Atmospheric ghost stories are never quite as well done as when they're written by Margaret Oliphant. Perhaps that's because she wrote like her life depended on it . . . which it kind of did.

Oliphant published profusely, even by the standards of the other prolific authors in this book, producing nearly one hundred novels, more than fifty short stories, and various nonfiction pieces, essays, and reviews. Her body of work reveals her as the shrewd voice of a generation, a skilled storyteller with a keen eye for social commentary. Why aren't more people talking about Margaret Oliphant?

Oliphant's critical reputation may have been killed by her copious output. Meaning, perhaps she wrote herself into obscurity. Her output was so great that critics of the day viewed her as a sensational writer, one whose writing was meant to be enjoyed quickly by the masses and then tossed aside, rather than as a true literary talent.

The truth is, Oliphant wrote furiously because she had no other choice.

Margaret Oliphant began her literary career in her Scottish homeland when she was only twenty-one years old, upon the publication of her first novel, *Passages*

in the Life of Mrs Margaret Maitland (H. Colburn, 1850). Shortly after, she married a stained-glass artist named Francis "Frank" Oliphant and moved to London, where she continued to write, becoming a regular in *Blackwood's Magazine*, famed for publishing the work of Percy Bysshe Shelley and Sir Walter Scott. Despite its ties to Romanticism, *Blackwood's* was an important publisher of horror fiction, and the stories in its pages would later influence Edgar Allan Poe and other masters of the genre.

When Oliphant's husband died of tuberculosis in 1859, leaving her to care for their three surviving children (three others had died in infancy), her writing took on a fevered speed. Given the dearth of career choices available to women in the late 1800s, Oliphant was forced to make money any way she could. She was good at writing and had proved that the family could live off her earnings while her husband was ill. Now her writing was the only income the family had. By the end of her life, Margaret Oliphant was taking care of an alcoholic brother and some of her nieces and nephews; by 1894, all her children had perished from illness.

God Is Silent

Though she wrote historical novels and other genres, Oliphant's talent shone brightest when she tackled horror and supernatural fiction. Her 1882 story "The Open Door" (*Blackwood's Edinburgh Magazine*, January 1882) is an atmospheric tale that relies on terror simmering just offstage. The format is familiar: A man takes his family to an old estate, where they are tormented by a ghostly voice on the other side of a doorway in a crumbling castle wall, crying to be let in. But Oliphant is masterful in crafting the suspense, pulling it tight, a bit like a noose around a throat, as a ghostly child calls for its mother: "Oh, Mother, let me in! Oh, Mother, let me in! Let me in!"

Though she hasn't been discussed by critics as much as her contemporaries, Oliphant had her fans. In his 1929 essay "Some Remarks on

Ghost Stories," the English author M. R. James wrote that "the religious ghost story, as it may be called, was never done better than by Mrs. Oliphant in 'The Open Door' and 'A Beleaguered City.'" Oliphant's use of religion and the supernatural is more complex than James suggests. Many of her ghost stories revolve around a supernatural element that presupposes a life after death, often one which seems incompatible with the Christian idea of heaven, or even the Christian deity.

Oliphant's characters tend to question God, or at least religious faith, when confronted with the supernatural. If the dead from the past return to haunt the present, then surely God, as compared to science, holds the answers. But in Oliphant's stories, there is no deus ex machina—no God will offer help. It's of note that Oliphant usually doesn't use the name of God in her supernatural stories or refer to anything explicitly religious. Rather, they hint at a Christian paradigm that's being tested.

Oliphant mixes these Christian elements with trauma. The spaces where her stories unfold—crumbling castles, old manor houses—are haunted by a long history of abuse. Her characters crave relief in comfortable constructs like religion, but often relief is not easily found. It would seem that, according to Oliphant at least, the past can never truly be conquered. It can only be confronted, no matter how painful doing so may be.

Reading List

Not to be missed: Over the past few decades several academic presses have published reprints of Oliphant's work. Canongate Classics compiled her ghostly tales in 2009 in *A Beleaguered City and Other Tales of the Seen and Unseen*, which includes some of her best work, such as "The Open Door" and the short novel *A Beleaguered City*, about a small town besieged by the dead returning. It's not quite the zombie apoca-

"Oh, Mother, let me in! Oh, Mother, let me in! Let me in!"

—"The Open Door"

lypse envisioned by filmmakers like George Romero, but it's an eerie read nonetheless.

Also try: "The Open Door" was adapted for television in 1966 for the BBC's *Mystery and Imagination* anthology series (season 1, episode 4).

Related work: Oliphant often draws comparisons to other female supernatural writers of her day. Her name is usually joined to Mary Elizabeth Braddon and Rhoda Broughton (though Oliphant openly criticized the latter for her purple prose). Broughton's story "The Truth, the Whole Truth, and Nothing but the Truth" (*Temple Bar*, February 1868), in which letters exchanged between women slowly build tension, and Braddon's "At Chrighton Abbey" (*Belgravia*, May 1871), about a cursed mansion in which would-be grooms are killed before their weddings, are worth a read.

❖ *The Spine-Tingler* ❖
Edith Wharton

1862–1937

Edith Wharton once wrote that a good ghost story should send "the cold shiver down one's spine." She called this the "thermometrical quality" of a supernatural tale. Wharton may have been more attuned than most to this spectral quality. According to an often-told anecdote, as a young woman she was so deathly afraid of ghost stories that she wouldn't even sleep in a house that had a book of them somewhere inside. So how did she end up writing some of the most spine-tingling tales of the twentieth century? Some suggest that she did so precisely to get over her fear.

Wharton was born Edith Newbold Jones on January 24, 1862, in New York City. The youngest of three children (and the only girl), Wharton was given a broad education, which was still unusual for girls at that time. Her family traveled across Europe, visiting France, Spain, and Italy, and young Edith learned languages, art, and history. In 1870 her parents took her and her siblings to Germany, where Wharton fell dangerously ill with typhoid fever. While recovering, she relied on books— mostly fairy tales and ghost stories—to stave off boredom. She was still petrified by these stories, but her dread had morphed into a kind of morbid fascination and she became entranced by what she feared. Wharton recovered for a while, but then suffered a relapse. She would ultimately regain full health, but this period changed her. In a biographical fragment she called "My Life and I," Wharton writes:

"When I came to myself, it was to enter a world haunted by formless fears. I had been a naturally fearless child; now I lived in a state of chronic fear."

She described her newfound terror as "some dark indefinable menace, forever dogging my steps, lurking and threatening."

A few years later, the family returned to New York City, where Wharton continued her education via private tutoring at home. Following her illness, Wharton suffered from anxiety and hallucinations that plagued her into early adulthood. They faded after a few years but would return when she was older, following the death of her mother. Though horrible to experience, these hallucinations and fears also provided inspiration as she penned her ghost stories.

In 1885, Wharton was twenty-three years old and nearly considered an old maid, so she settled into married life with Edward "Teddy" Robbins Wharton. Theirs wasn't a passionate affair, but married life suited her, and she began writing. She published her first novel at age forty. Wharton's career would outlast her marriage; the couple divorced in 1913.

The Other Works of Edith Wharton

Like many authors of the supernatural who preceded her, such as Elizabeth Gaskell and Charles Dickens, Wharton has been remembered primarily for her realist fiction, especially in the classroom (unless it's a class taught by one of the authors of this book). She was the first woman to win a Pulitzer Prize for literature, in 1921, for her novel *The Age of Innocence* (D. Appleton & Co., 1920). She was nominated for a Nobel Prize in 1927, 1928, and 1930. She wrote celebrated novels such as *The House of Mirth* (Charles Scribner's Sons, 1905) and *Ethan Frome* (Charles Scribner's Sons, 1911) and short stories, including "Roman Fever" (November 1934, *Liberty*). During her career, realist fiction was the fashion, and hers received more critical attention than did her ghost stories.

Like her contemporary and friend Henry James, Wharton often focused on the privileged upper class of America, and she was not afraid

to skewer the foibles of her own cohort. Also similar to James, who had a fascination with the Societies for Psychical Research (more on them in the next chapter) and wrote *The Turn of the Screw* (Macmillan, 1898) among numerous other supernatural tales, Wharton was intrigued by ghost stories. To ignore the ones she penned is to paint an incomplete picture of one of the twentieth century's great writers.

In 1937 Wharton collected her eleven supernatural stories in one volume, appropriately titled *Ghosts* (Appleton Century). These tales, and her characters, are often preoccupied with the past. In one popular story, "The Eyes," the main character is telling his dinner guests a story about a pair of ghostly eyes that followed him in his youth. The story takes a spine-tingling, and ironic, turn as the storyteller realizes the eyes belonged to him—his older self was looking (rather) disapprovingly on the adventures of his youth. "The Eyes" is indicative of Wharton's supernatural style; she likes the cozy setting of the Victorian Christmas ghost story (think fireside tales told in drawing rooms with snifters of brandy, or in Gothic-style libraries surrounded by stacks of dusty tomes). But though Wharton's staging is decidedly Victorian, her scares are not muted, and she often detours into unexpected territory. "Bewitched" is a creepy vampire tale set in a small, rural New England village reminiscent of Ethan Frome's neighborhood. "Kerfol" is a ghost story that adds spectral dogs into the mix, and "All Souls" takes on the possibility of witchcraft at the end of October, the spookiest time of year.

Anyone who has read "Roman Fever" knows that Wharton loves a twist ending, and her story "Afterward" has one of her best. The protagonist Ned Boyne wants to purchase a haunted house for fun. He and his wife buy a home that they are assured has a ghost, but they won't know for sure "till afterward." Ned is unimpressed—until his past catches up to him and he gets more than he bargained for.

Reading List

Not to be missed: It's no surprise to anyone who's taken a university literature class that Edith Wharton is still widely published today. Short-story collections abound, and our favorite is *The Ghost Stories of Edith Wharton* (Wordsworth Editions, 2009), which includes favorites like "Afterword" and "Kerfol." We especially recommend "Miss Mary Pask," another chiller that shows off Wharton's talent for unexpected endings.

Also try: Wharton's popularity has not waned since her death in 1937. Several collections of her short fiction are available, including books devoted entirely to her ghostly stories. Along with the ones mentioned above, we recommend seeking out "Bewitched," which originally appeared in *Here and Beyond* (1926). Farmer Saul Rutledge is cheating on his wife, who is understandably upset. Complicating matters is the fact that Saul's lover has been dead for quite a while. The love triangle between man, wife, and ghost only gets stranger as the story unfolds.

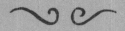

"The light went out, and I stood there—we stood there—lost to each other in the roaring coiling darkness."

—"Miss Mary Pask"

PART THREE

Cult of the Occult

When you consider the 1984 film *Ghostbusters*—or the 2016 romp of a reboot—and the glut of ghost hunter shows available on multiple cable channels any time of the day, any day of the week, ghost hunting seems like a modern enterprise. Not so! Fictional experts of supernatural investigation and battling negative entities go back all the way to Fitz James-O'Brien's character Harry Escott, who first appeared in "The Pot of Tulips" (*Harper's*, November 1855), Sheridan Le Fanu's occult detective Dr. Martin Hesselius from *In a Glass Darkly* (Richard Bentley & Son, 1872), and of course Bram Stoker's vampire hunter, Abraham Van Helsing, from *Dracula* (Archibald Constable, 1897). Following Sherlock Holmes's debut in 1887, the concept of an eccentric private detective with a sidekick was quickly adapted to stories of paranormal investigation. The resulting genre of occult detection owes its popularity to several women writers whom you're about to meet.

Outside the realm of fiction, fascination with the occult reached a peak by the late nineteenth century, in both England and the United States. This expanding interest was a result of the Spiritualist movement (see pages 50–52). Though Spiritualism was fading in popularity by century's end, its ideas never disappeared completely (in fact, the movement saw renewed interest after the First World War). Multiple groups formed to attempt the organized, scientific study of supernatural phenomena. Prominent examples include the Society for Psychical Research, founded in the United Kingdom in 1882, followed by the American Society for Psychical Research in 1885. These organizations originated with professors of philosophy, the sciences, psychology, and the classics at universities like Trinity College, Cambridge, and Harvard. But their membership reached beyond the halls of academe.

Writers of supernatural fiction were irresistibly drawn to these groups. Algernon Blackwood and Dion Fortune were members of the Hermetic Order of the Golden Dawn and its spin-off factions, which favored occult and magical interpretations of the unknown, as opposed to the psychical societies' more objective and skeptical attitudes. Another member likely familiar to our readers is the prominent occultist Aleister Crowley, whose belief system called Thelema incorporated ceremonial magic (with quite a bit of sexual "magick") and a blend of Eastern and Western religions and philosophies. Think mysticism mixed with Egyptian gods and goddesses, piled on top of an orgy, and you have a good, if not completely accurate, idea of what Crowley was experimenting with.

Other writers of fiction, including Henry James (whose brother William was a founder of the American Society for Psychical Research), Vernon Lee, Mark Twain, Arthur Conan Doyle, and Margery Lawrence, were members of the Societies for Psychical Research, or at least interested in their investigations. Ghost stories written in the late nineteenth century would commonly mention the society and its work. Arthur Conan Doyle disapproved of the psychical societies' skepticism, and he eventually aligned with Spiritualist groups.

The resulting literature is just as wild as one would expect. In these stories, ghosts are rarely dead people who can't find their way into the light. Sometimes they're not even ghosts; these writers imagined and experimented with more entities lurking in the great beyond. After all, it didn't have to be just your dead Uncle Frank reaching through the great veil of death. Who knows what might be hiding in the shadows where occultists go ghost hunting?

Scribe of the Supernatural
Marjorie Bowen

1885–1952

She was born, at least according to her autobiography, in the hour between All Saints Day and All Souls Day. She grew up in a haunted house. And, appropriately, she would become one of the most prolific writers of the ghost story and influence horror writers for decades to come.

Marjorie Bowen was one of the many pseudonyms of the British writer Margaret Campbell, author of more than 150 published books. She wrote her first, *The Viper of Milan* (McClure, Phillips, 1906), when she was only sixteen years old. The novel went on to be a best seller, setting the stage for her to emerge as a literary celebrity. Remarkably, her talent for writing was largely self-taught.

Born Margaret Gabrielle Vere Campbell in Hampshire, England, Bowen learned quickly to fend for herself. Her father was a kind man, but he struggled with alcohol addiction and walked out on the family when Bowen was only five years old. Around 1905 he died homeless on the streets in London, leaving Margaret to be raised by a single mother with limited savings and a volatile temper (though she was beautiful, charming, and smart). Any money available for education was allotted to her older siblings. Margaret was close to her nurse, Nana, who taught her to read, and she spent much of her childhood in the library. A favorite book was Alfred, Lord Tennyson's *Idylls of the King* (Edward Moxon, 1859–85). Nana also filled the girl's imagination with fairy tales that would keep Margaret enrapt for hours.

Throughout her childhood, Bowen's mother moved the family to several homes in and around London, with a constant parade of artists, actors, and writers marching in and out of the household. In her autobiography, Bowen writes about several encounters with haunted houses. She describes experiencing as a child what modern readers might consider night terrors—nightmares that prevented sleep. But as she grew older, she encouraged Nana to tell her stories of the rumored murders that occurred nearby.

With dreams of becoming an artist, Bowen enrolled in the Slade School of Arts in London. Her instructors deemed her talentless, so she left school and took work as a research assistant in the British Museum, an opportunity she made the most of, reading and learning as much as she could.

Next, Bowen's mother pushed her to go to Paris to pursue the arts. Bowen struggled to sell her artwork and sent home what little money she earned. Her mother mismanaged the family's finances, so Bowen cut short her artistic career yet again and returned home. She became the family's sole breadwinner by writing to help pay the bills. Unfortunately, Bowen's mother had a habit of spending the money as soon as it came in.

Bowen's first book, the Renaissance drama *The Viper of Milan*, was rejected by eleven publishers, who considered its violence inappropriate for a woman writer. Bowen persisted, and the book she had begun writing as a teenager was finally published in 1906, when Bowen was twenty-one years old. She turned her entire paycheck over to her struggling family, but her mother—who'd once had her own dreams of being a writer—quickly grew jealous of her daughter's success. Bowen wrote that her mother would discourage any dreams of literary achievement.

Certified Haunted

Bowen enjoyed writing dramas that involved history, a love she had cultivated since working in the British Museum. But the trajectory of her literary career took a sharp turn when she—along with her mother,

Nana, and her siblings—moved to a new home. Strange things started happening, and Bowen worried that her childhood troubles had returned. She quickly realized, however, that what she was witnessing was more than just nightmares. The family heard footsteps walking up and down stairs, all night long. Through the walls, they heard the soft shuffling of feet, as if someone was pacing back and forth, but when Bowen would investigate, the rooms were always empty. Groaning emanated through the house. Lights constantly flickered. Eventually the family contacted the Society for Psychical Research, whose members investigated and determined the house to indeed be haunted—by madmen who had committed murder there years ago.

Yet, in a way, the haunting was a boon, for now Bowen began to write ghost stories, which sold quickly.

And once she started, Bowen didn't stop, becoming one of the most prolific writers of her time and a best seller in both the United States and Britain. Still, she never felt as though the money was enough. She continued supporting her family and paying off the debts her mother incurred for squandering her daughter's earnings on frivolous things.

In 1912, Bowen married Zefferino Emilio Costanza, who died of tuberculosis four years later. She remarried, to Arthur L. Long. With her two husbands, Bowen had four children though one daughter died in infancy. Through it all, she kept writing, producing more than 150 works under the pen name Marjorie Bowen, which she initially chose to differentiate her work from her mother's literary attempts. She also published under the names

FLORENCE FLANNERY,
BORN 1500

Joseph Shearing, George Preedy, and Robert Paye; she used multiple aliases to confound literary critics, many of whom believed that the work of prolific writers was somehow cheaper than that of their less productive counterparts.

Among her notable horror works are the novel *Black Magic. A Tale of the Rise and Fall of the Antichrist* (Alston Rivers, 1909) and two excellent short-story collections, *The Bishop of Hell and Other Stories* (The Bodley Head, 1949; Wordsworth Editions, 2006) and *The Last Bouquet: Some Twilight Tales* (The Bodley Head, 1933). Bowen's horror fiction often mixes the supernatural with Gothic traditions. Her story "Scoured Silk" (first published in 1918 in *All-Story Weekly*, collected a year later in Bowen's *Crimes of Old Ludlow*) almost predicts the domestic themes in Daphne du Maurier's Gothic horror novel *Rebecca* (Victor Gollancz, 1938). It's the account of a young bride who becomes frightened when her husband-to-be insists on taking her to visit the grave of his first wife. Ghosts of the past and personal demons abound in Bowen's work, but she excels at writing female characters, particularly those who face real-life horrors such as violent men and suitors obsessed with youth and beauty.

The twelve-story collection *Kecksies and Other Twilight Tales* (Arkham House, 1976) republished some of Bowen's earlier stories with a few newer ones, serving to reignite interest in her work. "Florence Flannery" is a good example of her talent. The narrative seems to be a typical haunted house yarn about a young couple moving into a decrepit old home. But there's a twist: the wife quickly discovers that the house had been previously occupied by a woman of the same name born centuries earlier. The story demonstrates Bowen's flair for injecting life into a tired horror plot by putting women in dangerous situations that are rooted in the real world, with details like abusive spouses and the isolation that comes with a lack of access to education.

The threat in Bowen's stories is usually both supernatural and mundane, and her writing is best when that threat is directed toward women.

Women readers will find these dangers all too familiar, which adds delicious suspense to Bowen's tales.

Reading List

Not to be missed: Bowen remains a popular writer today, and many of her collected stories are readily available, including the Wordsworth Edition of *The Bishop of Hell and Other Stories* (a new edition was published in 2006). In addition to her hits, such as "Scoured Silk," check out "Ann Mellor's Lover," an atmospheric tale of a psychic bookseller who is intrigued by a sketch of a woman he finds in an eighteenth-century book.

Related work: Though Edith Nesbit is known for her children's books, such as *The Railway Children* (Wells Gardner, 1906), she also wrote ghost stories for an adult audience, earning her comparisons to Marjorie Bowen. Nesbit's story "John Charrington's Wedding" (in *Grim Tales*, 1893; 2012 edition available from Echo Library) is a good example of her ability to craft evil. The narrator is jealous of an engaged couple, so much so that he stalks them throughout the story. The ending is revealed to be his darkest wish come true.

"A peal of thunder rolled, the walls of the church shook, and an image of the Virgin was hurled to the marble pavement and shivered into fragments."

—Black Magic

L. T. Meade

1844–1914

Elizabeth Thomasina Meade Smith may not be a household name, but many who know her work have called her the J. K. Rowling of her day.

Born in 1844 in Ireland, Meade was raised by a Protestant clergyman and a devout mother. Her father took great pride in the fact that no woman in his family had ever had to work. One can imagine his horror when his daughter announced that she wanted a career—as an author, no less! Meade would not be deterred, however, and when her mother died and her father remarried, she set off for London: the big city, the place of dreams and opportunities. Like Marjorie Bowen (page 94), Meade found a place to pursue her dreams in the Reading Room of the British Museum, where she studied everything she could about her chosen craft.

Meade published more than 280 works, much of which would now be called "girl's fiction," with titles like *A Sweet Girl Graduate* (A. I. Burt, 1891), *Polly: A New-Fashioned Girl* (Grosset & Dunlap, 1889), and the oddly titled *Dumps: A Plain Girl* (W. & R. Chambers, 1905). These sound more like nineteenth-century precursors to the Baby-Sitters Club or Sweet Valley High than anything produced by an icon of horror or speculative fiction. But Meade's work offers more depth than these books suggest.

Her stories focused on young schoolgirls dealing with childhood issues, from making and losing friends to dealing with illness and grief. Often Meade's young heroines had lost their mothers, were left with distant fathers, and, therefore, looked to a schoolmistress for an adult role model. Meade's works in this mold were quite successful; one of her

books, *A World of Girls* (Cassell and Co., 1886), sold more than 37,000 copies. It's this vast contribution to children's literature, with books popular among readers of all ages, that has earned her the comparison to Rowling.

Meade also wrote crime fiction, particularly short stories, some of which appeared in *The Strand*, the magazine familiar to those fond of a certain detective who lived at 221B Baker Street (Sherlock Holmes, for the uninitiated). Fans of TV's *House* may want to seek them out; some critics consider Meade the godmother of the medical mystery subgenre.

Meade's crime fiction crossed over into horror when her detectives became intimately involved with the supernatural. Starting in 1898, she wrote a series of stories with the author Robert Eustace. That was the pen name of Eustace Robert Barton, a medical doctor who collaborated with numerous writers, including Dorothy L. Sayers on *The Documents in the Case* (Victor Gollancz, 1930). Together Meade and Eustace produced some eleven volumes of stories. One collection of occult detective tales titled *A Master of Mysteries* (Ward, Locke, 1898) focuses on the character John Bell, alternately called the "Ghost Breaker" or "Ghost Exposer." Bell is an independent and eccentric Victorian man of means who solves unsolvable mysteries reminiscent of the adventures of Scooby-Doo. To be clear, Bell's exploits are not written for kids, and he doesn't have a talking Great Dane as a sidekick. But most of his cases first appear to be supernatural but turn out to be intricate schemes orchestrated by villains using technologies new for the time period. As with the Scooby gang, the faux hauntings are intended to cover up criminal activity or scare away snoopers.

Meade and Eustace's other recurring characters are two unforgettably crafty women villains: Madame Sara and Madame Kalouchy. The latter appears in *The Brotherhood of the Seven Kings* (serialized in 1898 in *The Strand*, published in total the following year by Ward, Locke), and she remains one of the most diabolical criminal masterminds in literature. Madame Kalouchy is a smart, well-respected doctor whose reputation gains her entry into exclusive societies where wealth abounds. Charming, beautiful, and deadly, she is everything readers could want in villain. She's creative in her murder methods, too, attempting everything from homicide via injected diseases to a mass killing delivered by killer bugs. Of course, her plans are always foiled. Kalouchy's talent for escape and her position as head of a secret organization of criminals who follow her orders are reminiscent of another criminal mastermind who appeared just five years earlier in *The Strand*—Professor James Moriarty.

Madame Sara, who appears in the collection *The Sorceress of the Strand* (*Strand Magazine*, 1902), is in many ways Kalouchy's doppelgänger, also possessing brains and beauty that she uses for nefarious purposes. But Sara's a bit more exotic and a bit darker in both heritage (possessing Indian and Italian blood) and practice (she's described as a kind of underground abortionist in some stories). Most villains in Victorian literature are male, and Sara stands out not only because of her gender but also because of her intelligence, especially in the medical and scientific fields. The Sherlockian reasoning of the detectives who pursued her was no match for her fiendish mind. Madame Kalouchy was a nefarious villain, but Madame Sara was an evil genius, a true Moriarty—only wearing a skirt.

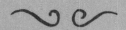

"Some of the country folk have declared that the tunnel is haunted. . . . That Pritchard saw some apparition, and in wild terror sought to escape from it by climbing the rocks."

—"The Mystery of the Felwyn Tunnel," in *A Master of Mysteries*

Reading List

Not to be missed: If you're looking for some supernatural fare by Meade, check out her and Eustace's story collection *A Master of Mysteries* (Ward, Locke, 1898), about John Bell the "Ghost Exposer." It's in the public domain as well as in print, notably in Volume 1 of Coachwhip Press's Supernatural Detectives series (2011).

Also try: Madame Sara appeared in season one, episode seven, of the British television show *The Rivals of Sherlock Holmes*, which aired on November 1, 1971. Meade was given a writing credit for the episode.

Related work: Sherlock Holmes may be the Victorian detective who gets all the love, but he wasn't the only investigator on the block. Another worth mentioning is Susan Hopley, a character created by the English writer Catherine Crowe. In *The Adventures of Susan Hopley; or, Circumstantial Evidence*, published in three volumes in 1841 by Saunders and Otley, Hopley is a maid suspected of murder who has to gather evidence to prove her innocence. The carefully designed crime story is ahead of its time both for the procedural aspect of the plot and for its depiction of a working-class woman as the detective and heroine. Readers may also be interested in Crowe's *The Night Side of Nature; or, Ghosts and Ghost-Seers* (T. C. Newby, 1848; reprinted by Wordsworth Editions, 2001), which was a best-selling nonfiction book examining ghosts and those who look for them. It also delved into occult topics like phrenology and mesmerism. Both books are in the public domain.

Casualty of War
Alice Askew

1874–1917

Séances sound like fun, don't they? Sitting around a candlelit room, maybe with a little mood music, holding hands with everyone and having a chat with dead loved ones. When solving mysteries is added to the mix, though, things can get complicated. The wife-and-husband writing team of Alice and Claude Askew describes occult detection as one part old-fashioned deduction, one part dogged sleuthing, and one part familiarity with the astral plane.

Such is the tone of their stories featuring the supernatural detective Aylmer Vance, the Askews' most famous literary creation. Vance travels around and solves cases involving all manner of ghosts and possessions, and, in one case, a vampire. He shares a last name with Eleanor Vance, the heroine of Shirley Jackson's 1959 novel *The Haunting of Hill House*, perhaps signifying Jackson's appreciation of the Askews' character.

The Askews likely saw plenty of blood while serving in World War I in Serbia as war correspondents attached to a British medical unit. The pair didn't stay on the sidelines and observe. They actively participated in the unit's work. Their lives ended tragically in 1917, when, in the Mediterranean, their ship was torpedoed by a German submarine. Both were reported lost at sea, though a body washed on shore at Corfu immediately afterward was thought to be Alice's. The couple left behind two children and more than ninety works (published as novels and as serialized "sixpenny" pieces of fiction) written before and during their war service.

The Askews' writing was adapted for six silent films, two of which were based on their novel *The Shulamite* (Chapman & Hall, 1904). The Hollywood adaptation, the Paramount-produced *Under the Lash*, came out in 1921 and starred Gloria Swanson. *The Shulamite* was a tragedy about a woman in a loveless marriage in South Africa who falls for an Englishman visiting the region to learn about agricultural techniques. During the course of the love triangle, the Englishman kills Deborah's overbearing husband and then reveals that he must return home to care for his ill wife. The Askews' most successful work was in romance, and *The Shulamite* is a prime example. Unfortunately, no copies of the film adaptations exist.

The pair's major contribution to horror is in the subgenre of occult detective fiction. Even before Dion Fortune's popular Dr. Taverner appeared in 1922 (see page 115), the Askews had created an eponymous occult detective in their story collection *Aylmer Vance: Ghost-Seer*, published in 1914 in the *Weekly Tale-Teller*. Vance and his sidekick Dexter are effectively Sherlock Holmes and Watson, only the cases they solve are weirder. The detectives are part of an organization known as the Ghost Circle, though the group is never clearly described. They're the ones to call if your problem is otherworldly—like when you think you might have fallen in love with a ghost or a vampire, but no one believes you.

In addition to being Vance's roommate, Dexter reports on the duo's paranormal investigations, and during the course of the series he develops his own psychic talents (unlike Holmes's partner Watson, who never transcended his role as the reporter of their cases). Aylmer Vance's adventures unfold over a series of "penny dreadful" stories, notably "The Invader" and "The Vampire." The duo faced scenarios that were familiar to readers of horror fiction: vampires, poltergeists, possessions, haunted houses. If all this sounds trite by today's standards, keep in mind that Vance and his occult detectives of the early twentieth century brought us several modern characters and stories: Constantine, Kolchak, *Ghostbusters*, *The Dresden Files*, *The X-Files* or any other supernatural files—Aylmer Vance is a common ancestor of them all.

Reading List

Not to be missed: For haunted fare by the Askews, read the Aylmer Vance tales that Wordsworth Editions reprinted as *Aylmer Vance: Ghost-Seer* in 2006. The Vance stories also can be found in volume two of Coachwhip Press's 2011 Supernatural Detectives series.

Also try: Film buffs may be interested to know that several of the Askews' works were adapted to silent movies, though they're not supernatural. *God's Clay* (published in 1913; adapted to film in 1919 and 1928) is about trysts, blackmail, and intrigue. The book can still be found in good used condition, for those willing to look.

Related work: For a notable psychic detective who predates Alymer Vance, try the adventures of Flaxman Low, who first appeared in 1899. This occult investigator was created by "E. and H. Heron," the collective pen name for the British authors Kate O'Brien Ryall Prichard and Hesketh Hesketh-Prichard . . . a mother-and-son writing team. Not much is known of the elder Prichard; her son was an army sniper, a cricket player, a journalist, and a world-traveling big-game hunter, in addition to being a writer. The character they created is a bit of a skeptic when he investigates a supernatural phenomenon; he's slow and careful, and sometimes the body count rises uncomfortably high while he's still deducing (bystanders don't fare well in these stories). "The Story of the Spaniards,

Hammersmith" is one of the most anthologized Flaxman Low stories, with truly goosebump-inducing imagery, like a "blotched, yellowish face, flanked by two swollen, protruding ears" that hangs around uninvited.

More recently, Flaxman Low appeared with Sherlock Holmes in the short story "The Things That Shall Come upon Them," by Barbara Roden, and was included in the anthology *The Improbable Adventures of Sherlock Holmes* (Night Shade, 2009), a collection that includes contributions by Neil Gaiman and Stephen King.

DYNAMIC DUOS

Alice and Claude Askew aren't the only married writing partners in the horror genre. *Frankenstein* author Mary Shelley collaborated with her husband, poet Percy Bysshe Shelley, on the travelogue *History of a Six Weeks' Tour* (Hookham, 1817). Husband-and-wife writing team C. L. Moore and Henry Kuttner wrote under the shared pen name Lewis Padgett (see page 130). Stephen King is married to writer Tabitha Jane King (see page 191). Legend has it that Stephen was ready to trash what would become his first published novel, *Carrie* (Doubleday, 1974), until Tabitha prompted him to continue writing it. And Jeff VanderMeer, one of the leading voices of the New Weird genre (which we discuss in Part 8), is married to Ann Kennedy VanderMeer, well known in weird fiction as an editor of *Weird Tales* (2007–11). The VanderMeers have coedited numerous anthologies.

"I do meet someone in the woods. I have never spoken to him, nor has he spoken to me; I have never even touched his hand, and I always call him the stranger to myself, except when I call him the—the god."

—"The Stranger"

Speaker to the Spirits ✦
Margery Lawrence
1889–1969

Margery Lawrence didn't just write paranormal fiction. She fervently believed in the supernatural. Although she was baptized and raised in the Church of England, upon the death of her parents in the 1920s, Lawrence became a dedicated Spiritualist. The loss of several friends and an early love in the First World War likely also contributed to her turn to Spiritualism. While writing about ghosts in her fantasy and horror stories, she communed with them in her everyday life, even claiming to speak with her deceased parents and, later, her dead husband. Her explanation of her introduction to Spiritualism resembles the plot of one of her stories: A family member died, and three days later his specter appeared to Lawrence and told her where to find some important papers (because why else do ghosts appear to the living, except maybe to solve their own murder?). She found the papers exactly where the ghost said they'd be and immediately desired to learn more about what was across the ghostly veil between our world and the place beyond death.

Lawrence lived a bohemian life, studying art in London and abroad in France. As a young woman, she traveled across Europe; when her mother died in 1921, the two were together in Monte Carlo. During World War I and the years leading up to World War II, she continued traveling through Europe and then into Africa. In 1936, she lived in Jamaica briefly before returning to London. In 1938 Lawrence married Arthur Edward Towle, and the couple remained in London, for the most part, until his death in 1948.

All that travel lent an air of authenticity to Lawrence's first novels, published in the 1920s, which were primarily adventure stories with romantic entanglements. (Several of her later ghost stories were set in locales outside of England or recounted hauntings that resulted from travel abroad.) She wrote romance novels, too, two of which—*Red Heels* (Hutchison & Co., 1924) and *The Madonna of Seven Moons* (Bobbs-Merrill Co., 1933)—were made into films. In both her adventures and her romances, Lawrence didn't shy away from describing women's experiences. Her 1928 novel *Bohemian Glass* (Hurst & Blackett) focused on the topics of sexual and artistic awakenings and was viewed by critics as scandalous. In *The Madonna of Seven Moons*, she wrote about a character with a split personality that resulted from witnessing sexual abuse. Her stories, primarily the supernatural ones that she wrote throughout her career, were popular both in British literary magazines, such as *The Tatler*, and in pulps, like *Hutchinson's Mystery-Story Magazine*.

Lawrence was headstrong in her opinions, and not just about the occult. In January 1929, she wrote an essay called "I Don't Want to Be a Mother" for *Cosmopolitan* magazine. According to the historian Daniel Delis Hill, when *Cosmopolitan* ran an advertisement for the article in *Good Housekeeping*, the latter published a disclaimer, stating that it could support Lawrence's right to an opinion without endorsing her ideas. She liked to push the boundaries of gender roles in her fiction, promoting issues like sexual independence and gender equality. She did marry but never was a mother, and she always valued her life of travel and freedom. Lawrence was a woman who wanted to follow her own path, and she certainly didn't believe a woman needed to rely on a man, financially or otherwise.

Perhaps inevitably, given her interest in all things occult, Lawrence's writing took on a supernatural bent. The shift was apparent first in her short stories, but soon her novels abandoned adventure and romance plots in favor of overtly Spiritualist themes. Her first novel to explore Spiritualism was *Madame Holle* (Jarrolds, 1934), in which an orphan is rescued from the clutches of the evil title character. Next came *The Bridge of Wonder* (R. Hale, 1939), which was a kind of morality tale warning against mediums using their powers for financial gain. Things got even more interesting with her 1966 novel *The Tomorrow of Yesterday* (Hale). In the author's foreword, Lawrence wrote that the story was dictated by its Martian narrator through a trance medium. The novel describes the utopian civilization on Mars that predated humanity on Earth but was destroyed because of power struggles and unfettered scientific development. It then turns to the development of humanity through the efforts of refugee Martians who left their home planet to escape the end of society. Oh yes, the lost city of Atlantis is also involved. What more could you want?

Reading List

Not to be missed: Lawrence wrote in many formats, but her short fiction is of greatest interest to supernatural and horror fans. Her first story collection, *Nights of the Round Table*, was published in 1926 by Hutchison & Co. Richard Dalby, an editor and relation of Lawrence, describes it as "one of the last remaining completely forgotten great ghost story collections of the 1920s." A favorite story within is "The Haunted Saucepan," which follows M. R. James's theory of the "malice of inanimate objects." The new tenant of a suspiciously low-rent apartment quickly realizes that there is something weird about the kitchen and a particular saucepan. The pot slightly raises its lid and looks as if it is watching him. Things get worse, but we won't spoil anything.

Also try: *Nights of the Round Table* was followed by *The Terraces of Night* (Hurst & Blackett, 1931) and *The Floating Café* (Jarrolds, 1936).

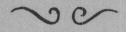

"The noise of the bubbling shaped itself into a devilish little song, almost as if the thing was singing to itself, secretly and abominably, chortling to itself in a disgusting sort of hidden way."

—"The Haunted Saucepan."

Both of these later collections go beyond ghosts and hauntings to explore more supernatural territory, namely, witches and vindictive mermaids and other sea creatures bent on raising hell and exacting revenge. All three collections have been reprinted by Ash-Tree Press.

Lawrence also wrote an occult-detective series, *Number Seven Queer Street* (R. Hale, 1945), and *Master of Shadows* (R. Hale, 1959), which features yet another psychic doctor, Dr. Miles Pennoyer. Pennoyer is a psychic doctor who solves the unsolvable with the help of ghost friends . . . how has no one turned this into a Netflix series yet?

Also fun: *Fifty Strangest Stories Ever Told* (Odhams Press, 1937), Lawrence's collection of true stories of the paranormal . . .

THE GHOST CLUB

Margery Lawrence referred to herself as a "ghost-hunter," not an exaggeration given her active participation in haunted house investigations and séances with famous mediums of the day such as Eileen Garrett. Lawrence was a member of the Ghost Club, an organization that began in London in 1862 and still exists as a place for discussion and investigation of psychic and spirit phenomena. Members have included Charles Dickens, Arthur Conan Doyle, Algernon Blackwood, W. B. Yeats, and Peter Cushing. In the 2015 Ubisoft video game *Assassin's Creed Syndicate*, players can accept side missions investigating the paranormal for Charles Dickens and the Ghost Club. We think Margery Lawrence would've been a cooler choice.

Britain's Psychic Defender
Dion Fortune

1890–1946

Writers of weird fiction have often turned to the occult for inspiration, and sometimes for personal motivation. Dion Fortune did one better than Margery Lawrence and other writers-turned-occultists: she grew a religion from her philosophies. Her occult beliefs informed her fiction, which in turn blended with her faith as she wrote mystical works.

Born Violet Mary Firth in 1890 in Wales, Dion Fortune grew up in a Christian Science home, and early in life she reported visions and psychic ability. Her more esoteric beliefs led her to join the Theosophical Society and, later, the Hermetic Order of the Golden Dawn. She was unique in that she connected occult practices to psychology—particularly Jungian studies—believing that magic could help seemingly untreatable mental disorders. One of her first books about occultist magic, *The Mystical Qabalah* (S. Weiser, 1935), was a kind of pseudoreligious guide to the good life that combined Jewish faith traditions with occult staples. Her ideas eventually evolved into the creation of her own occult order, the Society of the Inner Light. The organization is aimed at bringing people to their so-called divine intention, or true purpose in life.

Prior to her life as seeker of the inner goddess, Fortune wrote occult mysteries and weird fiction. The character of Dr. Taverner, from her 1926 short-story collection *The Secrets of Doctor Taverner* (Llewellyn Publications), reads like Sherlock Holmes meets a psychic Dr. House. Here's a typical plot: When traditional medicine fails fatally ill patients, it's Dr. Taverner to the rescue! With the help of a little magic, the good doctor is able to save the sick from a myriad of supernatural foes . . . like vampires who drain victims of life-giving energy, and mysterious stones that cause people to commit suicide. If the doctor is stumped, no worries. Secrets from the other side come to him in psychic visions.

The Taverner stories place Fortune firmly in the canon of occult detective authors, a subgenre that included few women writers (who produced exemplary work). Parallels between Dr. Taverner and Sherlock Holmes are numerous, from their similar appearances to their fascinations with seemingly unsolvable puzzles to their physician assistants who have returned wounded from war. But it's not a case of simple imitation; both Holmes and Taverner were modeled on real people. Holmes was inspired by Dr. Joseph Bell; Taverner was based on an Irish occultist and physician named . . . Dr. Theodore Moriarty, who had served in the Indian Medical Service and was Fortune's mentor in her study of the occult. (No, he didn't also inspire Arthur Conan Doyle's villain of that name; it's simply a delightful coincidence.) In the introduction to her story collection, Fortune writes that the cases of Taverner and his assistant, Dr. Rhodes, were composites of real investigations that she worked on with her mentor. She even claimed that she had to tone down a few of the stories to make them publishable. Whether or not that's true, it's a brilliant bit of showmanship.

Sexual Sorcery

Fortune's second work of fiction and first occult novel, *The Demon Lover* (Noel Douglas, 1927), has even more recognizable elements of modern horror. In the vein of films like *White Zombie* (1932) and others of the period that involved an evil sorcerer wielding black magic against innocent victims, *The Demon Lover* tells of a magician who plans to sacrifice a young woman. That goal becomes difficult when he falls in love with her. His fellow magicians (evil, of course, and interestingly a bunch of stodgy old white men) turn their dark arts against him and his lady love. There's also reincarnation and supernatural help from the other side (not unlike the aid that tended to arrive at just the right time for Dr. Taverner). With these stories and others, Fortune doesn't appear hostile to the idea of magic; rather, she asserts that formalized magical orders are disruptive, both to the practice of magic and, particularly, to the well-being of women who are involved with the men who practice it.

The Demon Lover was the piece of fiction that Fortune published under the name Violet Firth. The pen name she took was a pared-down version of her family's crest, *Deo, non fortuna* (by God and not by luck). The Latin phrase was also her so-called magical name when she was associated with the Hermetic Order of the Golden Dawn.

Her subsequent novels, *The Winged Bull* (S.I.L., 1935) and *The Goat-Foot God* (Samuel Weiser, 1936), continued to focus on women's experiences. In them Fortune explored the idea that a freer attitude toward sexuality can lead to gender equality and to freedom from the mental malaise—most commonly, depression and neurotic personalities—that often affected Dion's characters. These later novels presented sexual healing as magical healing.

Fortune turned up the heat in *The Sea Priestess* (Samuel Weiser, 1938) and its sequel *Moon Magic* (Weiser, 1957). Both are literary tornadoes of feminism, paganism, natural magic, and sex . . . with Atlantis thrown in for good measure. Fortune also published romantic thrillers, under the name V. M. Steele. (Perhaps she felt that romance fiction was separate from her work as a mystic and didn't want to use her own name on their covers.) In addition to her considerable fiction output, she penned nonfiction books that explained her brand of occult magic.

Some scholars assert that, more than developing her personal philosophies in these texts, she defined a kind of feminist-friendly magic that laid the foundation for modern Wicca.

Fortune's deep belief in magic and the occult continued throughout her life and was demonstrated most clearly in what she called "The Magical Battle of Britain." During World War II, Fortune marshaled her occultist colleagues and like-minded magicians to create protections for Britain against German invasion, via group visualizations of spiritual guards positioned along the country's coast. This practice may seem silly now, but let's remember: the Germans never set foot on British soil.

Reading List

Not to be missed: Weiser Books published an edition of *The Secrets of Doctor Taverner* in 2011, which includes a foreword about Fortune and her occult detective, by fantasy author Diana L. Paxson.

Also try: *Demon Lover*, which Weiser Books reprinted in 2010, is a good introduction to Fortune's occult fiction outside of the Taverner stories. If you're interested in learning the signs of psychic or paranormal attack and how to combat them, check out Fortune's *Psychic Self-Defense: The Classic Instruction Manual for Protecting Yourself against Paranormal Attack* (Weiser Books, 2011).

Related work: Fans of Dr. Taverner might also like the comics series *The Death-Defying Doctor Mirage* (2014) by Jen Van Meter (available in collections from Valiant Entertainment). Doctor Mirage, a.k.a. Shan Fong, can talk to the dead and uses her power to solve murders, assuage others' grief, and earn a little money. She's grieving the loss of her husband, Hwen, but no matter how hard she tries, she can't communicate with him. That is, until she becomes involved with a famous occultist who has gotten in over his head.

"I am not easily scared by anything I can see, but I frankly admit I fear the thing I cannot."

—"The Scented Poppies"

PART FOUR

The Women Who Wrote the Pulps

From the 1920s until the 1950s, fans of horror, science fiction, and fantasy got their fixes through pulp magazines, so named for the wood-pulp paper they were printed on. The pulps, along with dime-store paperbacks also made from cheap paper, got fiction into the hands of a wider audience because they were so affordable.

But the transitory nature of that low-cost material meant that unknown numbers of those stories were lost forever as the paper they were printed on decomposed to nothing. Pulp magazines often changed publishers, and during those transitions there was often no focus on preserving old inventory. Some pulps survive today in the hands of collectors, in university library archives, and in the Library of Congress, but despite sporadic collection and recovery work, entire careers of now-forgotten writers have been lost. Stories that have been anthologized tend to belong to the more popular—and often male—authors of the day, such as H. P. Lovecraft, A. Merritt, and Clark Ashton Smith.

All of which helps explain the accepted wisdom that few women wrote speculative fiction in the early 1900s and that, instead, the lineage starts in the 1960s and 1970s with writers like Ursula Le Guin and Joanna Russ. In fact, many pioneering women were writing during the pulps' heyday, and their work appeared in major speculative fiction magazines such as *Weird Tales* (the horror pulp most closely associated with Lovecraft), *Galaxy*, *Amazing Stories*, *Startling Stories*, and *Thrilling Wonder Stories*.

Historians and literary critics have mined collections of old material for references, such as readers' letters, to these early women writers. In his book *Partners in Wonder: Women and the Birth of Science Fiction, 1926–1965* (Lexington Books, 2005), the historian Eric Leif Davin catalogued women writers working in the pulps. His research produced a list of 203 women who wrote for science-fiction magazines from 1926 to 1960, as well as 127 women whose writing was published in *Weird Tales* from 1923 to 1954.

The award-winning science-fiction writer Connie Willis pointed to the presence of women in early pulps in her article "The Women Sci Fi Doesn't See," published in *Isaac Asimov's Science Fiction* magazine in October 1992. Willis asserts that she would not have become a successful science-fiction writer had she not read women writing science fiction in the early pulp magazines as a child. She points to C. L. Moore, Margaret St. Clair, Zenna Henderson, Shirley Jackson, Judith Merril, Mildred Clingerman, and Kit Reed as influences, all of whom predate the authors of the 1960s and 1970s.

Unfortunately, as readily available copies of pulp magazines disappeared from public attention, so, too, did these early women writing speculative and horror fiction. Also working against their legacy was the fact that reading tastes change with generations; literary critics and teachers tend to regard experimental literary fiction more highly than popular fiction, which disadvantages genre writers in the long game of reprints and academic study. With more women writing speculative fiction during the second-wave feminist movement, their foremothers faded into the past.

The women in question didn't just write for the pulps; they were in high demand. Two of the most popular writers in *Weird Tales*, based on readers' votes and mail, were women: Greye La Spina and Everil Worrell (see page 144). Mary Elizabeth Counselman (see page 134) was one of the magazine's most prolific writers, publishing thirty stories and six poems from 1933 to 1953. Other fan favorites were Eli Colter and G. G. Pendarves.

Women were also illustrating. Alternately known as "The Queen of the Pulps" and "The First Lady of Pulp Pinup Art," Margaret Brundage (a high school classmate of Walt Disney) was the most popular *Weird Tales* cover illustrator in the 1930s, known for macabre pastels of damsels in distress and strong women, usually depicted at least partially nude. She also had a tendency to include whips, ropes, and chains. All told, she created sixty-six covers for *Weird Tales*, including all nine of Robert E. Howard's *Conan the Barbarian* cover stories. In 2016, her original art for the 1937 story "The Carnal God" sold for $47,150 at auction.

In addition to writing and illustrating, women also filled editorial roles at these publications. Dorothy McIlwraith began as an editorial assistant at the literary magazine *Short Stories* and moved up to lead editor in 1936. When the magazine's parent company purchased *Weird Tales* in 1938, McIlwraith became editorial assistant of that publication, and in 1940 she took over as lead editor. McIlwraith brought new names, and new life, to the *WT* roster: Ray Bradbury, Manly Wade Wellman, Allison V. Harding, Margaret St. Clair, and Fritz Leiber Jr., to name a few. Fans of Wellman's occult detective John Thunstone have McIlwraith to thank; she worked with Wellman to create the concept.

Pulp writers such as Margaret St. Clair and C. L. Moore have clearly influenced science fiction, horror, and fantasy writing well into the twenty-first century. Ever played *Dungeons and Dragons*? Then you know St. Clair's work. Like your space operas with a debonair Han Solo type? Moore was writing that trope well before *Star Wars*. Are you a fan of dark fantasy? Gertrude Barrows Bennett is credited as the creator of that genre, and she is called "the mother of dark fantasy" even today.

Perhaps the weirdest tale is how we've managed to forget the women who created such amazing stories.

Exploring Our Depths
Margaret St. Clair
1911–1995

Tiny elvish people. Underground journeys in the midst of a world recovering from an apocalypse. Magic. All these story elements were the products of the imagination of one remarkable woman who embraced gardening, Wicca, and the Quaker value of charity.

Fans of *Dungeons and Dragons* will recognize the science fiction of Margaret St. Clair even if they don't recognize her name. Gary Gygax, one of the pioneering designers of the game, included her in Appendix N of the *Dungeon Masters Guide* (TSR, 1979), which is a list of his inspirations in creating his extensive world. Specifically, Gygax mentioned St. Clair's novels *The Shadow People* (Dell, 1969) and *Sign of the Labrys* (Mineola, 1963). Both involve a journey to, and an exploration of, an underground world that closely mirrors the dungeons of Gygax's creation. For a long time, this footnote, written more than a decade after St. Clair's death, was one of the few enduring traces of her extensive catalogue of stories. Fortunately, contemporary editors and authors are working to revive interest in her work, including Ann and Jeff VanderMeer, who included St. Clair's story "The Man Who Sold Rope to the Gnoles" in their anthology *The Weird: A Compendium of Strange and Dark Stories* (Tor, 2012).

The aforementioned is one of St. Clair's most anthologized stories. Its popularity kept her legacy alive, along with "Horror Howce" (*Galaxy*, 1956) and those of her stories adapted for television, such as "The Boy Who Predicted Earthquakes" and "Brenda" (both adapted for episodes in season two of *Night Gallery* in 1971). St. Clair's narrative about the gnoles is a reimagining of a well-known Lord Dunsany story, "How Nuth Would Have Practised His Art upon the Gnoles," which originally appeared in *The Book of Wonder* (William Heinemann, 1912). Dunsany's gnoles live in the forest and are extremely dangerous, but their appearance is never explicitly described. St. Clair's version are forest creatures born from the same dark fairy tales as the original Grimm fables, a strange mixture of trolls and fairies, with a dose of gnome thrown in for good measure. She describes them as looking like "artichokes made of India rubber," with red eyes. They have no ears, and their mouths are full of fangs. In Dunsany's tale, a skilled thief and his apprentice attempt to steal from the gnoles. (We'll let you guess how that turned out.) In St. Clair's version, the protagonist is a rope salesman trying to expand his customer base, but let's just say the gnoles don't understand the rules of commerce.

Born in Kansas in 1911 to a schoolteacher and a lawyer, Margaret Neeley devoured science fiction as a child. She attended the University of California at Berkeley, where she met the writer Eric St. Clair, whom she later married. Although Margaret was raised in the Quaker faith and supported the American Society of Friends throughout her life, she and Eric became interested in witchcraft and Wicca in the 1950s while in California, where Margaret was researching a novel. The Wiccan belief system quickly became part of the couple's household and lifestyle. It also became an integral part of Margaret's writing, particularly in the 1960s, as her novels turned toward more postapocalyptic subjects.

Enter the Labrys

The back cover copy on a 1963 edition of St. Clair's novel *Sign of the Labrys* is a sign of its times:

"Women are writing science-fiction! Original! Brilliant!! Dazzling!!! Women are closer to the primitive than men. They are conscious of the moon-pulls, the earth-tides. They possess a buried memory of humankind's obscure and ancient past which can emerge to uniquely color and flavor a novel."

Sexist flap copy notwithstanding (not to mention that excessive use of exclamation points), twenty-first-century readers will find many familiar elements in St. Clair's postapocalyptic imaginings. Her hero is trying to survive in a world that's been hit by a deadly pandemic with possible military origins, and in a search for answers, he journeys to an underground world of tunnels occupied by a community who seem to have supernatural psychic powers. It's as though our current concerns about pandemics and bioweapons have converged with *Dungeons and Dragons* and witchcraft.

Rather than her novels, St. Clair's prolific writing for the pulp magazines of the 1940s and 1950s made her, at the time, a household name in horror and speculative fiction. Her story "Brenda" (*Weird Tales*, March 1954), a tale of a young woman who torments a swamp monster on an island, was later adapted for Rod Serling's anthology TV series *Night Gallery*. But don't let that fool you into thinking she wrote soft science fiction, or the kind of gentle family-friendly fantasy that defined genre television and movies of the '50s and '60s, like *Lost in Space* and *My Favorite Martian*. She didn't constrain herself to one genre, preferring to blend science fiction, fantasy, and even aspects of the occult into a single narrative. And her stories always pack a punch.

When she was in her seventies, St. Clair wrote:

"Those who have lived through the Holocaust, Hiroshima, Coven-

try, Dresden, may be excused for forgetting that love, kindness, compassion, nobility exist. Yet in man's animal nature lie not only the roots of his cruelty, viciousness, sadism, but also of his perfectly real goodness and nobility. The potential is always there."

Throughout her more than one hundred short stories and nine novels, St. Clair used her speculative fiction to explore human potential, both our depths and our heights.

Reading List

Not to be missed: Margaret St. Clair is one of the more anthologized women from the pulp era. Martin H. Greenberg and Ramsey Campbell have collected her writings in *The Best of Margaret St. Clair* (Academy Chicago Pub, 1985) and *The Hole in the Moon and Other Tales* (Dover, 2019), respectively.

Also try: Even when set in the future or on other worlds, St. Clair's stories focus on the possibilities and dangers of her contemporary society. She found horror in everyday occurrences, such as a family adopting a bird that turns out to have otherworldly powers in "The Bird" (*Weird Tales*, November 1951). In "New Ritual" (*Mercury Press,* 1953), a threat underlies the promise of domestic ease when a wife buys a new freezer that's not just for preserving food. St. Clair refuses to shy away from human cruelty, as is evident in "The Pillows" (*Thrilling Wonder Stories*, 1950), in which humans mine an otherworldly resource without thought of the consequences, and "Brightness Falls from the Air" (*Mercury Press,* 1951), a devastating tale of violence suffered by native alien populations for the entertainment of human men. In one of her most recognized works, "Horrer Howce" (*Galaxy,* 1956), she blends the themes of entrepreneurship and alien contact, leaving the reader unsure of which characters deserve sympathy—the Voom, an alien race, or the businessman who is exploiting them. These stories are available in *The Best of Margaret St. Clair* and online in science-fiction databases such as the Unz Review.

If you're interested in her novels, Dover reissued *Sign of the Labrys* in 2016 as part of their Doomsday Classics Series.

Related work: Fans of St. Clair's postapocalyptic books may enjoy Margaret Atwood's MaddAddam trilogy, *Oryx and Crake, The Year of the Flood,* and *MaddAddam*, released as a boxed set by Anchor in 2014.

Connie Willis has cited St. Clair (along with a few other writers featured in this book) as an influence. Check out her award-winning story "A Letter from the Clearys" (July 1982), which looks at the possibility of surviving an apocalypse from a child's point of view. If you like St. Clair's humor and science-fiction themes, you may enjoy *To Say Nothing of the Dog* (Bantam Spectra, 1997), one of Willis's most popular books, which features time travel and showcases the author's wicked wit. Her *Terra Incognita* (Del Rey, 2018) and *Doomsday Book* (Gollancz, 2001) will appeal to St. Clair's fans for their strong female protagonists and, again, time travel.

"*From the sedan there came a wild burst of shrieking. It was like the flopping, horrified squawks of a chicken at the chopping block.*"

—"Horrer Howce"

— *Space Vamp Queen* —
Catherine Lucille (C. L.) Moore

1911–1987

A space pirate. A cat-eyed woman with squirming (yes, squirming) red hair. These are only small glimpses into C. L. Moore's short story "Shambleau," a Lovecraftian tale of cosmic porportions. It establishes Moore's affinity for global-scale storytelling as well as for the femme fatale. Her treatment of female characters in particular is what sets Moore apart in the world of speculative fiction; she may have written in the tradition of H. P. Lovecraft, but unlike him, Moore gave her female characters agency and depicted women who own their power, even when men do their best to rob them of it. "Shambleau" also introduced audiences to Northwest Smith, a hero who frequents many of Moore's tales. Smith is a space pirate of the best kind: a smuggler, a traveler, a lady's man, and a cynic with a "heart of gold" that guides his (sometimes illegal) activities and gets him into more trouble than not. Sound familiar? Many critics and fans credit Moore's invention as the prototype for the much-loved science-fiction scoundrels and rogues: Han Solo of Star Wars fame and Malcolm Reynolds of Joss Whedon's TV show *Firefly*.

C. L. Moore is the pseudonym for the American speculative-fiction writer Catherine Moore. Moore began to identify herself by her initials not to hide her gender but to allow her to keep her day job as a secretary without her employer knowing she was a writer. "Shambleau" was her first published story, appearing in *Weird Tales* in November 1933, and it immediately established her as a writer to watch.

Next, Moore wrote more stories for the pulps, both solo and in collaboration with her husband, Henry Kuttner. The pair used a num-

ber of pseudonyms, both
separately and together,
including Lewis Padgett,
Lawrence O'Donnell, and
C. H. Liddell, which made
it difficult for Moore's
growing fan base to find her
work. As Lewis Padgett—
Moore preferred gender-
neutral names to obviously

feminine ones—she wrote some of her most memorable stories,
including "The Twonky" (*Astounding Science Fiction*, September 1942)
and "Mimsy Were the Borogoves" (*Astounding Science Fiction*, February 1943) The former is a cautionary tale about a robot disguised as a
television set and the couple who unwittingly bring it into their home.
It was adapted to film in 1953.

"Mimsy," the better of the two, takes its title from Lewis Carroll's
poem "Jabberwocky" and depicts futuristic toys that travel back in time
to the year 1942. A brother and sister find some of the toys, which teach
them how to build a portal to another dimension. One character, a
nineteenth-century girl, shares her name with Alice Liddell, the inspiration behind Lewis Carroll's classic novel *Alice's Adventures in Wonder-
land*. Like "The Twonky," this story was adapted to film, as 2007's *The
Last Mimzy*, starring Joely Richardson and Timothy Hutton.

Sadly, Kuttner died of a heart attack in 1958, just a few years after
the couple moved to California to write screenplays. After her husband's
death, Moore gave up writing short stories but, using her married name
Catherine Kuttner, wrote for several television shows, including the detective series *77 Sunset Strip* and the Western *Sugarfoot*.

Not to be missed: Without question, fans of *Star Wars* and *Indiana Jones* should read Moore's Northwest Smith stories; paperback collections are readily available. The series follows the space hero as he travels the universe, helping damsels in distress and bedding them before escaping a fate worse than death. That sounds like standard science-fiction adventure fare (even his name evokes Indiana Jones, as many reviewers have pointed out), but Moore imbues her fiction with a good dose of horror. In "The Cold Gray God" (*Weird Tales*, July 1936), for instance, Smith takes on a heist job for a mysterious (and, yes, beautiful) woman but quickly discovers that she wants to take over his body—and destroy his soul. Smith finds himself in danger once again in "The Tree of Life" (*Weird Tales*, October 1936) when a gorgeous woman seduces him in order to feed him to her ruler. These plot elements make Moore's short fiction wonderfully unexpected. ("The Tree of Life" was recorded and produced as an episode of the fantasy fiction podcast *PodCastle* in 2013, read by Dave Robinson.) Planet Stories Library collected the entire Northwest Smith story collection in *Northwest of Earth* in 2008.

Also try: Moore's earlier weird fiction shines through in some of her television writing after her husband's death. Several episodes of *Sugarfoot* involve supernatural plot elements, like a reportedly haunted house and a medium who makes a foreboding prediction at a séance.

Related work: If space adventures are your favorite, treat yourself to the work of Moore's contemporary Leigh Brackett. Her hero is Eric John Stark, a kind of wild man from Mercury who's imprisoned by colonizers and taken on adventures through space. Many have compared Stark to Tarzan and even John Carter of Mars. Brackett also wrote novels, including *Shadow over Mars* (published in *Startling Stories* in 1944), about the conflict between Martians and colonizing Earthmen, and the postapocalyptic *The Long Tomorrow* (Phoenix Pick, 1955), for which she was nominated for a Hugo Award. Brackett tended to weave more than a few mystery/noir elements into her science fiction. She worked on screenplays for the iconic 1946 noir film *The Big Sleep* and *The Empire Strikes Back*, which won the Hugo for Best Dramatic Presentation in 1981. Some of Brackett's stories and *Shadow over Mars* are available in Kindle editions.

> "It was like a nest of blind, restless red worms . . . it was—it was like naked entrails endowed with an unnatural aliveness, terrible beyond words."
>
> —"Shambleau"

Deep South Storyteller
Mary Elizabeth Counselman
1911–1995

What does the term "Southern belle" bring to mind? Perhaps a young woman dressed in Sunday best with white gloves, fanning herself on a grand porch, speaking demurely while sipping on iced tea (sweet, of course)?

Mary Elizabeth Counselman and her version of the South, which was at times horrifying and beautiful, just may challenge that idea.

Counselman was born in 1911 on a plantation in Birmingham, Alabama, a setting that informed her particular brand of horror story. Sometimes called "the Stephen King of Alabama," she wrote eight novels and numerous short stories for pulp magazines, including *Weird Tales* (she was one of their most prolific contributors). Her short stories and poetry also appeared in national publications like the *Saturday Evening Post* and *Good Housekeeping*.

A born writer, Counselman reportedly was penning poetry by the age of six. In her teenage years, she wrote "The Three Marked Pennies," which was published in *Weird Tales* in August 1934 and was reprinted seventeen times in nine languages, making it one of the most popular stories in the magazine's history. Counselman continued to write while studying at the University of Alabama and what is now Montevallo University. Following graduation, Counselman worked as a reporter for the local Birmingham newspaper and occasionally taught creative writing at Gadsden State Junior College, but her passion remained producing her own fiction.

Her first professional sale was "The Devil Himself" to *Myself: The Occult Fiction Magazine* in November 1931. She married Horace Vinyard in 1941, and the two lived on a houseboat (a paddle-wheel steamboat, in fact, the *Leota*) in Gadsden, Alabama. One imagines her happily writing weird fiction as the *Leota* lolled lazily down the river.

"The Three Marked Pennies" is her most famous tale; the title refers to three coins that are circulated in a small town in the South. One coin is said to bring wealth, one travel, and one death. Each of the three bears a mysterious mark (a cross, a circle, and a square) but no one knows which coin grants which fate. Should one of the coins find its way to your pocket, would you dare to keep it and hope for a good result? The story was published in *Weird Tales* as filler material, but readers responded overwhelmingly with positive letters. It was adapted for the radio program *General Electric Theater*.

"Seventh Sister," published in *Weird Tales* in January 1943 and later collected in various anthologies, is another Counselman story that garnered effusive praise from readers and critics alike. It stands out both for its focus on voodoo, a subject typically taken on by male writers of the weird, and for its protagonist, a young albino African American girl who is ostracized by everyone, her family included, because of her appearance and her occult powers. Counselman treats the character with remarkable and careful attention. Stories that depicted racial minorities with such empathy were rare, especially from writers in the 1940s Deep South, but Counselman was never one to shy away from the taboo. Another example is her story "The Unwanted," which deals with a childless woman who becomes mother to a group of ghosts of aborted children.

Before her death in 1995, Counselman was recognized for her

"They burned a witch in Bingham Square

Her eyes were terror-wild.

She was a slight, a comely maid,

No taller than a child.

They bound her fast against the stake

And laughed to see her fear . . .

Her red lips muttered secret words

That no one dared to hear."

—"Witch-Burning"

talent and her contribution to the weird fiction canon. In 1976, the National Endowment for the Arts presented her with a $6,000 grant. And in 1981, she received a lifetime achievement award from the Southern Fandom Confederation.

Reading List

Not to be missed: Counselman's collection *Half in Shadow* (Arkham House, 1978) contains some of her best stories, like "Three Marked Pennies," "Parasite Mansion," and "Seventh Sister." A newer edition is long overdue, but inexpensive used copies are available. Several of her stories have also been anthologized in various *Weird Tales* collections. Her more popular stories are available online and in digital-only formats as well.

Also try: Counselman's story "Parasite Mansion," which was first published in January 1942, was adapted for an episode of the television series *Thriller* that debuted on April 25, 1961. The episode starred horror legend Boris Karloff, and it is well worth tracking down. "The Three Marked Pennies" was adapted for an episode of the show *The Unforeseen*, but as it does not feature Karloff, we cannot say that it is the better adaptation.

Related work: Writing nearly a century earlier than Counselman, Mary Noailles Murfree (pen name Charles Egbert Craddock) also crafted unforgettable Southern-style ghostly tales. A major name in Appalachian literature, Murfree is particularly known for her local-color fiction, descriptive of the mountain regions of eastern Tennessee. Murfree was often stereotypical in her character depictions; this was a common tactic of regional writers attempting to catalogue special details of the locations and people they wrote about. Plus, she framed her narratives from a privileged outsider's perspective, although she was native to the area. But like her contemporaries Sarah Orne Jewett and Mary E. Wilkins

Freeman, Murfree was adept at using regional folklore to describe people and history. She used ghosts as markers for traumatic history, not unlike Counselman in "The Unwanted." Murfree's most ghostly tales appear in *The Phantoms of the Footbridge and Other Stories* (Harper and Brother, 1895); reprints of the text are relatively easy to find.

WHO WAS
G. G. PENDARVES?

According to Terence E. Hanley, writer of the blog *Tellers of Weird Tales*, and the historian Eric Leif Davin, Mary Elizabeth Counselman was the second most prolific writer for *Weird Tales*. In fact, the top three names on the list are female . . . but number one, Allison V. Harding, is suspected to be the pen name of a male writer. Third place goes to English writer G. G. Pendarves, who's a bit of mystery; we know her real name, Gladys Gordon Trenery, but not much else. She was born in England, though no one can say for sure where (Cornwall, Liverpool, and Lancashire are frequent guesses). A census record has her living in Birkenhead, Cheshire, as a sixteen-year-old girl. She played piano, apparently—there's a record of a music exam. What's certain is that Pendarves wrote prolifically for the pulps. Fans of Counselman's brand of supernatural occult pulp might enjoy Pendarves's stories, which are sometimes anthologized. (A word of warning: Pendarves was not always as sensitive as Counselman in her depiction of characters of color.)

Seer of the Unseen
Gertrude Barrows Bennett
1883–1948

Gertrude Barrows Bennett, who published under the pseudonym Francis Stevens, was a pioneering woman writer of science fiction and fantasy in the United States. In his introduction to *The Nightmare and Other Tales of Dark Fantasy* (Bison Books, 2004), a collection of Bennett's work, the editor Gary Hoppenstand admits to previously arguing that H. P. Lovecraft invented modern American dark fantasy, but he now believes that Gertrude Barrows Bennett deserves credit. Unfortunately, we have little documentation about Bennett's life and work, other than the stories that have survived in archives and collections, along with her two novels, *Claimed!* and *Avalon*, published in a single volume by Black Dog Books in 2018. What we know of her life and publication record is largely thanks to the work of literary critics like Hoppenstand and the historian Eric Leif Davin's book *Partners in Wonder* (Lexington Books, 2005).

Born in Minneapolis in 1883, Bennett attended school through eighth grade and went to night school to study art. She had dreams of becoming an illustrator but instead took a job as a stenographer. She married the British journalist and explorer Stewart Bennett, who died a year into their marriage in a tropical storm while searching for treasure. Bennett worked in offices for the rest of her life to support herself, her daughter, and her ill mother. Although she published most of her stories and novels between 1917 and 1923, she started writing much earlier, publishing her first science-fiction story at age seventeen, while working as a department store secretary. In 1904, her story "The Curious Experience of Thomas Dunbar" appeared in the magazine *Argosy* (under

Bennett's real name); about a week later, the children's magazine *Youth's Companion* accepted some of her poems for publication.

The first story she published as Francis Stevens was "The Nightmare," for *All-Story Weekly,* in 1917. Curiously, she had submitted the story under a different pen name, but the editor used Francis Stevens instead (why, we don't know) and her career was cemented. Her novel *The Citadel of Fear*, published serially in *Argosy Weekly* in 1918, garnered high reviews, including a fan letter from one Augustus T. Swift, who was revealed to be the great H. P. Lovecraft. Lovecraft wrote this of the story: "If written by Sir Walter Scott or Ibanez, that wonderful and tragic allegory, would have been praised to the sky. . . . Stevens, to my mind, is the highest grade of your writers."

Although Bennett was a contemporary of Lovecraft and the weird-fiction writer A. Merritt, who also was a fan of her writing, she seems to have written in isolation, unconnected to Lovecraft's circle of writer friends. (Some critics have speculated that Lovecraft and Merritt were influenced by her work.) Bennett's stories, in particular "Unseen—Unfeared" (*People's Favorite Magazine*, February 10, 1919), imply that other dreadful universes, with physics different from ours and peopled by fearsome creatures, exist next to us all the time. Like Lovecraft, Bennett implied that certain shades of lighting, or sounds, or chemicals could make these worlds, separated from us by a thin barrier, visible in all their terrifying glory—and danger.

The similarities led to rumors that Francis Stevens's true identity was A. Merritt, until the critic Lloyd Arthur Eshbach set the record straight in his biographical sketch of Bennett in the 1952 reprint of *The Heads of Cerberus.* The false attribution of Bennett's pen name to a male writer is not the only instance in which her talent was overlooked. Another is related to a prize for alternate-reality fiction, the Sidewise Award, given by the website Uchronia. The award is named for the story "Sidewise in Time" by Murray Leinster (the pen name of William F. Jenkins), published in June 1934 by *Astounding Stories*. However, two of Bennett's works—the story "Friend Island" (*All-Story Weekly*, September 7, 1918), set in a world where strict gender roles have been abandoned, and the novel *The Heads of Cerberus* (*Thrill Book*, 1919; published by Polaris Press in 1952)—feature earlier, and perhaps the earliest, examples of parallel universes.

We may not be able to establish Bennett's influence on Lovecraft and his circle, but we know that she was popular with readers of her day. Mary Gnaedinger, editor of the pulp magazines *Famous Fantastic Mysteries* and *Fantastic Novels*, reprinted stories by Bennett in the 1940s, while Bennett was still alive. And praise for her writing has continued long past the end of her career. The science-fiction critic Sam Moskowitz called Bennett "the greatest woman writer of science fantasy in the period between Mary Wollstonecraft Shelley and C. L. Moore."

Reading List

Not to be missed: *The Heads of Cerberus* was first serialized in 1919 in the pulp magazine *Thrill Book;* it was published by Fantasy Press in 1952 as a complete novel and is now available in a Kindle edition. It begins with Robert Drayton returning to Philadelphia a ruined man after being framed for a crime in Cincinnati. Drayton reunites with his friend, Irishman Terry Trenmore, and the two embark on a bizarre adventure with Trenmore's sister Viola. Their wild ride—which involves parallel universes and a look at the authoritarian dystopia that Philadelphia apparently will become in the year 2118—results from Trenmore's procuring an old vial of strange dust sealed with concrete and bearing the image of the three heads of Cerberus, the mythical hell hound. Despite numerous warnings to leave it sealed, Drayton convinces Trenmore to open the bottle. What else would one do with a vial of mystery dust that had been associated with Dante and the netherworld?

Also try: "Unseen—Unfeared," published in 1919, is reprinted in Ann and Jeff VanderMeer's anthology *The Weird: A Compendium of Strange and Dark Stories* (Tor, 2012). That's an appropriate place for this bizzarre tale that out-Lovecrafts Lovecraft and first appeared around the time the latter was debuting his tales of dreadful horror. Bennett's narrator wanders around a working-class neighborhood, feeling abhorrence for the people who live there, when he is disturbed by an awareness of an "impending evil." He stumbles upon a sign above a doorway: "SEE THE GREAT UNSEEN! Come in! This means you! FREE TO ALL!" We'll just stop there and let you find out for yourself what he discovers.

Another strange artifact appears in Bennett's novel *Claimed!* (first published in 1920; later edition, Carrol & Graf, 1985). This time it's a green box found after a volcanic eruption in the Azores that brings nightmares and death to anyone who comes in contact with it. According to the VanderMeers, Lovecraft called the book "one of the strangest and most compelling science fantasy novels you will ever read."

Her novel *The Citadel of Fear* (Argosy, 1918) involves a lost world, and possible possession by the gods is involved, too. Look for the Kindle edition or the 2015 paperback reprint from CreateSpace Independent Publishing.

Related work: The best modern-day heirs to Bennett's work are dark fantasy graphic novels. *Monstress* (Image Comics, 2016), written by Marjorie Liu and illustrated by Sana Takeda, follows a "monster underground," similar to the mythos Bennett depicted so well.

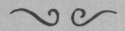

"Suddenly the man knew that he had seen too much."

—"The Citadel of Fear"

Night Writer
Everil Worrell

1893–1969

Many women who wrote for the pulp magazines in the mid-twentieth century lived a dual existence: by day, they worked in an office, typing memos for the boss and then rushing home in time to kiss their husbands as they come through the door; by night, they sat at their own typewriters, releasing their worlds of imagination onto paper.

Everil Worrell was one of those women.

According to legend (or at least the internet), Worrell was born one minute after midnight on November 3, 1893, in Loop City, Nebraska. After a childhood of moving around the country, she settled in Washington, D.C. In 1926, she married Joseph Charles Murphy and began her publishing career. She worked as a stenographer and secretary for the U.S. Department of the Treasury; at night, she penned weird, fantasy, speculative, and supernatural stories. Worrell and her husband had fun with her writing career. A playful couple, they would often describe the mundane household chores using Lovecraftian terms. For instance, if food burned on the stove, they would call it a "foul mephitic vapor."

Worrell wrote at least twenty-four stories, nineteen of which appeared in *Weird Tales* between 1926 and 1954. She also had two tales published in *Ghost Stories*, written under the name Everil W. Murphy, between 1926 and 1932. But these are just the ones we know about; she is believed to have been quite prolific, and more of her work may have been lost to time. According to the historian Eric Leif Davin, "The Bird of Space"—a 1926 *Weird Tales* cover story—was voted by readers one of the most popular stories to appear in the magazine.

One of Worrell's best-known works is her female vampire tale "The Canal" (1927), which is in the public domain. The story has shades of Le Fanu's novella *Carmilla* (serialized in the magazine *The Dark Blue,* 1871–72), in that the female vampire is seductive—that's her power and her danger. But the setting is unique: a riverbank at night, where fishermen make the perfect prey. The story was adapted for television in 1973 as the episode "Death on a Barge," appearing on Rod Serling's show *Night Gallery* (which—attention, *Star Trek* fans—was Leonard Nimoy's directorial debut). The vampire protagonist is played by Lesley Ann Warren.

"Leonora" (*Weird Tales*, November 1938) is another standout. Described as an "eldritch tale," the eponymous heroine meets a handsome but mysterious stranger by the light of the full moon on the night of her sixteenth birthday. Leonora's heart swells with the giddying emotion of first love, but things turn strange when she realizes she can only meet the stranger when the moon is full. (If you seek it out, be sure to read the entire story. There's a fun twist at the end.)

In addition to her fiction, Worrell wrote the lyrics to the song "Come to Me Dear," composed by Leo Friedman, who is best known for the tune to "Let Me Call You Sweetheart." She played the violin and was reportedly a talented painter as well. Through it all, she kept her day job, not retiring from her government position until 1957, when she was awarded the Albert Gallatin Award for her years of service.

Reading List

Not to be missed: Search the *Weird Tales* archive on the Pulp Magazine Archive website for "The Canal," "Leonora," "The Elemental Law" (June 1928), and "Deadlock" (September 1931). Worrell's mystery "The Gray Killer" (*Startling Mystery Stories*, 1969) can also be found in the Pulp Magazine Archive. She was one of the more popular *Weird Tales* writers—her stories made the cover three times—but Worrell did not find widespread fame. As a result, her fiction is not often anthologized, and to date no collection of her work has been published.

Also try: A biography by Worrell's daughter, Jeanne Eileen Murphy, was included in the first volume of Robert Weinberg's series *The Weird Tales Collector*, reprinted by Borgo Press in 1999.

Related work: If Worrell's version of a vampire story sounds enticing, then "The Antimacassar" by Greye La Spina (*Weird Tales*, May 1949) may be worth your time. You can find it in older *WT* anthologies, though it's not in the public domain. La Spina divorces her vampires from the typical Gothic types seen in Bram Stoker knockoffs. With its child vampire protagonist, "The Antimacassar" is a standout among pulp vampire stories. Also look for "My Dear Emily" by Joanna Russ, published in *Fantasy and Science Fiction* in 1962.

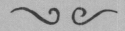

"It is the hour when Those outside must seek their dreadful homes, the hour when striking fleshless fingers against my window-pane is not enough."

—"Leonora"

Keeping the Wild West Weird
Eli Colter
1890–1984

Eli Colter begins "The Last Horror" with questions: "You wonder what happened to Bleeker? And to Remington? They aren't the same men any more, are they?" She doesn't tell us who these men are or what happened to them; instead she lets her ominous words work on our imaginations. And when her rich, evocative prose starts filling in the details, the true horror begins. Consider this next passage in the story:

"Bleeker: who once stood straight-limbed, straight-backed and full-fleshed, walked with high-carried head, clear-glowing eyes and ruddy blond skin; Bleeker, who now walks with a bent shuffle, whose cuticle is so tightly drawn over his emaciated features that it looks like dirty white rubber stretched over a skull; Bleeker, whose eyes have gone blank and sunken in their sockets, whose mouth is tightened in the middle and loose at the corners, whose nose is pinched, whose hands tremble when he isn't taking care to hold himself in."

Whatever happened to poor Bleeker is terrible indeed. He's gone from being the quintessential picture of health, the everyman's cowboy, a John Wayne prototype to . . . a walking skeleton. Few writers could describe a character so effectively.

Eli Colter certainly sounds like a fitting name for someone who writes Western fiction. The moniker evokes the image of a cowboy, muscular, with sunburned cheeks and strong features peeking out from beneath a weather-worn Stetson. But Eli Colter is a woman, of course, the pen name of May Eliza Frost, born and raised in Portland, Oregon. As a thirteen-year-old girl, Colter went blind. Though she eventually regained her sight, the temporary disability seems to have fueled her ambition. She set out to educate herself and began a career as a writer; to support herself while she followed her dream, she played piano and organ in movie theaters.

Colter published her first story around age thirty-two, in 1922, in *Black Mask* magazine, known for mystery and crime fiction. Tracing her career is difficult because not much has been written about her, save for her later standard Western stories. We do know that Colter had a productive writing career that included fifteen stories for *Weird Tales* magazine and several for *Strange Stories*. Among her *Weird Tales* work was a four-part serial that ran from January to April 1926, called "On the Dead Man's Chest." Readers voted it one of the most popular stories of the April issue. Other favorites are "The Crawling Corpse" (*Strange Stories*, December 1939), the aforementioned "The Last Horror," "The Man in the Green Coat" (*Weird Tales*, August 1928), and "The Golden Whistle" (*Weird Tales*, January 1928).

Colter's non-horror adventure publications include "The Pearl of Hahn" which appeared in *Super-Detective* (February 1945), "The Hell Cat" in *Detective Action Stories* (March 1931), "Not in the Evidence" in *Hutchison's Adventure-Story Magazine* (September 1925), and "Ozark Justice" in the *Liberty Quarterly* anthology *19 Tales of Intrigue, Mystery, and Adventure* (1950).

To return to Bleeker: "The Last Horror" is a great example of both Colter's mastery of language and her knack for sinking a hook of suspense into her readers . . . then pulling it tauter and tauter until the very last page. We won't disclose the story's secrets here. But we will say that Colter is a master of writing body horror. "The Last Horror" was ranked the second most popular story of January 1927 by *Weird Tales* readers and was reprinted in February 1939.

Weird Trails

Colter's stories were published frequently in *Weird Tales*, including "weird Westerns," which are just as they sound: supernatural stories set against a Wild West backdrop. It's interesting to look at the development of this subgenre. Writers like Robert E. Howard and Charles G. Finney are largely credited with writing the earliest such stories in the 1930s, publishing in magazines like *Weird Tales* and *Argosy*. Colter's weird Westerns predated them, and whether or not she was the very first, she certainly was one of the earliest pulp writers working the trend. The category started to gather steam in the 1970s with the success of the 1977 DC comic *Jonah Hex*, and its popularity continues today.

Following her foray into weird fiction and weird Westerns, Colter switched to writing straight-up Westerns as well as a few detective stories. "Something to Brag About" (originally published in the *Saturday Evening Post*) was adapted to film in 1948 as *The Untamed Breed*, directed by Charles Lamont (the man credited with "discovering" young Shirley Temple). After the 1950s, Colter seemed to largely stop writing; details from this part of her life are especially spotty; we don't know if she switched pen names or even careers.

Colter met her first husband, John Irving Hawkins, when she advertised for cowboys in order to do research for her writing. He was a ranch hand and aspiring writer with stories to share, and she was a writer in need of inspiration. Later she wrote stories in collaboration with another writer, Don Alviso, the pseudonym for Glenn FaGalde—who became her second husband. They were together until FaGalde's death in 1957. It would seem from her marriages that Colter's writing life and personal life were nearly inseparable.

Colter died in Los Angeles in 1984. Despite her successes, she was completely unknown at the time of her passing. Some fans still refer to her on websites and blogs devoted to classic Western novels as "he."

Reading List

Not to be missed: Eli Colter is one of the once-popular writers of weird fiction who have nearly been lost to obscurity. Her stories are listed in catalogues of pulp writers, but reprints are becoming increasingly difficult to locate. Her work deserves to be republished, reread, reloved.

"The Last Horror" (1927), "The Greatest Gift" (1927), "The Curse of a Song" (1928), and parts of her serials "The Dark Chrysalis" (1927) and "On the Dead Man's Chest" (1926) are available online in the *Weird Tales* magazine archive.

Also try: Compared to Colter's weird work, her not-so-weird Western novels are easier to find as used paperbacks. Check out *Blood on the Range* (Dodge Publishing, 1939), which was released in 2018 from Wildside Press in both paperback and Kindle editions. *The Outcast of Lazy S* (Grosset & Dunlap, 1933) and *Bad Man's Trail* (Mills & Boon, 1933) are available as reprints from Gunsmoke Westerns (1998) and Sagebrush Westerns (2005), respectively.

Related work: Since Eli Colter's *Weird Tales* days, popular culture has seen an explosion in the weird West subgenre. Standout examples include the work of Seanan McGuire and Nancy A. Collins. McGuire contributed to a series of books published by Tor based on the *Deadlands* role-playing games. Her *Deadlands: Boneyard* (2017) pits a traveling circus against the Clearing, a secretive community deep within the woods. In several books, Collins spins yarns about werewolves in a Western backdrop; we recommend *Walking Wolf: A Weird Western* (Mark V. Ziesing, 1995). Seek out the anthology *Dead Man's Hands* (Titan Books, 2014), which includes stories by McGuire, Beth Revis, and Elizabeth Bear. Also of note is *Six-Gun Snow White* by Catherynne M. Valente (reprint Saga Press, 2015), which reimagines the fairy tale princess as a Wild West gunslinger.

"The glaring, maniacal eyes glued to Rose's face. The thin mouth twisted in a hideous sneer. It was horrible, menacing, gloating. I felt a chill go over me and the hair raised on my scalp."

—"The Curse of a Song"

PART FIVE

Haunting the Home

I t's nighttime. You are home, tucked into bed, and you feel safe. But are you? You hear a creaking outside your door. Bumps in the walls. A low keening wail. Is it coming from down the hall? No, it's in the attic. What's that scratching the window? Did that shadow move?

Domestic spaces have long been the preferred setting for horror fiction. Nothing screams creepy like an old, isolated house in a desolate landscape, especially on a dark and stormy night. The haunted house is the epitome of the uncanny—the familiar and safe becoming strange and dangerous. Homes should be places of comfort and family, where we and our loved ones are sheltered from the world's pressures. Owning a home is a signal of financial security; losing it is the biggest threat in a sour economy.

Beginning in the Gothic period of the eighteenth century, horror storytellers gave us lonely haunted castles on moors or in foreign lands, complete with secret passageways, animated portraits whose eyes seem to follow the viewer, clanking chains, and the requisite dungeon (and if it's constructed as a maze, so much the better).

When writers in pre- and post-revolutionary America turned their hands to fiction, the stage was changed slightly. Writers like Washington Irving, Charles Brockden Brown, and Nathaniel Hawthorne added uniquely American elements to their horror stories, informed by the early settlers' Puritan faith and fears of indigenous peoples: eerie woods, the devil, and witches. Even today, much of American horror fiction reckons to varying degrees with fears that are tied up in the nation's history, fears of supernatural evil, of the racial other, and of the frightful consequences of the violent past coming home to roost.

American horror fiction transforms the home into a battleground for these phobias and hauntings. Homes can be sites of intimate family violence, trauma, and painful secrets. Homes can imprison people. Homes can be besieged by invaders. Homes can become twisted mimics of their owner's or builder's minds, like Edgar Allan Poe's House of Usher and Shirley Jackson's Hill House.

As weird fiction moved away from Gothic castles and crumbling mansions, writers—many of them women—evolved this subgenre in a few important ways. They showed readers that domestic horror needn't be isolated in the countryside or off the beaten path. A prime example of this phenomenon is Anne Rivers Siddons's *The House Next Door* (Simon and Schuster, 1978), set in an upper-middle-class suburb of Atlanta, Georgia.

And these writers used the image of the haunted house to represent internal as well as external horror. From the 1930s through the 1960s, in the United States and across the pond, Dorothy Macardle, Shirley Jackson, and Daphne du Maurier developed haunted house fiction that presented the supernatural as a psychological effect.

Historically, women have been consigned to the domestic realm, running the household and caring for children. Even today, when many families have two parents working outside the home, we are socialized to associate women with nurturing and housework. Another cultural belief exists that women can "have it all," meaning a joyous family life and a rewarding profession. Many of the women profiled in this book struggled with that dichotomy: the pressure to care for home and family, and the need to tend their writing career. Haunted house fictions play upon the complex fears and concerns about domestic issues that women have long grappled with.

The hauntings in these houses are bound to families and their attendant tensions. Secrets and broken relationships fuel the supernatural activity. The focus is on mothers and daughters for Macardle and Jackson and on marriage in du Maurier's *Rebecca*. Intimate spaces within the larger homes also play important roles: nurseries in Macardle's Cliff End and Jackson's Hill House (and, later, Susan Hill's Eel Marsh House in *The Woman in Black*); the second Mrs. de Winter's bedroom, boudoir, and writing room in du Maurier's Manderley.

Just as every home and its past are different, every domestic horror story approaches haunting via a different angle. Toni Morrison's *Beloved* focuses on mother-and-daughter relationships and a secret, painful past, compounded by the profound trauma her characters, formerly enslaved African Americans, live with in post–Civil War Ohio and Kentucky. Elizabeth Engstrom used the home as a place to explore the monstrous nature of domesticity itself. She masterfully examines the connection between mother and child, a bond that is unbreakable even in the most horrific circumstances.

Let's enter some of these houses of the damned. No need to knock, the doors are always open . . . at least, until you're inside.

Chronicler of Pain and Loss
Dorothy Macardle

1889–1958

In his introduction to the Tramp Press Recovered Voices Series 2015 edition of *The Uninvited*, scholar Luke Gibbons calls the Irish writer Dorothy Macardle a woman of contradictions. She was a feminist and humanitarian who also was an ardent nationalist and republican. She supported Irish neutrality during World War II, only to move to London to fight the spread of fascism. She was fascinated by history and psychology but loved a good ghost story. But she was steadfast in standing up for her political beliefs. For her republicanism and antitreaty stance in the Irish Civil War, Macardle was fired from her teaching post at Alexandra College in Dublin and jailed. While imprisoned, she participated in a hunger strike to oppose the poor conditions the inmates lived in. She was also an investigative journalist, and after serving her sentence, she wrote powerful exposés about the harsh treatment of prisoners, especially women.

Macardle was born in 1889 in Dundalk, Ireland, to a family that enjoyed financial security from their well-known brewery business. She grew into a woman with diverse interests, all of which played a role in her fiction and nonfiction writing. Macardle wrote plays and was a theater and film critic. She worked with the prominent psychoanalyst Anna Freud to chronicle the horrific effects of the Holocaust on Jewish orphans and other children liberated from World War II concentration camps, documenting their stories in her book *Children of Europe* (Victor Gollancz, 1949). Macardle's journalism reveals her empathy for others and her awareness of the effects of poverty and violence on families. It's not surprising that she wrote fiction concerned with a yearning for home (usually Ireland) and with trauma and loss. And she used the supernatural to represent such scars.

Today Macardle is known by historians for her huge tome *The Irish Republic* (Victor Gollancz, 1937; Farrar Straus & Giroux, 1965 reprint), a history of the Irish War of Independence. But she also wrote two uncanny supernatural novels: *The Unforeseen* (Doubleday, 1946) and *Uneasy Freehold* (Peter Davies, 1941). The latter, which was released in the United States as *The Uninvited* (Doubleday, Doran, 1942), follows Stella Meredith, a young woman who is simultaneously haunted by a traumatic childhood and the loss of her mother and dealing with a domineering grandfather in the present day. Both the book and the film adaptation, released in 1944 under the book's American title, were compared to Daphne du Maurier's *Rebecca*, which Alfred Hitchcock had adapted to the silver screen in 1940. Both films focus on homes haunted by a dead woman who is seemingly an icon of perfection and control.

Wife after Death

Macardle was a feminist, and her writing doesn't shy away from the dark sides of friendship, marriage, and parenthood.

She delves into the psychological depths of twisted love and loss, the horrors of obsession and neglect, the vagaries of memory, the dangers of misperception, and the damage women suffer at the hands of the men they love. In *Uneasy Freehold*, Stella's father, the artist Lyn Meredith, exhibits a near-demonic narcissism and cruelty and is drawn to extremes. Macardle creates a kind of Dorian Gray situation, in which the male artist vampirically sucks the life out of the two women he's put in competition for his love—his wife Mary and his mistress Carmel, who lives with the family. He paints various portraits of the two women, slowly wearing them down until they are merely objects of his gaze.

Macardle once wrote a feminist response to Oscar Wilde's *The Picture of Dorian Gray*. Her version, "The Portrait of Roisin Dhu," was published in *Earth-Bound* (Swan River Press, 1924; reprint, 2016), a collection of her short stories, most of which Macardle wrote while in prison. In that tale, a male artist inadvertently steals his female subject's vitality. But in *Uneasy Freehold*, Meredith intentionally uses the women's beauty for his art and then paints portraits that emphasize what they perceive as their faults, in order to manipulate and, ultimately, break them.

The Unforeseen is not as well-known as *Uneasy Freehold* but is enjoying a bit of a resurgence. In November 2017, the journalist Arminta Wallace called it a "page-turner" in an *Irish Times* article. Like Macardle's other novel, the story presents a mother–daughter relationship and has a twist ending. But, Wallace writes, its real strength is its uncertainty. The main character, Virginia Wilde, experiences visions that she thinks might be a sign that she's going insane. The novel alternates between supernatural and rational explanations for the visions as they grow more disturbing. Like *The Uninvited*, this is a story that takes the romance of the Gothic and mixes it with a little Victorian ambiguity, modern psychology, and a dash of Ireland.

Reading List

Not to be missed: Both of Dorothy Macardle's novels are easy to find and make for rewarding reading. *Uneasy Freehold* is one of our favorites.

Also try: Along with the 1944 film *The Uninvited*, Macardle's work has benefited from a number of worthy adaptations for the small screen. Two of her stories were adapted for the Canadian anthology television series *General Motors Presents* (called *Encounter* in the United States): "The Unforeseen," which aired in November 1956, and "The Watchers," which aired in 1960. A made-for-television movie called *Fantastic Summer*, based on one of Macardle's novels, debuted in 1955 and starred the actress Fay Compton, who played Mrs. Sanderson in *The Haunting*, Robert Wise's 1963 film adaptation of the Shirley Jackson novel.

Related work: Some readers and critics have drawn similarities between *Uneasy Freehold* and Elizabeth Bowen's 1945 story "The Demon Lover," which plays with the kind of psychological horror that Macardle renders so well.

> ## "Someone out of the world of the dead was moving about the house."
>
> —The Uninvited

• *The Queen of Horror* •
Shirley Jackson

1916–1965

In 1948, the *New Yorker* published a short story by a then-unknown writer. The tale, about an ordinary town with a sinister secret, so outraged readers that the magazine reported receiving more negative mail than ever before, including many subscription cancellations.

That story was "The Lottery" by Shirley Jackson, which went on to become one of the most famous short stories in American literature.

Though Jackson had been an obsessive writer since her youth and began publishing her writing during college, "The Lottery" made her a household name. For decades she received letters about it, which typically fell into one of three categories: bewilderment, speculation, and "plain old-fashioned abuse."

The New England setting of the story was an integral part of Jackson's writing, which often features main characters who are outsiders and find themselves persecuted in a hostile small-town environment. This was an experience familiar to Jackson.

Born in 1916, Jackson spent her childhood in California. She met her husband, the literary critic and professor Stanley Edgar Hyman, at Syracuse University, where they were students. The couple married in 1940 and moved several times before settling in 1945 in North Bennington, Vermont, where Hyman took a faculty position at Bennington College. She wrote, in what has become a famous anecdote from her life, that when checking into a hospital for the birth of her third child, the nurse asked Jackson what her occupation was. Jackson replied that she was a writer, to which the nurse said, "I'll just put down housewife."

The truth was that Jackson always struggled against her roles as wife and mother—or, to be more accurate, the roles that others cast her in. Professionally she was a successful author, but at home in North Bennington, she was Hyman's wife and the mother of four children. Her husband expected her to play the part of faculty wife: to maintain the household, to rear the children, to cook, to clean, and to entertain people he brought into their home. The residents of the college town never quite accepted her as one of their own, which likely informed how she wrote about various groups' intolerance of outsiders (see: the stone-wielding townsfolk in "The Lottery").

Hyman controlled the family's finances, but often it was Jackson's income that kept them afloat. Jackson's posthumously published collection *Come Along with Me* (Viking, 1968; Penguin, 1995 reprint) contains an anecdote about a time the family needed a new refrigerator. So she wrote a story, was paid, and bought the fridge. In this way, writing was, for Jackson, a real kind of magic. Hyman encouraged his wife's work, especially because it supplemented his income. But when eventually her career eclipsed his, Hyman no longer tolerated her success and belittled her in front of his university colleagues. What's more, he was frequently unfaithful, being particularly fond of his former students.

It's no wonder that Jackson wrote about women who were lonely and ostracized. Her characters are haunted, sometimes literally and sometimes figuratively, by pasts they can't escape. Jackson became a master of both types of hauntings, the supernatural and the psychological, the interior and the exterior.

Haunted Housekeeping

Haunted house stories are a staple in horror literature; nearly every writer of the genre has told one or two. None have come as close to perfection as Jackson in creating houses that loom larger than their actual size, describing a past that haunts the present. What also sets her domestic stories apart is how quickly and effectively the mundane scenarios she depicts turn violent. Even a setting as seemingly humdrum as a grocery store transforms into a downright bloodbath in *We Have Always Lived in the Castle*, her 1962 novel about two sisters living in a family home following an infamous multiple murder.

"The Lottery" established Jackson as reigning queen of the horror genre, though she wrote everything from campus novels to darkly comic domestic sketches about family life. These sketches were first published in magazines like *Good Housekeeping* and *Woman's Day* and, later, in the books *Raising Demons* (Farrar, Straus & Cudahy, 1957; Penguin Books, 2015) and *Life among the Savages* (Farrar, Straus & Cudahy, 1953; Penguin Books, 2015). She cemented her status as a titan of terror with the 1959 publication of *The Haunting of Hill House* (Viking), which was adapted in 1963 into the film *The Haunting*, which then developed a cult following of its own. Director Jan de Bont brought a less popular adaptation to the screen in 1999. And in 2018, the Netflix series *The Haunting of Hill House* took the bare bones of Jackson's story into new territory.

Hill House is a lovely work of ambiguity. Four characters from different walks of life converge on the titular property, which has a bad past and a bad reputation. Eleanor Vance, the protagonist, has answered an advertisement posted by Dr. Montague seeking assistants for a haunted house investigation. She sees it as the first adventure of her life, which until that point she has spent taking care of her invalid mother. Once the action begins, it's hard to tell if the four people are cracking under the strain of their isolation in the bizarre mansion, or if the house truly is haunted. It doesn't help that every angle in the building is off by a few degrees, and the decorations are . . . well, let's just say, strange. In addition to the usual cold spots, bangs and knocks, and even a séance of sorts, Jackson adds Eleanor's internal monologues in which she struggles to understand her morbid attraction to Hill House.

With this book and others, Jackson drafted a blueprint for the modern haunted house in both literature and film. Stephen King modeled his Overlook Hotel in *The Shining* after another of Jackson's creepy settings, the Halloran house in *The Sundial* (Farrar, Straus & Cuddahy, 1958). Moreover, King wrote at length about his debt to Jackson in his nonfiction ode to the horror genre, *Danse Macabre* (Gallery Books reprint, 2010), and in *On Writing* (Scribner reprint, 2010), his memoir on his chosen craft. Other authors who have cited Jackson as an influence include Neil Gaiman, Richard Matheson, and Sarah Waters.

If *The Haunting of Hill House* was the definitive haunted house novel, then Jackson's final completed novel, *We Have Always Lived in the Castle* (Viking, 1962), cemented her in the Gothic and horror traditions. *Time* magazine named it one of the ten best novels of 1962. The story focuses on the Blackwood sisters, Constance and Mary Katherine (nicknamed Merricat), who live with their infirm Uncle Julian in their fenced-in family estate outside of a New England town. Uncle Julian's poor health and the scorn the townspeople feel for the surviving Blackwoods are the result of a tragedy that occurred six years earlier. One night at supper, four members of the Blackwood family—the girls' parents, brother, and aunt—were poisoned and died. Constance, who hadn't used the arsenic-laced sugar on the dinner table, was arrested for the crime but not indicted. The townspeople believe she got away with murder. Her younger sister Merricat had been sent to her room without dinner on that fateful night and now is the only member of the household who ventures outside; she also practices magic rituals in order to keep Constance safe. Out of the blue, their cousin Charles swoops in, believing he is the rightful inheritor of the estate, and establishes himself as patriarch.

Castle is often praised, especially for its protagonist. Merricat Blackwood is an outsider, like many of Jackson's women, but she maintains an imaginative spirit and a fierce devotion to defending her sister and her home. Fans of the horror writer Paul Tremblay will recognize similarities in his protagonist Merry in *A Head Full of Ghosts* (William Morrow, 2015).

The Blackwood sisters' existence at the margins of their community reflects Jackson's own experience. She didn't quite fit in with the other wives of her small university town; she spent her days writing and tending children, but her nights were filled with more exotic fare. A lover of the occult, Jackson gave tarot readings to friends and family. She claimed not to believe in ghosts but she owned a crystal ball and a Ouija board and seemed to relish her reputation as a "witch." Whether or not she practiced witchcraft is debatable.

Shirley Jackson may not have been understood by the people who knew her, but her literary legacy is indisputable. As an example, consider the Shirley Jackson Awards, a juried accolade that has been given annually since 2007 for excellence in horror, thriller, and dark fantasy fiction.

Reading List

Not to be missed: Need some Shirley Jackson in your life? Honestly, who doesn't? Jackson is best known for her novels *The Haunting of Hill House* and *We Have Always Lived in the Castle*, both available from Penguin Classics. "The Lottery" can be found in *The Lottery and Other Stories*, a 2009 Penguin reprint, among other editions. But Jackson's other novels are criminally underread. *The Sundial* is an apocalyptic tale with all the Gothic trappings: a family with a sordid past, a manor house with secrets, and a storm blowing in. Yet it avoids cliché thanks to a unique exploration of family relationships. The narrative quickly turns into psychological suspense, and readers must question whether the end of the world is, in fact, near. It is available in a 2014 Penguin edition, with a foreword by Victor LaValle.

Also try: As mentioned, the 1963 film adaptation of *Hill House* has gained a fandom of its own. The ten-part 2018 Netflix series provides a fantastic reimagining (not a straight adaptation) of the novel that is well done and worth viewing.

Judy Oppenheimer's *Private Demons* (Ballantine Books, 1989) was the first full-length biography of Shirley Jackson. Oppenheimer interviewed Jackson's family and friends for a more complete portrait than a mere blurb on a book jacket could offer. In it she focuses on Jackson's supposed witchcraft and occult leanings . . . maybe a little too much. Ruth Franklin's more recent and thoroughly engaging *Shirley Jackson: A Rather Haunted Life* (Liveright, 2016) dives deep into Jackson's personal papers and notes from the Library of Congress archive and interweaves insightful readings of her works into a sharp yet sympathetic biographical portrait. If you read only one biography of Jackson, make it Franklin's.

Related work: In a testament to Jackson's enduring allure, Susan Scarf Merrell's murder mystery *Shirley* (Blue Rider Press, 2014) features Jackson as a character. Like so many of Jackson's novels, this is a psychological thriller, with a young girl at the center. When the girl disappears, Jackson is a suspect. The director Josephine Decker began adapting the novel to film in 2018, with actress Elisabeth Moss playing Shirley Jackson.

"I'm going to put death in all their food and watch them die."

—We Have Always Lived in the Castle

The Dame of Dread
Daphne du Maurier

1907–1989

Unusually independent women. Dangerous obsessions. A flock of seagulls. Sexual intimacy with a male robot. Many women named Rebecca. Welcome to the mind of Daphne du Maurier.

Du Maurier was primed for a literary career from birth. Born in 1907 in London to a wealthy couple with a bohemian lifestyle, du Maurier grew up surrounded by riches and art. Her grandfather was the famed cartoonist and author George du Maurier, known for his work in the British satire publication *Punch* and his novel *Trilby* (Osgood, McIlvaine, 1895), which introduced the world to the character of Svengali. Her father, Gerald du Maurier, was a theater critic and an actor. Her mother, Muriel Beaumont, was an actress who often brought the dramatic arts home; Daphne and her two sisters grew up to write or to paint. Maybe the most intriguing detail is a connection to another literary legacy: Daphne's cousins were the Llewelyn Davies boys, who famously inspired J. M. Barrie while he was creating the character Peter Pan. Barrie and other writers were often visitors to the du Maurier family home in London during Daphne's childhood.

She was an unusual child. Though often called a tomboy, she mused that she may have been a boy soul placed in the wrong body (calling herself a "disembodied spirit"). As an adult, du Maurier often said that she had two personas: the female energy that she presented to the world, and a male energy, which she called "lover," that controlled her writing. Many critics have pointed to her tendency to use male narrators, even in stories with a female protagonist. She had early crushes on women and same-sex relationships (though she despised the term "lesbian") prior to her marriage to Frederick "Boy" Browning, a military man from a middle-class background. Rumors abound of same-sex flirtations even after her marriage, including an unrequited crush on her publisher's wife, Ellen Doubleday, and a relationship with the actress Gertrude Lawrence.

Though she kept her maiden name for her writing career, du Maurier became Lady Browning in 1946, when her husband was bestowed the title of Sir Browning and made a Knight Commander of the British Empire for his service in the South East Asia Command during World War II. In 1969, she was elevated to Dame Daphne du Maurier DBE, Fellow to the Royal Society of Literature.

The couple had three children, and du Maurier was the breadwinner, supporting the family with her writing. Her success eventually allowed for the purchase of Menabilly, a manor house in Cornwall, which provided the inspiration for Manderley, the setting of her most famous novel, *Rebecca* (Gollancz, 1938). Du Maurier's marriage may also have inspired the plot. According to their youngest child, the union was far from ideal, and du Maurier worried that Boy was still in love with a former flame. Perhaps her real experience being haunted by her husband's old love was transformed into the literal haunting of her fiction.

Birds and Dolls

Rebecca is a Gothic tale with domestic horror at its heart. The plot centers on a young wife—a shy, naive waif of a woman—who moves into a cold and vast mansion with her new husband. At first glance, the narrative appears to be typical ghost story fare, though deliciously steeped in Gothic elements: there's a vicious servant who refuses to accept the new wife, a husband with a murky, and perhaps dangerous, past, and a haunted house with entire wings that are off limits to the protagonist (and the reader by proxy). But beneath the ghostly trappings await the complicated identities of the two Mrs. de Winters: the deceased, who was vivacious and outgoing but cruel and manipulative, and the living, who is shy and submissive but dangerously obsessed with the woman who came before her.

In *Rebecca*, the tension is not in what the husband might be hiding, but in whether the two female forces can learn to inhabit the same space. The struggle to belong is a common thread in du Maurier's work; her female characters never quite fit into the roles they've been given, and often, as a result, pay the ultimate price. Though the novel was poorly received by critics, *Rebecca* earned du Maurier a National Book Award. The tale has become so popular that, some eighty years after its publication, it still sells around 4,000 copies a month.

Beyond du Maurier's most enduring work, readers would be remiss to ignore her other writing, which pushed the boundaries of what female characters could do. Her short story "The Doll" (written when du Maurier was twenty-one and then buried in a sheaf of work rejected by editors, lost for nearly seventy years) tells the story of a woman—curiously also named Rebecca—who enjoys a life of luxury and independence, a life that she happens to share with a mechanical doll named Julio. Like the novel *Rebecca*, much of the story's plot revolves around secrecy and the strangely cloistered life of the strong-willed and self-sufficient main character. The story is narrated not by Rebecca, but by one of her suitors, who is driven mad with jealousy and anger over her relationship with Julio. The unnamed narrator, who flies into a murderous rage when confronted with a love interest who rejects him, is the story's most fascinating element. That a woman would not need him—that she doesn't need any man for financial stability or sexual pleasure—confounds him.

The story was republished in 2011 in an anthology of the same name by William Morrow Paperbacks.

Du Maurier often takes what would likely be clichés in the hands of lesser writers—haunted houses, environmental catastrophes—and cooks them down into terrifying morsels. A perfect example is "The Birds," a short story that was first published in her collection *The Apple Tree* (Penguin, 1952) and is also found in *Don't Look Now* (Doubleday, 1971). It is an environmental horror tale about birds that unleash a kamikaze-style killing mission on the denizens of Cornwall. The premise—apocalypse by seagulls—doesn't quite inspire horror at first blush; yet du Maurier maintains a taut tension unlike any other thriller writer of her time. Alfred Hitchcock directed the film adaptation in 1963.

Of all the du Maurier adaptations, none garnered as much scandal as the 1973 Nicolas Roeg–directed film *Don't Look Now*, mostly due to a graphic sex scene between its stars, Donald Sutherland and Julie Christie, which nearly earned the picture an X rating. Du Maurier's story originally appeared in her collection *Not after Midnight* (Gollancz, 1971). It deals with the aftermath of the death of a child and the complicated grief that plagues a married couple, complete with psychic visions, a creepy shadow child, and a serial killer. Both the story and Roeg's film remain among the best psychological thrillers ever written.

Reading List

Not to be missed: *Rebecca* lives up to its reputation. Follow that with *My Cousin Rachel* (Doubleday, 1951), which packs a whirlwind of questions about identity, intent, and intrigue; it is a predecessor to novels that blur the lines between victim and killer, good and bad, such as Gillian Flynn's *Gone Girl* (Crown, 2012). Also highly recommended is the short story "Blue Lenses," which is as thrilling as du Maurier's novels. You'll find it, along with "The Birds" and several other unsettling stories, in a reprint of the abovementioned collection *Don't Look Now: Selected Stories of Daphne du Maurier* (NYRB Classics, 2008).

Also try: Du Maurier penned masterful Gothic romances, including *Frenchman's Creek* (Doubleday, 1941) and *Jamaica Inn* (Doubleday Doran, 1936). Skip the 1939 Alfred Hitchcock adaptation of the latter—it's universally panned as his worst movie. Stick with *The Birds* to get your film fix.

Related work: The thriller writer Patricia Highsmith is frequently compared to Daphne du Maurier, and for good reason: both are masters of suspense. Highsmith wrote horror as well, but those stories are not as frequently anthologized as her thrillers. If "The Birds" got under your skin, take a look at Highsmith's snail stories "The Snail Watcher" (*Gamma 3*, July 1964) and "The Quest for *Blank Claveringi*" (*Saturday Evening Post*, June 17, 1967). Yes, snails are the predators. And, yes, Highsmith makes them terrifying. Both were collected in *Eleven* (Grove Press, 2011 reprint).

"And slowly, softly, with no one there to see, the house whispers her secrets, and the secrets turn to stories, and in strange and eerie fashion we are one, the house and I."

—"The House of Secrets," in The Rebecca Notebook and Other Secrets

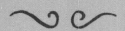

Haunted by History
Toni Morrison

1931–

Toni Morrison is one of the best-known authors in American history. If you weren't assigned one of her novels for English class, perhaps you've seen her being interviewed by Oprah Winfrey or on *The Colbert Report*. She's the recipient of high-profile awards and accolades, including the 1988 Pulitzer Prize, the 1993 Nobel Prize in Literature, the Presidential Medal of Freedom in 2012, and the 2016 PEN/Saul Bellow Award for Achievement in American Fiction. She's one of the most written about authors, up there with the two Wills, Shakespeare and Faulkner.

Toni Morrison is awesome. But is she a horror writer? Is she part of the tradition of weird fiction?

Our answer is yes, and our proof is her fifth novel, *Beloved*, published by Knopf in 1987.

Toni Morrison was born Chloe Wofford on February 18, 1931, in Lorain, Ohio. Her parents, George and Ramah, were migrants from Southern states. She studied the classics and humanities at Howard University, where she earned a bachelor's degree, and Cornell, where she earned a master's. She gained critical attention with her first novel, *The Bluest Eye*, published by Holt, Rinehart and Winston in 1970, and she hasn't slowed down since. She has published ten additional novels and worked as an editor for Random House and then as a professor at several universities. She has influenced numerous writers, including Angela Davis, Henry Dumas, Toni Cade Bambara, Gloria Naylor, Amy Tan, and Louise Erdrich. Morrison retired from teaching in 2006, and her papers and manuscripts are archived at Princeton University. But Morrison maintains an active literary life through writing and speaking and

by recording audio book versions of her novels.

Toni Morrison may not be a horror writer in the vein of Shirley Jackson or Anne Rice or Tananarive Due. But in addition to being a great historical novel of twentieth-century American literature, *Beloved* is a horror tour de force that evokes every trope of the genre while peeling back the bandages from the wound of slavery on Americans' collective psyche. Writing within the horror genre affords authors an opportunity to show the most violent and terrifying parts of real life, and *Beloved* is a master class in that technique. Morrison tells a ghost story that makes visible the gut-wrenching true horror of slavery, especially as experienced by African American women, and forces readers to reckon with an often-ignored part of U.S. history and its haunting effects.

Morrison is also no stranger to the supernatural. Several of her novels, including *Song of Solomon* (1977), *Jazz* (1992), *Paradise* (1997), *Love* (2003), and *Home* (2012), feature ghosts of the past. Her play *Desdemona* (Oberon Books, 2011) focuses on the ghost of Shakespeare's character, giving her a voice (finally!) to explore what went wrong in her relationship with Othello; in letting this character speak, Morrison calls attention to the issues of race and class that Shakespeare glossed over in his play.

Beloved, however, is a full-on ghost story from top to bottom. Morrison centers the story on the title character, the ghost of a deceased girl called Beloved, in order to explore the effects of trauma. It is a fictionalized reimagining of the life of Margaret Garner, an enslaved woman who, in 1856, attempted to escape her northern Kentucky slaveholder, along with her children, husband, and in-laws. The family crossed the frozen Ohio River into Cincinnati, where they were ambushed and recaptured. Because Garner believed that death was preferable to slavery, she tried to kill her children, and succeeded in slaying one of them.

The subsequent trial, and accompanying fiery speeches, protests, and violence, presaged the Civil War. Testimony revealed that Garner's owner had physically and sexually abused her. Ultimately she was returned to enslavement but sold to a planter in Louisiana. She and one of her children were traveling there by riverboat when their vessel sank in a fiery crash with another boat. Her child died but Garner survived; she died two years later in Louisiana of typhoid fever. Her husband recalled that her last words to him were: "live in hope of freedom."

Chains of Memory

Morrison read a news clipping about Margaret Garner while doing research for another book, and she decided to try to imagine what caused a woman to commit infanticide. What does it mean to be a mother to children who literally belong to another person? What does it mean to face, every day, the possibility that your loved ones could be abused, tortured, maimed, killed, or sold away? What she created was a novel in the tradition of ghost stories, but in which the ghost represents more than just a person returning from the afterlife. The spirit also stands for the estimated sixty million people who died in the so-called land of the free during the time of enslavement.

Beloved begins with the protagonist, Sethe, and her daughter Denver living in a home troubled by an angry ghost-child, whose torments prompted Sethe's two older sons to run away. Mother and daughter attempt to communicate with the spirit because they believe it belongs to Sethe's youngest daughter, whom Sethe killed, as Margaret Garner had done, after the family escaped slavery and was faced with recapture. Both

Sethe and Denver find comfort in the haunting presence of the lost two-year-old child. Then the ghost comes back in physical form.

Or does it? Like all good supernatural fiction, Morrison's story can be explained one way or the other . . . or both. Regardless, as the women interact with the seemingly full-grown Beloved, each is gripped by memories of a past full of trauma—physical, emotional, and sexual—experienced and witnessed. Ultimately, Denver learns about the painful past despite her mother's attempt to protect her by refusing to speak about slavery.

Reading List

Not to be missed: After *Beloved*, turn to *Song of Solomon* (Knopf, 1977), which is probably Morrison's next most spectral read; it features a protagonist who is haunted by his parents' and aunt's pasts. By facing the ghosts, he learns where he came from and who he is. *Love* (Knopf, 2003) is a story of the strength of female relationships in the face of trauma and abuse, in which at least one of the narrators is a ghost.

Also try: *Beloved* (1998) was adapted to the screen in 1998 by Akosua Busia and directed by Jonathan Demme, starring Oprah Winfrey and Danny Glover. It was not well received, perhaps because there's something special in Morrison's prose that can't quite be translated to film. We think it's worth a watch nonetheless.

Related work: Steven Weisenburger's *Modern Medea* (Hill and Wang, 1998) outlines the events surrounding Margaret Garner's escape, recapture, and trial. It's history that is as riveting as any modern-day drama. For more fiction centered on strong African American women living in a world tinged with supernatural possibilities, read Gloria Naylor's *Mama Day* (Ticknor & Fields, 1988). Like Morrison, Naylor also explores the haunting past of slavery and how it ruptures family histories.

Tananarive Due's novel *The Good House* (Atria, 2003) is on our required reading list. Due explores how family histories haunt homes by focusing on the titular residence and its place in the nexus of African American and Native American history. As in Naylor's *Mama Day*, the story's paranormal elements may have roots in an ancestor's curse. Due's story collection *Ghost Summer* (Prime Books, 2015) is an exemplary group of varied paranormal and apocalyptic tales; the title novella is a great follow-up to *Beloved*. In it, Due explores how we are haunted by history, whether we learned about it or not. She doesn't shy away from violence; like the protagonist of Octavia Butler's *Kindred* (Beacon Press, 1979; reprint, 2009), Due's characters are physically injured by encounters with the past.

Speaking of *Kindred*, if you haven't read Butler's time-travel novel about slavery, what are you waiting for?

"She moved him. Not the way he had beat off the baby's ghost—all bang and shriek with windows smashed and jelly jars rolled in a heap. But she moved him nonetheless . . ."

—*Beloved*

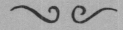

Monstrosity in the Mundane
Elizabeth Engstrom
1951–

Elizabeth Engstrom was born Betty Lynn Gutzmer, known to some as Betsy, in Elmhurst, Illinois, in 1951. She spent her childhood in two places: the Park Ridge suburb of Chicago, when living with her father, and Kaysville, Utah, north of Salt Lake City, where she lived with her mother. After a move west in search of warmer weather, she worked in advertising in Hawaii and eventually opened her own agency in Maui.

In 1984 her life took a sharp turn after she signed up for a writing workshop on Kauai with Theodore Sturgeon, a prolific and Hugo Award winning American science-fiction and horror author. Sturgeon was a mentor to writers of the weird; rumors abound that he was the inspiration for Kurt Vonnegut's recurring character Kilgore Trout. In 1986, Engstrom moved with her husband and two children to Oregon, where she was able to foster her writing career. She served for ten years as the director of the Maui Writers Retreat and was on the board of the nonprofit Wordcrafters. Engstrom holds a master's degree in applied theology from Marylhurst University and works with Love and Mercy Ministries, a nondenominational outreach organization.

It was in the workshop that Engstrom wrote her novella *When Darkness Loves Us*. Sturgeon loved the story and urged Engstrom to pair it with another of her works, *Beauty Is*. The two novellas were eventually published in a single volume by William Morrow in 1985, with an introduction by Sturgeon.

When Darkness Loves Us is the tale of a dim-witted, or perhaps just naive, farm girl named Sally Hixon. She is high on life, pregnant and still in the newlywed glow of marriage. The honeymoon ends, however, when she becomes trapped in an underground cave. Literally trapped. There is no rescue, no happy ending. Sally must confront her deepest fears down in the cold darkness. And the pregnancy? Let's just say that cave birth isn't easy. What's astounding about this particular story is that Engstrom was hit with inspiration at the happiest place on earth. She described the moment the story was conceived in a 2009 interview with *Apex Magazine*:

"Strangely enough, *When Darkness Loves Us* came to me almost fully formed while in the midst of an excruciating bout of claustrophobia while riding the submarine in Disneyland. I'd always known I didn't care for small, closed-in places, but being stuck in one with my kids almost had me clawing my way out."

Trauma and What Comes After

Engstrom finds inspiration in the most mundane moments of life. In many of her works, the domestic space is one of both safety and danger. In *Beauty Is*, the main character, Martha, is a woman born without a nose. The world treats her with horrible hostility, but it's memories of her home life—notably her father's rejection and her faith-healer mother, who was taken advantage of by a group of drunk men—that truly haunt her. Engstrom's writing as been called everything from speculative fiction to erotica, and these labels are not necessarily wrong. But she is also a writer of the best kind of horror fiction: stories that present the human condition coming to grips with the aftermath of trauma and grief.

Engstrom's horror fiction often draws comparisons to Anne Rice, largely because she wrote a book in the mid-1980s about vampires titled *Black Ambrosia* (Tor Books, 1986). But her writing covers many subjects. Another standout is *Lizzie Borden* (Tor Books, 1991), about the infamous unsolved ax murders committed in 1892 in Fall River, Massachusetts.

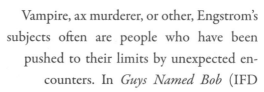

Vampire, ax murderer, or other, Engstrom's subjects often are people who have been pushed to their limits by unexpected encounters. In *Guys Named Bob* (IFD Publishing, 2018), a middle-aged woman is carjacked and must fight for survival. In *Lizard Wine* (Headline, 1995), university students find trouble in an abandoned campground when their car breaks down. Whatever the details, Engstrom's characters are thrust into a world that they don't know; often it's so unfamiliar that they question their very reality. Her characters dig deep to find the person they didn't know they could be—if that person is good or bad is left for the reader to decide.

Engstrom was nominated for a Stoker Award in 1992 for best fiction collection, and her story "Crosley" was included in *The Year's Best Fantasy and Horror: Thirteenth Annual Collection* (St. Martin's Griffin, 2000), edited by Ellen Datlow. We think her body of work deserves more critical attention.

Reading List

Not to be missed: Engstrom's talent sings in her short stories. Several collections are available, including *Suspicions* (Triple Tree 2002), *Nightmare Flower* (Tor Books, 1992), and *The Alchemy of Love* (Triple Tree, 1998), with an introduction by horror writer Jack Ketchum.

Also try: Her novel *Candyland* (IFD Publishing, 2012) follows a couple who meet in a bar and embark on a nightmarish journey. It was adapted into the film *Candiland* in 2016, starring Gary Busey.

Related work: Something Engstrom does well is explore how women push and pull against the roles that society has given them. Her literary successor may be Zoje Stage, whose novel *Baby Teeth* (St. Martin's Press, 2018) is a nightmarish look at how far a mother will go to protect her daughter, who, by the way, may be trying to kill her. *Entertainment Weekly* called it "*We Need to Talk About Kevin* meets *Gone Girl* meets *The Omen.*"

"She managed one scream, drowned by the earth-vibrating essence of the great engine above."

—*When Darkness Loves Us*

PART SIX

Paperback Horror

I n the 1980s, horror went mainstream in America. Children who grew up during this decade may recall such pop-culture touchstones as Freddy Krueger and the Garbage Pail Kids. Personally, we have vivid memories of walking through Blockbuster Video, shielding our eyes so we wouldn't see the covers of certain VHS tapes. (It didn't work.) We first became acquainted with Pinhead and Jason Voorhees years before summoning the courage to see their movies. And video-rental stores weren't the only spaces where terror reigned. Horror lived on the covers of paperbacks that lined the shelves of every B. Dalton. Even grocery store aisles weren't safe.

For all the talk of horror and weird fiction taking over the new millennium—more about that in Part Eight—an earlier horror revolution occurred beginning in the 1970s. Highly successful horror chartbusters like *The Exorcist* triggered a deluge of lurid, bloody paperback horror fiction. Now-defunct trade publishers and imprints like Zebra and Leisure spat out novels at a dizzying pace, filled with Satan, sex, monsters, and murder.

All of which was boldly displayed right on the book covers. It seemed that every paperback needed disturbing art to make it stand out against the competition. The two artists who beckoned readers better than anyone were women: Lisa Falkenstern and Jill Bauman.

Falkenstern's signature was a balance of the macabre with the innocent. Her cover for *Piper*, the 1987 novel by Brett Rutherford and John Robertson, published by Zebra, features two blonde children dancing around a jester clown that has a skull for a face. She also created the beautiful and creepy blonde children who populate the covers of V. C. Andrews's books. Our favorite is her cover image for Ken Greenhall's *Childgrave* (Pocket, 1982; reissued in 2017 by Valancourt Books), which depicts a wide-eyed girl—blonde again—hovering over a small town, the steeple of a church dangerously close to her cherubic blue eye.

Jill Bauman created covers that often featured thin—even skeletal—portraits and dark, gloomy atmospheres. Our favorite is her cover for Elizabeth Engstrom's *When Darkness Loves Us* (Tor, 1985), featuring a broken baby doll that's missing a nose. As if dolls aren't creepy enough, Bauman's looks as if it is reaching out, almost grasping for the reader. Bauman has worked with some of the biggest names in the genre, including Peter Straub and Stephen King, and her work has earned her several World Fantasy Award nominations.

Another horror cover artist, Rowena Morrill, achieved close to rock-star fandom. And like Cher or Madonna, her fans sometimes referred to her by just her first name. Her artwork for the original printing of Jane Parkhurst's *Isobel* (Fantasy Fiction, 1977) launched her career. The book's premise is simple: in the year 1630, Isobel Gowdie is accused of witchcraft, but unlike her contemporaries, who professed their innocence as they met a fiery death (or a watery one, or a hanging-by-the-neck one, depending on the executioner), Isobel proudly *admitted* she was a witch, confessing in great detail. There's lurid sex and the devil and everything else you might imagine. Morrill's cover is everything a '70s horror novel deserves: a naked woman reaches up to her lover, who is a horned blue-skinned goat-man.

Morrill created covers for horror and science-fiction books, wild scenes filled with monsters and epic battles not unlike the work of Frank Frazetta. Her art visualized the stories of authors like Philip K. Dick and Anne McCaffrey and earned numerous awards, including a Hugo for best professional artist. Her work graced other mediums, including album covers, and was even plagiarized for the evangelical literature of a cult. An original piece was found in one of Saddam Hussein's palaces.

Horror in the latter half of the twentieth century underwent a major identity shift. In previous decades, horror belonged to the monster roster of Universal Studios and, later, to British monster makers Hammer Film Productions. But the '70s and '80s paperback boom pushed the genre away from the Dracula-meets-Frankenstein-meets-Wolfman plot generator and into new territory. Authors of this era redefined the horror novel, exploring increasingly gory and, well, sometimes trashy material. The audience was relatively small at first. But as more horror paperbacks found their way onto more shelves and into more hands, the readership grew. And women authors were part of that trend.

Lois Duncan wrote about teens in peril in books like *I Know What You Did Last Summer* (Little, Brown, 1973). Betty Ren Wright scared the youth of America with titles like *The Dollhouse Murders* (Holiday House, 1983). Patricia Wallace penned books whose covers featured every possible combination of creepy child and skeleton. Clare McNally wrote *Ghost House* (Bantam House, 1979), *Hear the Children Calling* (Penguin, 1990), and *Cries of the Children* (Penguin, 1992), among others. Apparently, readers—and authors—in the 1980s were afraid for, and more often afraid *of*, the tiny humans in their lives.

Like the women horror writers of the pulp-magazine era (see Part Four), the contributions of women authors to this horror paperback boom tend to be overlooked. Yes, readers flocked to every new release from Stephen King, Dean Koontz, and Peter Straub (and still do). But women writers were also making names for themselves, among them Suzy McKee Charnas, Sharon Ahern, Kit Reed (aka Shelley Hyde), Florence Stevenson, and Melanie Tem. If you haven't read *The Man on the Ceiling* (Wizards of the Coast Discoveries, 2008), which Tem co-wrote with her husband, Steve Rasnic Tem, you need to. There's a good reason it won a Bram Stoker Award, a World Fantasy Award, and an International Horror Guild Award.

Another woman writing during this boom was Tabitha King (yes, *that* King—she is the wife of Stephen). Her talent was put to good use when her agent brought her an exciting opportunity: the completion of an unfinished manuscript by the late Michael McDowell, a great and underappreciated horror writer of the late twentieth century. Her completion of his novel *Candles Burning* (Berkley Books, 2006) proved she could match him word for word. We also recommend *Small World* (Macmillan, 1981), which involves a lusty woman and adult daughter of a former U.S. president. Oh, and there's a shrinking machine. It's schlocky at times but a fun read.

Every boom has its bust, and by the end of the '80s, paperback horror no longer dominated store shelves. Small publishers like Zebra closed up shop. As with the pulps, once these paperbacks ceased to be printed, we lost access to much of the work of women authors who grew horror from a niche genre to the force that it is today.

Fortunately, interest in these bygone books is on the rise. In 2017 the horror author Grady Hendrix offered an exhaustive look back at the gems of the era in *Paperbacks from Hell*, published by Quirk Books. Will Errickson's *Too Much Horror Fiction* blog is an excellent source for this heyday as well. And publishers such as Valancourt are looking to republish some titles; we hope others will follow suit.

Meanwhile, let's explore the days when paperback horror novels were on every bookshelf, their garish covers demanding our attention. Don't cover your eyes—you'll want to see this.

• Recipes for Fear •
Joanne Fischmann
1943–

Teens of the 1980s and '90s were well acquainted with horror. Slasher movies of the day presented all manner of terrifying, deadly scenarios to keep young people up at night. They couldn't go to summer camp without Jason Voorhees breathing down their neck (or skewering their hearts like roasted marshmallows). They couldn't babysit the bratty neighborhood kid on Halloween without Michael Myers stalking them. Not even sleeping was safe if you lived on Elm Street.

Alongside all the teen slasher movies, the 1980s saw a spike in horror books written with a young adult audience in mind. Christopher Pike started the trend with such titles as *Slumber Party* (Scholastic, 1985) and *Chain Letter* (Lightning, 1989). By the end of the decade, R. L. Stine joined in with his Fear Street series.

Another writer creating stories about blade-wielding maniacs for teens was Joanne Fischmann. As the daughter of an undertaker, perhaps Fischmann was destined to write murder mysteries. She was born in 1943, grew up in small-town Minnesota, and attended St. Cloud State University before transferring to and ultimately graduating from California State University in San Bernardino. She married and settled in Southern California with her husband, a screenwriter. Fischmann had a passion for writing and worked a variety of odd jobs to support her dream, including stints as a cook, a teacher, a florist, and a party planner.

After publishing several mystery novels in the 1980s, many under the name Joanne Fluke, Fischmann began writing a series of "suspense thrillers" (translation: horror) for a young adult audience. The first was for Kensington Books' Scream series. As Jo Gibson, she wrote the fourth book in the series, *The Dead Girl*, which was published in 1993. The cover, whose artist is unknown, is quintessential '90s teen horror: a young girl wearing head-to-toe denim clutches her chest and steps on a grave—as a skeleton hand reaches up and grabs her ankle. The plot is simple: a teenage girl moves to a new town where everyone keeps mistaking her for her dead cousin, and she begins to fear that the same dead cousin may be trying to possess her living body.

Fischmann continued writing YA horror with *My Bloody Valentine* (Zebra, 1995), which follows a group of teen girls all vying to be the belle of the Valentine's Day dance. The competition is deadly. A year later she published *The Dance of Death* (Scholastic, 1996), a retelling of Hans Christian Andersen's tale about cursed dancing shoes. Fischmann also penned three Christmas-themed horror novels: *Slay Bells* (Z-Fave/Kensington 1994) and *The Crush* and *The Crush II* (Z-Fave/Kensington, both 1994). In 2014 Kensington rereleased *Obsessed*, which collected *The Crush* and its sequel; *Twisted*, which contains *My Bloody Valentine*, *The Séance* (originally published by Zebra in 1996), and *Slay Bells*; and *Afraid*, which includes *The Dance of Death* and *The Dead Girl*. Unfortunately, the covers—close-up photographs of half-obscured faces—are less intriguing than what appeared on the originals.

Jo Gibson's career ended in 2014 with those three books, but Fischmann's did not. She returned to writing as Joanne Fluke and cooked up an entirely new career, this time penning a series of cozy (meaning no blood or gore) mysteries about a lovable baker named Hannah Swensen. Dead bodies keep interrupting her as she tries to run her bakery, the Cook-ie Jar. The first book, *The Chocolate Chip Cookie Murder*, was original-ly published in 2000 by Kensington. It was an immediate hit, not only due to the likeable protagonist but also thanks to recipes interspersed throughout. By 2018 Fluke had published twenty-two titles in this se-ries, which spawned spin-off cookbooks and a made-for-TV movie se-ries, starring Alison Sweeney as the titular baker.

We love a good chocolate chip cookie (and so do Fluke's fans, appar-ently), but we love teenage slasher horror just a little bit more.

Reading List

Not to be missed: Joanne Fischmann wrote horror that seems down-right cheery when compared to work by Lisa Tuttle, Ruby Jean Jensen, or V. C. Andrews. She wrote for a teen audience, and her books are more light suspense than anything else. But if you suffer from '80s nostalgia (and have a soft spot for the shopping mall setting of so many teen '80s movies), *Slay Bells* is your best bet.

Also try: Before launching the Hannah Swensen books, Fischmann wrote a few adult psychological thrillers using the Fluke surname. *Win-ter Chill* (Kensington, 1984) is about a snow-buried Minnesota town and a series of horrible "accidents" claiming its citizens. There is nothing cozy about this book—the tone is as dark as winter nights in the Upper Midwest.

Related work: One of the biggest names on the Scholastic Books teen horror roster was Caroline B. Cooney, who has written more than seventy-five books. Though she is adept at writing mysteries—*Hush Little Baby* (Scholastic, 1998), *Safe as the Grave* (Coward, McCann & Geoghegan, 1979), and the Janie Johnson series, which started with *The*

Face on the Milk Carton (Bantam Doubleday Dell, 1990)—she shines best in the horror genre, particularly with novels like *Fog* (Scholastic, 1989), about a strange mist that descends upon a small town and causes the students at the local school to behave oddly.

Diane Hoh also has an impressive backlist and contributed numerous titles to the Point Horror series, which was published by Scholastic beginning in 1991 and included R. L. Stine and Christopher Pike. Hoh's titles include *The Accident* (1991) and *The Fever* (1992), but her best work may be the standalone novel *Funhouse*, which tells the story of a horrible, and possibly intentional, accident on a carnival rollercoaster. Critics compared it to work by Stephen King as well as the *Final Destination* movies.

> "After all, there was no way that they could elect a dead girl as Valentine's Day Queen."
>
> —*My Bloody Valentine*

◆ *Where Evil Meets Innocence* ◆
Ruby Jean Jensen
1927–2010

In the 1980s, Zebra Books made sure that every bookstore had access to a flood of horror paperbacks. Readers were tempted with covers that featured skeletons screaming (or laughing—who can really tell with a skinless skull?) or baby dolls on a black background, staring blankly. These books came fast, one right after the other. Readers couldn't get enough. Neither could writers, who produced a deep catalogue of titles for the "skeleton farm," as Zebra was sometimes called.

By the 1990s Zebra had largely slowed its manic production of horror titles, and many of their most inventive authors have drifted into obscurity. One such writer is Ruby Jean Jensen.

The Missouri-born Jensen spent most of her life in Arkansas. Little is known about her, with the exception that she was a prolific writer for Zebra and Tor. She produced thirty novels, beginning with *The House That Samael Built* (Warner), published in 1974. We have to assume that at some point she made the acquaintance of an extremely creepy child, because her books established her as the horror author for stories about tiny demon spawn, picking up a tradition started by Mary Shelley. If an ominous phrase includes the word "child" or some variation, it's probably been considered as a Jensen title; her books have names like *Child of Satan House* (Manor, 1978), *Hear the Children Cry* (Leisure, 1983), *Such a Good Baby* (Tor, 1982), and *Vampire Child* (Zebra, 1990).

Jensen wrote about both evil children and innocent children in the clutches of evil. *Home Sweet Home* (Zebra, 1985) is about sweet little Timmy (can you imagine a more innocent name?) who finds himself on a mountain vacation with the perfectly friendly Mr. Walker. As the summer progresses, though, Mr. Walker turns menacing.

Some critics have labeled *Home Sweet Home* cozy horror or even young adult horror, perhaps because of Jensen's tendency to feature younger protagonists. We're not sure this label is earned. Jensen might not be as explicitly violent or gory as other writers of her day. But she never keeps her young characters safe. They can—and sometimes do—meet violent ends.

Toying with You

When Jensen wasn't writing about children in peril (or causing the peril), she turned her pen to more overtly supernatural fare, especially possessed children's toys. Recognizing the plain fact that dolls, whose glass eyes refuse to blink and gaze at you while you sleep, are creepy. Jensen wrote more than one novel about them.

Mama (Zebra, 1986) is a standout in the killer doll category because of the care Jensen takes in crafting her characters. Dorrie has lost her father to cancer, and as a grieving child will do, she forms an attachment to her dolly. Dorrie chooses a doll that is dented and dirty and has seen better days; she wants to heal it, to make it better, because she couldn't make her dying father well. The appeal of Jensen's story lies in her ability to use a tired trope—a child's doll haunted by a supernatural entity—to craft a tale with empathetic characters. Her other doll novels include *Baby Dolly* (Zebra, 1991), *Annabelle* (Zebra, 1987), and *The Living Evil* (Zebra, 1993), whose tagline read, "She Walks . . . She Talks . . . She *Kills*!" (FYI, these killer dolls have nothing to do with the current *Annabelle* movie franchise. And it's too bad, because in our opinion, Jensen's dolls are superior.)

It's not all dolls, though. Jensen also wrote a book called *Jump Rope* (Zebra, 1988) about—you guessed it—a killer jump rope. Doesn't sound like good horror material, but in her hands, the concept is downright creepy. A young girl finds her dead father, who has apparently committed suicide, with a jump rope wrapped around his hands. Then she sees her own doppelgänger take the rope and jump away, sweetly humming a nursery rhyme.

Clearly, Jensen could use any mundane object to give readers chills that would last for days.

Reading List

Not to be missed: Ruby Jean Jensen was prolific and she amassed a following of loyal horror fans. Yet she never won awards (at least none that we could find) or received critical praise. Her extensive library has fallen out of print and her books are becoming increasingly difficult to find, but talent like hers deserves to be read. Used copies are available, and thanks to the internet, readers can find some of her titles at a reasonable price. Read *The Haunting* (Zebra, 1994) if you can snag a copy. Its plot is familiar: a family moves into a house possessed by evil, unaware of the past horror that occurred there. But this book is anything but formulaic and it will leave readers contemplating the story long after turning the final page.

Also try: *House of Illusions* (Zebra, 1988) is a funhouse horror book worth reading if you can find a copy. Jensen writes just as brilliantly about the uncanny carnival as she does about creepy baby dolls.

Related work: Patricia Wallace is another Zebra author worth searching for. Her book *See No Evil* (Zebra, 1988) is about a young girl who undergoes a cornea operation to correct her sight. We shouldn't have to tell you that eye transplants are never a good thing in horror fiction. Wallace's writing skills are not up to par with Jensen's, but the book is a fun read, and it's available in a Kindle edition. Wallace wrote several novels for Zebra, which sport some of our favorite covers in the publisher's backlist. These include *The Children's Ward* (1985), about a sick girl staying in an evil hospital, whose excellent cover depicts a young girl being held by a skeleton doctor wearing a surgical mask across its skull. Another title worth seeking out for the cover alone is *Water Baby* (1987), with a skeleton mermaid holding a fat cherublike infant.

> *That face that looks so pure and so fine and so handsome, eyelashes as long as a girl's. That is the face of a killer, my good people.*
>
> —The Haunting

Nightmares in the Attic •
V. C. Andrews

1923–1986

Ann Radcliffe wrote Gothic novels that caused a craze in the 1790s, and no author since then has whipped readers into such a frenzy with deliciously dramatic horror set in gloomy forests and crumbling mansions. Not until V. C. Andrews took the literary stage, that is. Andrews combined the elements of Gothic horror with soap-opera-style family drama. And she included more than enough incestuous plot lines to keep her audience mesmerized.

Born and raised in Portsmouth, Virginia, Cleo Virginia Andrews had a difficult childhood. From a young age she suffered from crippling rheumatoid arthritis that was unresponsive to surgical treatments; at times she was wheelchair bound or dependent upon crutches. Still, she excelled at her studies and earned an art degree via a correspondence program that allowed her to work from home. She started her career as a commercial artist, but her writing became her lifeline to the outside world. Andrews never married or had children. Due to her health problems, which left her in pain and largely immobile, she lived with her mother for most of her life.

Andrews started writing in the early 1970s, producing what she called "confession stories" in order to "finance [her] more serious efforts," as she wrote in a pitch letter to the literary agent Anita Diamant. Those serious efforts included the first novel she wrote, though not her first to be published, a science-fiction work called *Gods of Green Mountain* (published posthumously in 2004 by Pocket Books). The book is set on a distant planet that has been ravaged by two suns and endless storms, and it's packed with typical space-opera fare such as a princess, a reckless hero, outlaws, and civil war, plus a mysterious plant that can solve the world's problems. But Andrews's so-called confession stories that paid the bills early in her career are more interesting. The titles alone are packed with tawdry details. Take, for example, "I Slept with My Uncle on My Wedding Night," which has become practically apocrypha for Andrews fans. It was published in a pulp magazine, but the publication details have been lost and no copies exist. Certainly the story anticipates Andrews's most famous book: *Flowers in the Attic* (Simon and Schuster, 1979), which introduced the Dollanganger family, whose saga would unfold over five novels. That first book was a runaway hit right out of the gate, staying on the *New York Times* Best-Seller List for fourteen weeks. The sequel spent nineteen weeks on the list.

It's a Family Affair

The plot of *Flowers* is Gothic horror in its purest form: four children—beautiful, blonde cherubs all of them—are locked in the attic of Foxworth Hall by their wealthy, abusive, emotionally frigid grandmother. The scenario is a bizarre attempt by their mother to keep her virginal reputation intact so she can secure the family fortune. The book is full of twisted relationships, especially the grandmother's to religion, which is terrifying and the reason for the abuse that borders on torture. She can yell about sin as well as Carrie's mother (no mention of "dirty pillows" in this book, though). But the relationship that scandalized readers the most was between the two oldest Dollanganger children, who fall in love while trapped in that lonely attic, their teenage hormones raging.

It could be a sweet story, really, but the horror is real. The mother, who at the beginning of the novel seems to be a loving and protective caregiver, becomes a monster, willing to sacrifice her daughters for wealth. The youngest child dies. There's also rape. And rats.

The child incest was sufficient to get Andrews's book banned from several libraries, but the story was popular enough to support immediate

sequels, in which readers learn that the Dollanganger family had a long history of incestual romance. Andrews created other franchises that were just as juicy. The Audrina series, beginning with *My Sweet Audri-*
na (Simon & Schuster, 1982), involved another child locked away in a Gothic mansion, this one haunted by the ghostly memories of a sister who is long dead (or *is* she?). Andrews's books about the Casteel family, beginning with *Heaven* (HarperCollins, 1985), offer more dead children, a wealthy elite who scorn the impoverished family, and a creepy doll made to look just like a dead woman.

Andrews's writing career was lucrative. She sold her first book to Simon & Schuster's Pocket imprint for $7,500, and two sequels were immediately ordered, with a $50,000 advance. *Heaven* brought in $2 million and was part of a two-book deal. In addition to making her wealthy, Andrews's novels served as a rite of passage for would-be Goth girls. The lure of secret incest in an old manor house is too great to resist. But Andrews's work is more than a guilty pleasure. It's Gothic fiction directly descended from the lineage of Anne Radcliffe. Her work is melodramatic, yes, but it's also packed with compelling characters, especially women, caught up in villainous schemes.

Unfortunately, Andrews could not keep up with her growing career. Her already fragile health declined, and she was in constant pain. While writing *Heaven* and its sequel, which were her final books, she discovered a lump in her breast that turned out to be cancer. She didn't want to seek medical treatment until the books were finished, by which time the illness had spread to other parts of her body.

After Andrews passed away in 1986, her estate kept her literary legacy alive through a ghostwriter. Andrew Neiderman stepped in to pen mass-market paperbacks under her name, using some of her unfinished outlines as inspiration. Her novels continue to sell well decades after her death. Some readers speculate whether her salacious plots have a basis in her life. Maybe her early "confession stories" have something to do with that rumor.

HALLMARK MOMENTS

Newcomers to V. C. Andrews's novels can expect the following elements:

- **The drinking of blood.** In *Flowers in the Attic*, food becomes scarce and so the children turn to feeding on the blood of the oldest brother.

- **Incest.** The most famous example is between the blonde cherublike siblings in *Flowers in the Attic*. But Andrews's work also depicts problematic scenes in which consent is neglected.

- **Child torture and slavery.** Children don't fare well in Andrews's novels; they're often drugged, poisoned, tarred (yes, you read that right), and sometimes sold for moonshine money. Who are these parents?

- **A tiger mauling a kid.** In the United States of America. We don't need to say more about this, do we?

Reading List

Not to be missed: If *Flowers in the Attic* leaves you wanting additional melodramatic horror, read the rest of the Dollanganger series. The subsequent books feature possession by the spirits of dead relatives and, perhaps more disturbingly, one of the children becoming a televangelist.

Also try: *My Sweet Audrina* features a classic 1970s keyhole cover (in which a portion of the cover is cut out, revealing an elaborate illustration underneath); the original paperback is worth tracking down for that alone, never mind the story's sweet twist ending. *Flowers in the Attic* has been adapted for the screen several times; the 1987 version, starring Kristy Swanson (the original Buffy the Vampire Slayer) as the oldest sister Cathy, has a strong fandom, although it gets some of the book's key details wrong and nearly erases the incest, leaving only a few longing looks. In 2014, Lifetime made a television version starring Ellen Burstyn as the grandmother and Kiernan Shipka (of Netflix's *The Chilling Adventures of Sabrina*) as Cathy. Although not perfect, this version is a closer adaptation and plays up the book's Gothic and horror aspects.

Related work: Andrews fans may also like the work of Lois Duncan, who wrote young adult horror and thrillers. Duncan's work never deals with sex or incest in quite the same way that Andrews's does, but Duncan does push boundaries. In *Killing Mr. Griffin* (Little, Brown, 1978), a group of teenagers accidentally kills one of their high school teachers. Similarly, high school friends find themselves hiding a murder—and running from a murderer—in *I Know What You Did Last Summer* (Little, Brown, 1973), which was made into a well-known movie in 1997. Duncan's Gothic horror novel is *Down a Dark Hall* (Little, Brown, 1974).

～◌～

"We don't anticipate accidents, nor do we expect to die young."

—Flowers in the Attic

～◌～

Kafka of the Weird
Kathe Koja

1960–

In 1991 Dell Publishing debuted the Abyss Books imprint with *The Cipher* by the Detroit-born author Kathe Koja. The novel, Koja's first, is about a black hole in a basement floor, which the book's two main characters dub the "Funhole." Things that are dropped into the hole—including a live mouse—come back changed, rearranged. The plot is as bizarre and wonderful and horrifying as that premise suggests, and the novel's release immediately cemented Koja as a horror creator to watch.

Koja's writing has a strange, indefinable quality that's hard to categorize; in the introduction to his 2012 interview with Koja for *Weird Fiction Review*, Jeff VanderMeer, author of the Southern Reach series, aptly called her work "Kafkaesque." Take, for example, her description of the Funhole:

"Black. Not darkness, not the absence of light but living black.... Pure black and the sense of pulsation, especially when you looked at it too closely, the sense of something not living but alive, not even some*thing* but some—process."

Koja's diction is precise and uncomfortable; her tone is often irreverent and confrontational. Not unlike the Funhole, Koja's writing style has a way of pulling you in completely and not letting go until "The End."

The Cipher garnered copious praise from critics. It won a Bram Stoker Award and a Locus Award, both for best first novel. It was also nominated for a Philip K. Dick Award. A year after its release, Koja published her second novel, *Bad Brains*, again with Abyss, which is just as strange as her first. It features an artist who, when his wife divorces him, becomes too depressed to create new work. That's only the start, of course. He then suffers a head injury that leads to hallucinations and other schizophrenic-like behavior. A nightmarish road trip follows.

Koja quickly followed up with a string of other books: *Skin* (Dell, 1993), *Strange Angels* (Bantam, 1994), *Kink* (Henry Holt, 1996), and *Extremities* (Four Walls Eight Windows, 1998). Her writing was the voice of '90s horror—raw, edgy, and any other adjective you'd expect to hear ascribed to a rock star. In *Skin*, for example, the main character is a metal-welding artist who discovers an underground art group that uses body horror as art, displayed on a Grand Guignol–style stage. The book features plenty of blood, mutilation, cutting, pain, and sadomasochism.

Exploring the Edges

For all the inventively grisly imagery, Koja's writing earned plenty of praise from critics. In a review of *Skin*, *Kirkus Reviews* compared it to William Burroughs. *Publishers Weekly* likened some of Koja's short stories in her 1998 collection *Extremities* to Edgar Allan Poe. Like her *Skin* protagonist, Koja pushes the boundaries of fiction, taking her audience along with her characters to an uncomfortable place. Those uncomfortable places are where her talent shines.

In 2002, Koja wrote her first book for a young adult audience, *Straydog* (Speak). The plot follows Rachel, a loner, who finds friendship with a feral dog whom she names Grrl. The novel is told from the dog's point of view, detailing a harsh life on the streets, and at times it is dark. But the novel offers hope about the possibility of finding friendship in the unlikeliest of places. Six more books followed.

In an interview for Macmillan's website, Koja discussed writing for young adults: "Many of the characters I love best in fiction—Louise Fitzhugh's Harriet, J. D. Salinger's Holden and Franny and Zooey, Francesca Lia Block's Witch Baby—are people who struggle with hard ideas, say what they think, show their bewilderments, love with all their hearts. They are exasperating, funny, intense people. Young people."

Koja's husband, the illustrator Rick Lieder, has designed covers for several of her novels, which play up the artistic nature of her many loner, creative-type characters. Koja's own creative work extends beyond her books; she formed Nerve, an "immersive performance group," which credits her as writer and director. She still lives—and writes—in Detroit, and we're always excited to see what she's come up with next.

Reading List

Not to be missed: If you read one Kathe Koja book, make it *The Cipher*.

Also try: In 2010, Koja published *Under the Poppy* (Small Beer Press), a historical novel that tells the story of two brothel-owning friends, Decca and Rupert. Decca loves Rupert, but Rupert loves Decca's brother, who disrupts Decca's life when he returns to town with his traveling puppet theater. Koja's love for performance and the artistry of the theater shines brightly in this novel. The book took the title of best novel at the 2011 Gaylactic Spectrum Awards, which honor queer-positive work in science fiction, fantasy, and horror.

Related work: Koja has referred to Shirley Jackson as one of her primary literary influences. Jackson certainly shared Koja's affinity for nightmarish journeys and characters who exist just outside of normal society. For companion pieces to Koja, try Shirley Jackson's short stories "The Bus," "Charles," and "One Ordinary Day, with Peanuts."

"Anne, bent like a coat hanger, it hurt to see the angle of her back, her eyes wide and empty and some stuff coming out of her mouth like spoiled black jelly but it was too late . . ."

—"Angels in Love"

Adversary for the Devil
Lisa Tuttle

1952–

George R. R. Martin is famous for creating an entire kingdom with a vast mythology in his Song of Ice and Fire saga. But before the dragons and incestuous romance, Martin collaborated with Lisa Tuttle, a feminist voice in the world of science fiction and horror.

Born in Houston, Texas, but based in the United Kingdom since 1981, Tuttle is a writer whose creative output spans continents and genres. Although she leans toward horror, she has published science fiction and fantasy, always with a dash of feminism, and many of her stories feature complex female characters. She began her career in short fiction; her first published work was the short story "Stranger in the House" (published in the anthology *Clarion II* in 1972). She won the John W. Campbell Award for Best New Writer in 1974. She wrote her first novel, *Windhaven* (Timescape Books, 1981), with Martin. The novel was nominated for a Locus Award.

In a 2015 interview with the writer Angela Slatter for her website, Tuttle said, "I can't actually remember a time when I didn't want to write, as well as read, stories." This is not surprising coming from an author who has written over fifteen novels, a series of children's books, several short story collections as well as numerous uncollected short stories, and four works of nonfiction, including the *Encyclopedia of Feminism* (Facts on File, 1986) and the more recent *Writing Fantasy and Science Fiction* (A & C Black, 2002). When Slatter asked if she feels at home in the horror genre, Tuttle expressed unease with being boxed in, but admitted, "I have always been drawn to the weird, the strange and the supernatural in fiction. That is certainly my natural territory."

This affinity for the weird is evident in her story "The Dream Detective," which appeared in March 2013 in *Lightspeed* magazine. In an interview published with the story, Tuttle cited Sax Rohmer's 1920 story collection *The Dream Detective, Being Some Account of the Methods of Moris Klaw* (A. L. Burt) as having sparked an idea about the un-

canny and dreams. Rohmer is famous, or perhaps infamous, for having created the villainous and racially insensitive character Fu Manchu. He also tried his pen at occult detective fiction, which was all the rage at the beginning of the twentieth century. His eccentric character Moris Klaw believed that violent criminal actions left behind palpable thought and emotional residues, and, in essence, he solves crimes by taking a nap at the scene. While he dozes, residual psychic impressions from the crime affect his dreams, and he wakes up with the solution.

Tuttle admitted to not remembering much about Rohmer's book other than the title, which she borrowed for her story. Her other inspiration was a dream in which she committed a crime and got away with it, which deeply affected her. To avoid spoilers, we will simply say that "The Dream Detective" is an unsettling read with an appropriately weird, slow build-up. The story's narrator is told by his dinner date that she's a dream detective who solves crimes committed *in dreams*. The narrator is shocked and becomes defensive. (We wonder why.)

Strange Familiar

After *Windhaven*, Tuttle wrote the horror novel *Familiar Spirit*, published in 1983 by Tor. A young woman, Sarah, moves into a new home

"It was about the size of a cat, naked-looking, with leathery, hairless skin and thin, spiky limbs that seemed too frail to support the bulbous, ill-proportioned body."

—"Replacements"

that happens to be inhabited by an angry demonic spirit that wants to possess her soul. What's a girl to do?

Familiar Spirit could easily be just another demon-possesses-girl story, but Tuttle's interesting choices make the novel feel fresh. For one thing, she avoids casting as her main character a young waif who is helpless to battle the demon until a priest shows up to tie her down and fight the spirit for control of her body. A male priest (or father figure) fighting the (usually male) demon for control of a woman's body is patriarchy at its worst, and Tuttle, a feminist, wants no part of it.

Instead, Tuttle creates a protagonist who's a worthy adversary. Sarah is level-headed and smart. She makes a plan to vanquish the demon because she can, and she feels a sense of duty and responsibility to banish it from her home.

Feminist politics aside, in *Familiar Spirit* Tuttle has written a flat-out good horror story. She's a superior storyteller. And if you think the title is a reference to a cat, as in a witch's familiar, you won't be surprised to find cats in this story. And demons. And one killer toad.

Tuttle's other books blend genres and incorporate horror with psychological suspense and dark fantasy. *The Pillow Friend* (White Wolf Games Studio, 1996; later edition from Spectra in 2005) blurs the boundaries between dreams and reality, as a young woman encounters a strange porcelain doll, her "pillow friend," who offers wonderful dreams that come at a cost. It's every bit as eerie and uncomfortable as you might imagine. *Gabriel* (Tom Doherty, 1988) also mingles horror with weirdness. A woman returns to the city where her husband had died shortly having a threesome with her and another woman. Now, the other woman is back—with a young boy in tow, who claims to be the reincarnation of his dead father. And that's just the beginning.

Reading List

Not to be missed: The out-of-print *Familiar Spirit* should be your first Lisa Tuttle book if you can find a used copy. In 2018, Penguin Random House released a graphic novel adaptation of *Windhaven*, Tuttle's collaboration with George R. R. Martin. Tuttle cowrote the adaptation, and the book is gorgeously illustrated by Elsa Charretier of Marvel Comics.

Also try: In her novel *The Mysteries* (Bantam, 2005), Tuttle dips her pen into the well of the weird detective. Ian is a private investigator who specializes in finding missing people (his own father mysteriously vanished when Ian was just a boy). He's tasked with finding a young woman named Per, a search that leads him to the Scottish Highlands and a world where Celtic mythology might be more fact than fiction.

Interested in Tuttle's short fiction? She has published several collections, including *Stranger in the House* (Ash Tree Press, 2010).

Related work: A few new writers seem to be following in Tuttle's feminist horror footsteps. The Argentinian writer Mariana Enriquez's collection *Things We Lost in the Fire* (Hogarth, 2017) is at times horrifying and skin-crawling; her supernatural stories are set against the backdrop of a brutal dictatorship. Like Tuttle, Enriquez renders her cast with powerful empathy, making them heartbreakingly human. The British author Naomi Alderman's speculative novel *The Power* (Viking, 2016) imagines a world in which women have the ability to physically dominate men; her characters are reminiscent of the powerful women that Tuttle writes so well. An honorable mention goes to the 2009 film *Jennifer's Body*, written by Diablo Cody and directed by Karyn Kusama; while not perfect, the film tries to push back against the patriarchal message in so many female possession stories, as Tuttle did in her books.

Rewriting Snow White •
Tanith Lee
1947–2015

The British writer Tanith Lee was the prolific creator of more than ninety novels and two hundred short stories in various genres for both adults and young adults. She was a regular contributor to *Weird Tales* magazine and also wrote science fiction, horror, gothic, fantasy, crime, spy fiction, erotica, and historical fiction. She wrote two episodes for the British science-fiction show *Blake's 7*. Nevertheless, in Lee's obituary for the *Guardian* in 2015, the British writer Roz Kaveney stated that "all her work shares a tone . . . a gothic, not to say goth, sensibility in which the relentless pursuit of personal autonomy and sensual fulfillment leads her characters to the brink of delirium, as well as to a fierce integrity that can co-habit with self-sacrificing empathy." Her career spans more than half a century, but she did some of her best work during the paperback boom of the 1980s.

Lee was born to professional dancers Hylda and Bernard Lee (no, not the Bernard Lee who played M in early James Bond films). When asked in a 2012 interview for *Weird Fiction Review* if she was exposed to weird fiction while growing up, she said:

"I was often up at midnight in glittering dance venues. And my parents and I would frequently discuss *Hamlet*, or *Dracula*—or Rider Haggard's *She*. I've no doubt all this had its due effect."

As a result of then-undiagnosed dyslexia, Lee didn't learn to read until age eight. She was an avid fan of radio dramas until she could read independently, and then she became a voracious reader. She read science fiction such as Theodore Sturgeon's "The Silken Swift," weird stories by Saki, and books by Dickens, Shakespeare, and Chekov. In the 2012 *Weird*

Fiction Review interview, Lee recognized differences among the labels horror, gothic, and weird. But not surprisingly, considering her prolific output that encompasses numerous genres, she expressed greater interest in how those genres can intersect and meld with one another than in what separates them.

Her story "Yellow and Red," anthologized in the VanderMeers' collection *The Weird: A Compendium of Strange and Dark Stories*, feels like a nineteenth-century Gothic-tinged haunted house story, although it is set in the 1950s. The VanderMeers note an echo of "Casting the Runes" (published in 1911 in the collection *More Ghost Stories* by Longmans Green) by M. R. James, the early twentieth-century British ghost-story master. The narratives share a creeping dread, narrators who think themselves unshakably rational and faced with something out of their ken, and the presence of those always bothersome archaeological sites. (When will horror characters stop digging up artifacts and bringing them home?)

Lee's tale calls to mind another James story, "The Mezzotint," published in the 1904 collection *Ghost Stories of an Antiquary* by Edward Arnold; both feature photography as a weird medium for spirits. Lee's narrator employs whiskey to reveal the horrors that are somehow captured in his family's snapshots, or, as he says, "using a spirit to show a spirit." A mysterious undiagnosed malady has caused every member in his family, no matter how young, to waste away. He slowly learns the story behind what may have happened to his vanished relatives.

Lee is probably best known for her award-winning Tales from the Flat Earth series, published by DAW, which comprises novels and stories beginning with *Night's Master* from 1978 through "The Pain of Glass" from 2009. It chronicles life on a world that is literally flat, square, and composed of four layers, or realms: the Underearth, occupied by demons; the Flat Earth, where the people live; the Upperearth, realm of the gods; and the Innerearth, where the dead roam. The series features interconnected stories in the vein of *One Thousand and One Nights*. Its popularity prompted Penguin to rerelease twenty of Tanith Lee's most popular DAW-published novels, starting in 2015 with *The Birthgrave*.

The Birthgrave begins with a nameless woman waking up in the center of a dormant volcano, unsure of who she is. She sets off on an adventure of self-discovery through a brutal and dangerous landscape. The book, the first of a trilogy, is a prime example of how authors transcended the horror boom of the 1970s and 1980s to create something wholly new—in this case, haunting speculative fiction.

Lee was still writing at the time of her death from cancer, leaving work unpublished and incomplete. She was the first woman to win the British Fantasy Award, for her 1979 book *Death's Master* (DAW). She won the World Fantasy Award several times, including the Life Achievement Award in 2013; her other numerous honors include the World Horror Convention's Grand Master Award, in 2009, and two Nebula Awards, in 1975 and 1980.

Reading List

Not to be missed: *White as Snow* (Tor, 2000) is Tanith Lee's retelling of Snow White, which earned her comparisons to Angela Carter's reworking of fairy tales. Lee's story is dark and mixes the familiar elements of the story—an angry aging queen, a huntsman, an innocent young woman, and small forest-dwelling folk—with the mythology of the goddess

Demeter and her stolen daughter Persephone, creating a book about the complicated relationships between mothers and daughters.

Also try: Along with Lee's Flat Earth books, her Birthgrave trilogy— *The Birthgrave*, *Shadowfire*, and *Quest for the White Witch* (DAW, 1975, 1978, 1978; reissued by Penguin)—is finding popularity with twenty-first-century readers.

In *Disturbed by Her Song* (Lethe Press, 2010) Lee shared a byline with her two characters, Esther Garber and Judas Garbah. Each tells their own story, and Lee and Esther tell a few together. This ambiguity between characters and author, or even the idea of writing as channeling, unmoors readers' expectations about narrators. The stories focus on queer love and sexuality, and the collection was nominated for a Lambda Award for best LGBT science fiction, fantasy, or horror.

"You see, it looked to me like a funny sort of animal—a sort of snake thing, with hands—and a face."

—"Yellow and Red"

PART SEVEN

The New Goths

Gothic is back.

But what exactly is it? The term's meaning is slippery or, perhaps more appropriately, foggy. More often than not, it is used interchangeably with "atmospheric" or "haunting" or some other equally vague adjective. Usually, the phrase "Gothic horror" describes a creative work whose atmosphere is gloomy and whose main characters are brooding, moody, and most likely clad in black. A blend of romance, costume drama, and dreariness also comes to mind. Imagine a sad girl wearing velvet, hanging around her dismal manor house. Her boyfriend might be a vampire, or at least strongly resemble one. Also Gothic: if the aforementioned manor house is haunted by a bevy of ghosts.

However, as we discussed in Part One, Gothic fiction has both a strong literary tradition and a set of core characteristics that extends beyond moping around a dark, crumbling castle. Fiction that deals with themes of isolation, vulnerability, family strife, and the bubbling up of hidden secrets is undoubtedly Gothic, whether the story takes place on the moors, or in a country farmhouse, or in a city.

Modern stories based on this literary tradition, which we call the new Gothic, leave behind the strict rules of the eighteenth-century Gothic novel and instead center on the main character's struggle to understand reality in a world that embraces the supernatural. In the traditional Gothic story, a female protagonist's virginity was endangered; in the modern Gothic, the protagonist is still (usually) female, but what's now at stake is her psyche, as she struggles against paranormal forces and risks losing her grip on reality.

New Gothic writers also offer a "fix" for some of the sins of their foremothers. In the Gothic novel of the eighteenth century, for instance, being Italian or Spanish (or non-English, or nonwhite) was shorthand for being the villain. Modern Gothic writers challenge this tradition by creating a broad spectrum of characters that resonate better with twenty-first-century readers.

The Gothic never really went out of style, but this new brand of Gothic horror began to emerge in the middle of the twentieth century, with novels like Shirley Jackson's *We Have Always Lived in the Castle* (Viking, 1962), Michael McDowell's *The Elementals* (Avon Books, 1981), and Stephen King's *The Shining* (Doubleday 1977). The new Gothic is exemplified by films such as Guillermo del Toro's *Crimson Peak* and television series like Showtime's *Penny Dreadful* and Netflix's *Alias Grace*. The trend is also visible in comics and graphic novels, such as Emily Carroll's highly praised *Through the Woods* (Faber & Faber, 2014), a collection of five graphic horror stories that read like dark fairy tales.

In literature, the most Gothic contemporary author is probably Anne Rice. Her work is full of the lush atmospheres of the old South (think manor houses decorated with candelabras, and tree-lined drives framed by hanging Spanish moss). But she updates the Gothic narrative by swapping the love story of the poetic hero and virginal damsel for a romance between two men, and she places stories in the grimy urban underbelly of New Orleans.

Writers like Helen Oyeyemi, Susan Hill, and Sarah Waters each create their own distinct versions of a Gothic heroine trapped inside a space with a mind of its own. Angela Carter has established herself as the reigning queen of fairy tale Gothic. And Jewelle Gomez, with her Afrofuturistic vampires, could be considered an heir to Anne Rice. In many ways, the rules no longer apply. Any place can be haunted by the supernatural, including the protagonist's own mind.

That's not to say that these writers forget where the Gothic got its start. In particular, new Gothic authors writing for young adults seem to embrace the connection of the Gothic to the teenage experience, with its surging hormones, changing emotions, and deep tendency toward brooding and melancholy. Kiersten White's *The Dark Descent of Elizabeth Frankenstein* (Delacorte Press, 2018) is a retelling of Mary Shelley's classic novel for a young adult audience. Orphan Elizabeth has lost everything when she is brought to the Frankenstein home, where she befriends the lonely Victor. As they grow up, the friends grow closer, but Elizabeth finds that romance with Victor pulls her life into a dark spiral. White has revisited Gothic material before; she wrote the YA novels *And I Darken, Now I Rise, and Bright We Burn* (Delacorte, 2016, 2017, 2018), a trilogy that follows the Dracul siblings. We think Bram Stoker would be proud.

Another new Gothic author writing for young adults is Madeleine Roux. Her Asylum series (*Asylum, Sanctum,* and *Catacomb*; 2016, Harper Collins) is set in a dormitory, formerly a psychiatric hospital, that is haunted by the past. Her novels that most embrace the Gothic setting, however, are the House of Furies series (Harper Collins, 2017–19), in which a seventeen-year-old girl finds work as a maid at Coldthistle House, a manor that would be at home in any Charlotte Dacre or Mary Shelley novel. The house and its owner, Mr. Morningside, are full of secrets, and all guests are judged for past sins and punished, making the house a nightmare prison for its inhabitants.

For adult fiction that embraces the new Gothic, consider Ania Ahlborn. As a child, Ahlborn was fascinated by cemeteries and was concerned with making sure all the gravestones had flowers. (This sounds to us like a second coming of Mary Shelley, whose fascination with graveyards is well documented.) Ahlborn's horror novels unmistakably reveal her Gothic sentimentalities. *Brother* (Gallery Books, 2015) is about an impoverished Appalachian family with dark secrets. *The Bird Eater* (47

North, 2014) and *Within These Walls* (Gallery Books, 2015) feature haunted homes, but the true Gothic nature of the books is at work in the haunted protagonists, who have pasts to overcome before they can confront anything supernatural. The renewed interest in Gothic horror may be a response to modern fears, especially as technology advances at such a dizzying a rate that it is difficult to predict what consequences these new innovations will have (hello, *Black Mirror*). Horror has always been cathartic; it allows a safe space for readers to experience fears and confront danger. Although the world is constantly changing (in sometimes frightening ways), in new Gothic fiction the ghosts that haunt us are familiar. So are the possessed spaces, which are overgrown and decaying reminders of the past that can distract us from worries about the future.

Whatever the reason, two and a half centuries after *The Castle of Otranto*, it seems that neither readers nor authors have tired of Gothic tropes yet.

Queen of the Damned
Anne Rice

1941–

Anyone who has been to New Orleans can tell you that the city possesses a strange magic. The place is a melting pot of cultures, a hazy mix of religious icons and voodoo dolls. The nights are long—hot and humid—rolling with loud music and booze-fueled revelers. The days are bright. Mornings in the French Quarter smell of soap and horses. Afternoons hold promises of gumbo and crawfish boils and magnolia blossoms.

Then there is the city's folklore. New Orleans is a city of vampires, of voodoo queens, of witchcraft, of ghost pirates. It's where Madame La-Laurie allegedly tortured and killed enslaved people in the early 1800s. It's where the jazz-loving serial killer known as the Axman roamed the streets looking for victims in 1918 and 1919.

No author is more closely associated with New Orleans lore than Anne Rice. Born and raised in the city, Rice was named Howard, after her father, but began using Anne in first grade. After moving to Texas with her family in high school and attending several universities there, Rice dropped out and moved with a friend to the Haight-Ashbury section of San Francisco. She kept in touch with Stan Rice, whom she met in high school, and the two would reconnect during her visits back to Texas. They married in 1961 and moved to California, where Anne returned to school; she received a master's in English and creative writing in 1972 from San Francisco State University.

In 1966 the couple had their first child, a daughter named Michele, who passed away from cancer just five years later. Rice has said that she threw herself into writing after the devastating loss, creating vampire characters in part because of the alluring possibility of life after death. In 1978 Rice gave birth to a son, Christopher, who is a successful novelist like his mother. In the midst of raising a family, Rice worked odd jobs—waitress and insurance claims examiner, among them—before she turned to writing full-time.

Her first book, *Interview with the Vampire*, was published by Knopf in 1976. The novel was an immediate success and set off Rice's popular Vampire Chronicles series, which, as of this book's publication, totals fifteen books. And it breathed new (unending) life into this quintessentially Gothic character.

Gone were the soapy storylines; no maiden withering in the hands of a bloodthirsty fiend here (or, at least, that isn't the main plotline). Instead, Rice's vampires face existential dilemmas, struggling to cope with the realities of their undead nature. Rice's character Lestat de Lioncourt is a fairly straightforward throwback to Bram Stoker's Dracula: he loves his power, his immortality, his wealth and privilege. But his companion Louis de Pointe du Lac grapples with his conscience and expresses guilt and remorse for taking human life. Perhaps the best example of vampire existentialism is seen in the character Claudia who, having become a vampire when she was a child, is horrified to realize that she will never physically age. Though her mind matures to adulthood, her undead body will forever be that of a prepubescent child.

Rice's readers loved it all.

The books were so popular that Hollywood took interest. The film rights were sold immediately, but it took almost twenty years for a movie to be produced. (Pop culture critic Eric Diaz speculated in a July 2018 *Nerdist* article that the delay was due to concerns about the novel's erotic content.) Finally, in 1994, Tom Cruise and Brad Pitt starred in the film adaptation of *Interview with the Vampire*. Rice was skeptical of the decision to cast Cruise as the lead character (and outspoken about her doubts), but she loved the movie once she saw it. One of the sequels, *The Queen of the Damned*, was brought to the big screen in 2002, starring Stuart Townsend. In July 2018, Hulu announced that a television adaptation of *The Vampire Chronicles* is in the works, for which Rice will collaborate with her son Christopher, who will serve as writer and producer. Nearly three decades of adaptations starring Rice's most famous character, Lestat, proves that a vampire truly never dies (in Hollywood at least).

Beyond Belief

Rice is a prolific writer who has authored thirty-six books, including a Christian series called *Songs of the Seraphim* (Penguin Random House, 2011–12), which features time travel, angels, *and* hit men; a series about the Mayfair family of witches; books about magical wolves; and reimagined fairy tales that often have an erotic bent. When looking at her body of work as a whole, it's difficult to identify a singular pattern or put Rice in a single category. Broadly speaking, she writes supernatural fiction, particularly with Gothic overtones, sometimes with erotic elements.

For a time, Rice abandoned vampire stories and wrote books de-

fending her religious beliefs. After being raised in a Catholic family, she had become an outspoken atheist until 1998, when she renewed her faith. During this period she wrote a memoir, *Called Out of Darkness: A Spiritual Confession* (Knopf, 2008), and her Christ the Lord series, two novels that portray the life of Jesus Christ (Knopf, 2005 and 2008). Then, on July 28, 2010, Rice announced on Facebook that she was leaving organized religion. She wrote, "I remain committed to Christ as always but not to being 'Christian' or to being part of Christianity. It's simply impossible for me to 'belong' to this quarrelsome, hostile, disputatious, and deservedly infamous group." One reason for Rice's ultimate break with the Catholic Church was its refusal to accept same-sex relationships.

Having parted ways with religion, Rice returned to her supernatural beginnings, writing *Prince Lestat and the Realms of Atlantis* (Knopf, 2016) and, with her son, *Ramses the Damned: The Passion of Cleopatra* (Penguin Random House, 2017). In an interview with the *Guardian* on July 27, 2016, Rice called *Prince Lestat and the Realms of Atlantis* "one of my greatest personal adventures."

Anne Rice's personal struggle with her religious faith coloring her fiction can be seen as analogous to the arc of Gothic imagery as a whole. Traditional Christian mythology has long played a role in depictions of vampirism (see: crucifixes), and since its beginnings, Gothic literature has been full of evil monks and women who are sent to live in convents. But, like Rice's stories, religion isn't a fundamental component of new Gothic stories and monsters, vampires or otherwise. Today's vampires are afraid of bigger, badder things than crucifixes and holy water. Just as these relics are losing their hold on our culture, so are the old Gothic vampires who cared about them.

Reading List

Not to be missed: Anne Rice wrote about far more than vampires. *Violin*, published in 1997 by Knopf, is her take on the ghost story. Like much of her work, it is rich with history, moving through time from nineteenth-century Vienna to modern New Orleans and Rio de Janeiro, and tells a story of three musicians.

Also try: Largely overlooked is Rice's chronicle of the Mayfair witches, beginning with *The Witching Hour* (Knopf, 1990). This novel takes the familiar plot of a woman who discovers she has magical powers and weaves in history and folklore to make the story feel fresh. *The Feast of All Saints* (Simon & Schuster, 1979), a historical novel about free people of color in 1840s New Orleans, was adapted as a miniseries for Showtime in 2001, starring James Earl Jones, Forest Whitaker, Eartha Kitt, and Pam Grier.

Related work: Fans of vampires set amidst a rich historical tapestry may enjoy the writing of Chelsea Quinn Yarbro. She created the character of the Comte de Saint-Germain, who was introduced in the novel *Hotel Transylvania* (St. Martin's Press, 1978) and developed over a series of novels and stories.

"Evil is always possible. And goodness is eternally difficult."

—Interview with the Vampire

Teller of Feminist Fairy Tales
Helen Oyeyemi

1984–

Fairy tales are ubiquitous. Until recently, we have told them to children without a second thought about the message we might be spreading, for good or ill. The tales so many of us have recited or heard as children—about a mermaid who trades her voice in order to be human, about a brother and sister hiking in the woods who meet a witch—were once much darker, more disturbing stories. In the Grimm brothers' version of Cinderella (titled "Aschenputtel"), her stepsisters are punished for their foul deeds by having their eyes pecked out by birds (and this is after they cut off parts of their feet to fit into those infamous slippers).

Helen Oyeyemi understands that fairy tales are essentially horror stories—cautionary tales that tell us about ourselves and our place in society. Oyeyemi emigrated from Nigeria to Great Britain when she was four years old. Growing up in Lewisham, South London, she was a voracious reader. But when a book had an unsatisfying ending (she has mentioned Beth's death in *Little Women*, for example), she simply rewrote the conclusion for herself. Her love of writing turned into a full-blown career while she was still a teenager. She wrote her first book, *The Icarus Girl* (Bloomsbury, 2005), while a student at London's Cardinal Vaughan Memorial secondary school. The novel is a play on a Nigerian folktale: There once was a girl who didn't quite fit in. Then she made a friend. But that friend—the ambiguous, near-doppelgänger girl TillyTilly—isn't all that nice, especially when it comes to the neighborhood bullies. Oyeyemi's debut was met with critical praise and set the tone for her work that followed, which also draws upon folklore and fairy tales, masterfully distorting her characters' realities so that nothing is ever quite as it should be. The tension in Oyeyemi's writing between the real world and the supernatural places are at the forefront of the new Gothic. Her follow-up to *The Icarus Girl* is *The Opposite House* (Penguin, 2007), a story inspired by Cuban mythology about two girls and two doors that open to alternate worlds.

White Is for Witching, her third book (Nan A. Talese, 2009), has all the trappings of a modern Gothic novel. A young woman is plagued by pica, a peculiar eating disorder that drives her to consume things that aren't food, like chalk and dirt. Following the death of her mother, her mental state only worsens and she moves to a house with her father and twin brother. Her father hopes to turn the house into a bed-and-breakfast, but the home seems to have a . . . personality, and it's not a nice one. The novel addresses contemporary concerns such as xenophobia and includes traditional Gothic aspects like the haunted house, a woman struggling with insanity, and the uncanny doubling that exists with twins.

In a 2014 interview with the *Guardian*, Oyeyemi said *White Is for Witching* is "about expanding the genre of the haunted house story." The narration switches between characters—even the house is afforded its own voice—and Oyeyemi's prose is as experimental as it is beautiful. She received much critical attention for the book, including the 2010 Somerset Maugham Award and a finalist spot in the Shirley Jackson Awards.

Oyeyemi's other works explore stories that are likely familiar to her readers. In *Boy, Snow, Bird* (Riverhead Books, 2014), she tackles the tale of Snow White, though this time the setting is 1950s America, and the name Snow White is a reference to racial passing. The book was a finalist for the *Los Angeles Times* Book Prize. *Gingerbread*

(Riverhead Books, 2019) overtly borrows its name from the ubiquitous cookie of fairy tales, folklore, and fantasy.

Oyeyemi's novel *Mr. Fox* (Riverhead Books, 2011) is a retelling of the French Bluebeard folktale. Mr. Fox is a British author in love with his wife, Daphne. But he also loves another, Mary Foxe. Further complicating matters, Mary Foxe is imaginary—and Mr. Fox's muse. The novel is dark and haunting; Mary Foxe isn't the only spectral-like character. Once again, Oyeyemi wisely and deftly joins a dark fairy tale with a story of human relationships, in all their magic and disappointments. Both Gothic fiction and traditional fairy tales typically depict the victimization of women or children and comment on disturbing family situations. Women writers have used both forms to fight against oppression by reimagining vulnerable characters as more formidable protagonists.

Reading List

Not to be missed: If you're in the mood for a Gothic haunted house tale, you can't go wrong with *White Is for Witching.* Oyeyemi's other novels described above are more in the camp of the unsettling weird.

Also try: Although young, Oyeyemi has already carved out a reputation as a writer of literary horror. She published two plays in 2005, *Juniper's Whitening* and *Victimese.* They are available in one volume from Bloomsbury's Methuen Drama imprint. In 2016, she published a collection of short stories, *What Is Not Yours Is Not Yours,* which won the PEN Open Book Award.

Related work: Fans of Oyeyemi's fairy-tale reimaginings might enjoy Carmen Maria Machado's short-fiction collection *Her Body and Other Parties* (Graywolf Press, 2017). A finalist for the National Book Award,

"But then, maybe 'I don't believe you' is the cruelest way to kill a monster."

—White Is for Witching

Her Body embraces the often antifeminist nature of some of the most enduring fairy tales and urban myths, giving them updated twists.

The Argentinian author Samanta Schweblin doesn't write fairy tales so much as nightmares. Her novel *Fever Dream* (translated by Megan McDowell; Riverhead Books, 2017) focuses on the relationship between mothers and children, in a nightmarish, and—well—fevered dream kind of way. The past and the present bleed together as they do in *White Is for Witching*. If you like Oyeyemi's writing for its near-poetic quality, try Linda Addison, the Bram Stoker Award winning writer of dark poetry.

In interviews, Oyeyemi has cited Kelly Link as an inspiration, calling Link's story "The Specialist's Hat" a particular favorite. It shares with Oyeyemi's stories such tropes as precocious children, twins, and a touch of magical realism (albeit dark magical realism).

Modern Gothic Ghost Maker
Susan Hill

1942–

When critics and readers consider the great writers of ghost stories, they usually think of nineteenth-century names such as Henry James or M. R. James, Elizabeth Gaskell or Charles Dickens. Some may call to mind the more recent horror maven Shirley Jackson. But Susan Hill deserves to be included on any such list. The prolific contemporary writer has, to date, penned the Simon Serrailler detective series, a sequel to Daphne du Maurier's *Rebecca* titled *Mrs. de Winter* (Sinclair-Stevenson, 1993), and numerous books with a Gothic flavor. But she will always be remembered for her first ghost story, the ever-adaptable *The Woman in Black* (Hamish Hamilton, 1983).

Hill was born in 1942 in Scarborough, England. As a child, she says she "was always wanting to tell stories, to my friends, to my dolls. I was always writing." She studied English literature from a young age, publishing her first novel, *The Enclosure* (Hutchison, 1961), when she was fifteen years old. The book made a splash; although, Hill says, "it wasn't a sex novel," it dealt frankly with adult relationships. Hill's headmistress told her, "You have brought shame and disgrace to this school."

But Hill was determined to write. She attended King's College in London and then began her writing career. She married Stanley Wells, a Shakespeare scholar, in 1975, and the couple had three daughters, one of whom died in infancy. In 2013, Hill caused the gossip mills to turn when she reportedly left her husband for Barbara Machin a screenwriter. Today, Hill writes everything from children's books to crime fiction. Within her impressive body of work, *The Woman in Black* and her mysteries are most popular among her fans.

Called "a rattling good yarn" by the *Guardian*, *The Woman in Black* opens on Christmas Eve. A lawyer named Arthur Kipps is gathered with his family to tell ghost stories, placing us in that British tradition as well as riffing on the frame story of Henry James's *The Turn of the Screw*. Kipps is reminded of the trauma he experienced at Eel Marsh House, the home of his late client, where he stayed in the course of settling her affairs; he refuses to share a story and leaves the room in a panic.

Of course, as with all good ghost stories and all terrifying experiences, Kipps can't let it lie. He decides to write out everything that happened; thus begins a slow burn of a tale in which Kipps recounts his experience of the Woman in Black who haunts Eel Marsh House. Hill pulls out all the traditional supernatural stops—his narrative includes secretive townspeople, cries in the night, a child's scream in the fog, and a haunted nursery. The ultimate creepy detail, however, is Eel Marsh House itself, a residence that is surrounded by water when the tide is high, leaving Kipps unable to escape whatever haunts the property. Being stuck in a haunted house is one thing; being stuck in a haunted house on an isolated island is another turn in the screw of anxiety.

Reading List

Not to be missed: *The Woman in Black*'s Gothic atmosphere and chilling ghost story make a great read, and it has been adapted many times. The stage adaptation by the English playwright Stephen Mallatratt de-

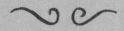

"And as I stood
I felt a small hand creep
into my right one, as
if a child had come up
beside me in the dimness
and taken hold of it."

—*The Small Hand: A Ghost Story*

buted on Christmas 1987 at the Stephen Joseph Theatre in Scarborough, England; it is the second longest running stage play in the West End of London, after *The Mousetrap*. A movie version starring Daniel Radcliffe and written by Jane Goodman was released in 2012. (Another film adaptation was made in 1989 for the British television network ITV, which Hill did not like.) In February 2012, when asked by a reporter for the *Guardian* if the 2012 film would be the final version of her famous ghost story, she said, "Who knows? I can see her as an opera."

Also try: Hill's 1970 novel *I'm the King of the Castle* (Hamish Hamilton, 1970), which won the Somerset Maugham Award, exemplifies her ability to craft a Gothic setting. Also check out *The Bird of Night* (Hamish Hamilton, 1972), shortlisted for the Booker Prize and a winner of the Whitbread Prize for fiction.

Hill's supernatural tales all share a similar slow-burn quality so if you like *The Woman in Black*, you will most likely enjoy her ghost stories, including *The Mist in the Mirror* (Sinclair-Stevenson, 1992) and *The Man in the Picture* (Overlook, 2008).

In her 2012 review of Hill's short novel *Dolly* (Profile Books, 2012), the English writer Sadie Jones notes a parallel between this tale of two children living alone in an old house and Henry James's 1898 novella *The Turn of the Screw*. But instead of a Jamesian psychological exploration of the ambiguity of evil, one of the children in Hill's story believes herself to be truly evil, and she certainly acts like it. Of course there's also a doll.

Related work: Elizabeth Hand's *Wylding Hall* (PS Publishing, 2015) provides a modern spin on the Gothic. This time a folk band, not a young woman, comes to an old house to write and record an album. Events suggest that something supernatural is going on, but the novel never reveals anything truly haunting.

◆ *Welcome to the Dark Séance* ◆
Sarah Waters

1966–

It's probably not hard to figure out how the Welsh writer Sarah Waters grew up to be a novelist. In a 2009 interview with the *Guardian's* Robert McCrum, she noted that having a much older sister made her feel at times like an only child. She was close to both of her parents, especially her father, who told her science-fiction and ghost stories of his own creation. McCrum described her childhood as happy, though often solitary; Waters told him she spent her time reading and watching "an awful lot of telly, sci-fi, horror and *Doctor Who*." Waters began her literary career in 1998 with her novel *Tipping the Velvet* (Virago), a Victorian drama with a lesbian love story at its center. The novel caused scandal— in New Zealand, for example, it was shrink-wrapped and labeled with a warning that it was only for readers eighteen and older—which seemed to only add to its allure. Waters was a bona fide literary star. Twenty years after its publication, she wrote of her debut novel:

"'What's it about?' people sometimes asked me, when they had heard I'd written a novel—and I always had to brace myself, slightly, to answer. There was the awkwardness of explaining the rather risqué title. There was the fact that I outed myself the moment I began to reveal the plot."

That first novel grew out of her identity and her academic work on lesbian and gay historical fiction, and it signaled her transition from scholarly study to representing lesbians in fiction.

Waters returned to lesbian drama in *Fingersmith* (Virago, 2002), a novel about a couple caught up in crime and class struggle. But Gothic themes recur throughout her body of work. She writes in the tradition of the Victorians, crafting classic ghost stories set in gloomy mansions and haunted by ghosts of the past that are hell-bent on being heard by the present. Her keen attention to the development of her female characters and her exploration of feminist and queer themes put her horror in the new Gothic school.

A terrific example of Waters's marriage of traditional Gothic horror and modern feminist sensibilities is her second novel, *Affinity*, published in 1999 by Virago. It's the story of Margaret Prior, a single woman of means in Victorian England who is recovering from a suicide attempt. She devotes herself to charity, working in a women's prison, in an attempt to heal her wounds by helping others. There she meets a spiritualist medium named Selina Dawes who is charged with fraud and assault after one of her séances leaves a woman dead. Margaret is drawn to this mysterious woman, and the attraction leads to a romantic relationship. Soon, pulled under the seer's control, Margaret becomes convinced of Selina's mysterious powers.

The novel lacks the mirth of *Tipping the Velvet*; it's a mystery at its core, ominous and imbued with the terror of what Selina calls a "dark séance." Waters goes deeper than the table taps and spirit guides of a nineteenth-century séance and captures the intricacies of the Spiritualist movement, balancing the mysteries that came together in those darkened rooms. Is the medium communing with the dead? Is she a fraud? Is she a criminal seeking to take vulnerable people's money? Is she a victim of a patriarchy that is systematically stripping women of their livelihood? The book is a puzzle, and it provides no easy answers. But Waters builds the sinister suspense beautifully, as well as the love story.

Perhaps Waters's best-known supernatural yarn is *The Little Stranger* (Virago, 2009), which was her third novel to be short-listed for the Man Booker Prize. In it, Waters raises questions about post–World War II class changes, but, remarkably, she didn't set out to write a horror story. Initially she wanted to write a novel that explored the experience of working-class people after the war. In a 2010 article for the *Guardian*, Waters wrote that the book's tone shifted after she woke "with a shriek in the middle of the night" during a stay at Dartington Hall, an estate that was hosting a literary festival. On that night, she had her recurring nightmare of seeing a figure at the end of her bed. The dream prompted Waters to start thinking about how a ghost, particularly a violent poltergeist, could heighten the class tensions in her book project. She noted in the *Guardian* article that the incident seemed to be an appropriate spark for an unsettling horror story. Reviewers have noted influences of Edgar Allan Poe, Henry James, Shirley Jackson, Charles Dickens, and Wilkie Collins on this Gothic tale, which never loses Waters's intended focus on class conflict.

The narrator is a doctor named Faraday who constantly reflects on his working-class roots and the sacrifices his parents made for him to become a physician. During his childhood he developed a preoccupation with the Ayres family, at whose estate, Hundreds Hall, his mother worked. His obsession continues into adulthood, when he becomes the family's doctor. In the course of treating Roderick Ayres's physical and mental wounds from the war, Faraday realizes the family cannot afford to keep Hundreds Hall up to its former glory. He then proceeds to overstep the bounds of his professional role: he pursues Caroline Ayres romantically, discounts the family's plans to escape their debt, and simultaneously dismisses their fears of supernatural attack from the home.

Waters builds suspense gradually; each member of the family faces a separate supernatural embodiment of their past and their fears. Dr. Faraday is an unreliable narrator, so the reader is always guessing at what's happening. Many of the book's supernatural events can be categorized as what ghost story scribe M. R. James called "the malice of inanimate objects." Ordinary items become projectile weapons; strange writing emerges from the plaster. A seemingly harmless Labrador retriever is psychically affected by the disturbing environment, as are other animals and people. *The Little Stranger* was a *New York Times* best seller, and Stephen King wrote that "several sleepless nights are guaranteed."

Reading List

Not to be missed: Our favorite Waters novel is *The Little Stranger*, which was adapted for the screen in 2018, starring Domhnall Gleeson and Ruth Wilson. Read the book, and then watch the movie. Let the chills linger.

Also try: Waters wrote a historical novel in 2006 called *The Night Watch* (Virago), which was short-listed for the Man Booker Prize and the Orange Prize. The novel follows a group of people—two lesbians, a straight woman, and her brother—whose lives interconnect in World War II–era London. The horror comes from the realities of life in wartime. A television adaptation was made for BBC2, starring Claire Foy and Jodie Whittaker. In 2014, Waters released *The Paying Guests* (Virago), a part satire, part drama, with more than a little sex appeal, set in post–World War I England. The *Sunday Times* named it "fiction book of the year."

Related work: Fans of Waters who appreciate her ability to develop characters' relationships against a historical setting might enjoy *Frog Music* (Little, Brown, 2014), set in 1876 San Francisco, by Emma Donoghue, who is the author of the thriller *Room* (Little, Brown, 2010).

"You're supposed to grow out
of horridness, aren't you?
I don't think I ever grew
out of mine. Sometimes
I think it's still inside me,
like something nasty
I swallowed, that got stuck."

—The Little Stranger

Teller of Bloody Fables
Angela Carter
1940–1992

The arts and entertainment blog *Vulture* has called her "the feminist horror author you need to read immediately." Joyce Carol Oates, Jeff VanderMeer, and Neil Gaiman, among many others, have cited her as an influence. The horror author Brian McGreevy wrote that his novel *Hemlock Grove* (Farrar, Straus and Giroux, 2012) "was one extended piece of Angela Carter fan-fiction."

That might be enough to convince you to read her books. Nevertheless, let's talk about Angela Carter.

Born in 1940 in Eastbourne, England, Angela Olive Stalker—which admittedly is a better last name for a horror writerr—grew up in a middle-class family. Her father was a night editor for a newspaper and her mother was attentive . . . sometimes too attentive for the rebellious Angela, who longed for a life outside her family's home. She married Paul Carter when she was nineteen years old; in 1972 they divorced. She later married Mark Pearce, with whom she had a son. As a child, she was shy; as an adult, she was the opposite. She traveled. She pursued a career as a journalist. And she reveled in the freedom she found while exploring writing in the 1960s.

Carter cannot be pinned down in a single genre and is known for writing unconventional fiction and nonfiction. Feminist views of sex and the female body are recurring themes in her work; for example, her nonfiction book *The Sadeian Woman and the Ideology of Pornography* (Pantheon Books, 1978) examines the writings of the Marquis de Sade through a feminist lens.

Carter's best-known collection of stories is *The Bloody Chamber* (Gollancz, 1979), all of which are based on traditional fairy tales. In

her 2006 introduction to the collection, the author Helen Simpson discusses Carter's love for ornate stories—what Carter described as "Gothic tales, cruel tales, tales of wonder, tales of terror, fabulous narratives that deal directly with the imagery of the unconscious"—over humdrum accounts of everyday life. Simpson also cites Carter's complaints about how her work was interpreted. Carter insisted that she did not intend to create "versions" of fairy tales, or fairy tales rewritten for adults. She wanted, rather, to "extract the latent content from the traditional stories and to use it as the beginnings of new stories." In other words, she wanted to use fairy tales as thematic inspirations for her original, contemporary stories.

The Bloody Chamber was groundbreaking upon its release in the late 1970s, and it inspired numerous writers to pursue magical or speculative fiction. To quote Helen Simpson again, the collection is "a multi-faceted glittering diamond reflecting and refracting a variety of portraits of desire and sexuality—heterosexual female sexuality—which, unusually for the time, 1979, are told from a heterosexual female viewpoint." Simpson also notes that Carter would later come under fire for that focus on heterosexual relationships. The book has since become a staple of British and American high school and university classrooms.

What Big Eyes You Have

The stories in *The Bloody Chamber* are of varying length. The title story clocks in around forty pages; others are more like sketches, although potent ones. For example, "The Snow Child" may be just a few pages long, but its tale of a magical girl born from snow bites as fiercely as the rose that spells doom for the titular character. The lush descriptions of the worlds Carter creates sharply contrast with intense moments of physical, sexual, and emotional violence. Her multiple reworkings of Little Red Riding Hood, "The Werewolf," "The Company of Wolves," and "Wolf-Alice," upend readers' expectations of the familiar story: women are sometimes victims, sometimes not, as they grasp at unknown powers and reserves of courage. The wolf stories never turn out well for Granny, but Little Red at times finds herself in a better place by the end. Sometimes she gets a house; sometimes she prospers; sometimes she sleeps soundly. Sometimes she doesn't.

Carter's style may be best classified as "feminist revisionist." In her novel *The Infernal Desire Machines of Doctor Hoffman* (Picaresque Fiction, 1972), she reimagines the Doctor Faustus legend less as horror and more as surrealist fiction, or perhaps surrealist weird fiction. The book cemented Carter as one of the strongest literary feminist voices of the twentieth century. In an article for the *Atlantic* published in 2017, forty-five years after the novel's release, the author Jeff VanderMeer said that it "still [feels] fresh and dangerous today."

Another testament to Carter's enduring legacy: In 2015, a *New York Times* reporter asked Margaret Atwood who she would invite to a literary dinner party. Among Atwood's picks was Angela Carter, saying: "What an inexhaustible source of strange details and worldly wisdom she was. How instructive, how fundamentally helpful. How like the white-haired fairy godmother you always wished you had."

Reading List

Not to be missed: *The Bloody Chamber* should be first on any reader's Angela Carter list. Each fairy tale is as horrific and thought-provoking

"And I almost tripped over a poor corpse on the floor in a purplish jacket of balding velvet, her worn, wax face raddled with age, only a few strands left of all that honey-colored hair . . . "

—"The Snow Pavilion"

(and sometimes disarmingly sexy) as the last. Carter's version of Little Red Riding Hood was adapted to film in 1984 as *The Company of Wolves*. Carter wrote the screenplay with the director Neil Jordan, and the movie starred Angela Lansbury as the grandmother.

Also try: In 1984 Carter published *Nights at the Circus* (Chatto & Windus, 1984), a novel about an aerialist who tells people she hatched from an egg. The story follows a fairy-tale structure and has a good dose of postfeminist magical realism, much like *The Bloody Chamber*, but the tone is not as dark. It won the James Tait Black Memorial Prize for fiction and was adapted as a play. Carter returned to the setting of the theater in her last novel, *Wise Children* (Chatto & Windus, 1991), which also plays with magical realism and the carnivalesque. In 2016, Chatto & Windus published *The Invention of Angela Carter: A Biography* by Edmund Gordon.

Related work: Werewolf fans may enjoy *St. Lucy's Home for Girls Raised by Wolves* (Knopf, 2007), a story collection by Karen Russell about nuns, wolf-girls, and alligators set in the Florida swamps.

If dark fantasy and horror mixed with the carnivalesque is your brand of fiction, we suggest Katherine Dunn's *Geek Love* (Knopf, 1989), the story of a traveling circus and the family of freaks that thrives there. Word of warning: although the novel is a cult classic and a perennial favorite among writers and readers, it's not for the faint of heart. It is a moving story that challenges perceptions of what is odd and what is normal.

Afrofuturist Horrorist ❖

Jewelle Gomez

1948–

What do queer activism and vampires have in common? Turns out, a lot.

Jewelle Gomez was born in 1948 in Boston and raised by a great-grandmother who was Native American (of Ioway heritage) and African American. Gomez attended Northwestern University, where she first became involved in the civil rights movement. She began her long career as an activist and worked in public television in Boston. In 1971 she moved to New York, where she earned a master's degree in journalism from Columbia University. Gomez conducted research and interviews for the 1982–83 PBS documentary series *Before Stonewall*, which told the history of queer communities prior to the 1969 riots that kickstarted the gay rights movement. She was also one of the original writers for the PBS educational show *The Electric Company*. In 1984 she sat on the founding board of the Gay and Lesbian Alliance Against Defamation (GLAAD); she also sat on the boards of the Astraea Lesbian Foundation, the Open Meadows Foundation, and the Human Sexuality Archives of Cornell University. Her résumé includes working to legalize gay marriage in California, where in 2008 she married her partner, Dr. Diane Sabin. Gomez was sixty years old at the time of their wedding, though she had known Sabin since the early 1980s. According to the couple's wedding announcement in the *New York Times* (published October 31, 2008), Gomez knew that she and Sabin were valuable to the movement, saying, "We had an important face to put on this issue. Would you tell your grandmother she doesn't have the right to marry?"

In addition to her extensive activist work, Gomez is the author of seven books. Her vampire novel, *The Gilda Stories* (Firebrand Books, 1991) offers an inspired take on the age-old horror trope. Unlike previous popular vampires, Gilda is a woman, she is black, and she is a lesbian.

Through Gilda's journey from life as a runaway slave girl to eternal life as a vampire, Gomez takes the reader through the history of African Americans from the nineteenth-century plantations of Louisiana and Mississippi to the dystopian Earth of the year 2050. By presenting a progressive, and transgressive, future that is both distinctly feminine and black, *The Gilda Stories* became an important pillar in the Afrofuturism genre. Afrofuturist literature and film imagine a future that not only includes people of color but is shaped by African and African American identity and culture. Examples range from the work of the poet and musician Sun Ra to the novels of Octavia Butler to the 2018 superhero film *Black Panther* to the music of Janelle Monáe.

Gomez's portrayal of vampires focuses on issues of race, gender, and sexual consent, as well as the beauty and terror of a life that does not end. Rather than existing as isolated predators, most of her vampires create communities to stave off loneliness and seek to live life on their own terms for as long as they choose. Their relationships, both with one another and with humans, are long and powerful, and they practice a nonviolent way of taking blood from humans. These vampires may be as hungry as Stoker's iconic count, but they use their superior physical and mental powers to protect humans and leave them with a gift in gratitude for the snack. As Gomez repeated in *Bones & Ash* (1996), her theatrical adaptation of *The Gilda Stories* that was performed by the New York–based dance troupe Urban Bush Women: "We take blood, not life, and leave something in exchange." While writing *Gilda*, Gomez worried that the popular Bela Lugosi–style image of the vampire was so entrenched in the collective consciousness that her creations might seem too strange, but she was heartened by the example of Octavia Butler's speculative fiction.

In a foreword to a 2016 edition of *The Gilda Stories*, Gomez describes an experience of being verbally abused by two men while in a phone booth in Manhattan. Feeling her isolation and powerlessness, she exploded in anger at the strangers, who in turn accused her of overreacting to their lewd threats. The experience inspired her to write the first chapter of her novel. In Gilda, she envisioned a woman who gains the ultimate power over life and death yet still lives in a world hostile to her gender, skin color, and sexuality.

Gilda may be an immortal creature, but she looks like a woman. Plus, she must adhere to the rules of vampires: she needs to avoid human food and feed on blood at night; she must carry the soil of her homeland with her; she must sleep during the day to avoid direct sunlight. She and Gomez's other vampires worry about many big issues that we mortals contemplate: life, family, community, and memory. But they also live for centuries and experience more than is possible in a human lifespan.

In a 1991 *Ms.* magazine article Gomez said that she created Gilda as a direct contrast to "exploitative and patriarchal" elements in horror. In correcting the wrongs she saw so clearly, Gomez created something completely new.

Reading List

Not to be missed: *The Gilda Stories* is Gomez's best-known foray into horror. An expanded twenty-fifth anniversary edition was published in 2016 by City Lights Publishers, at which time several literary luminaries praised the novel for its groundbreaking reimagining of the vampire myth, including Sarah Waters, Dorothy Allison, and Tananarive Due. In 2018, 13th Gen, a San Francisco–based independent film company, acquired the rights to the work for a possible television show.

Also try: Gomez's other Afrofuturist writing includes the collection of stories *Don't Explain: Short Fiction* (Firebrand Books, 1998), in which she imagines a dark future America where the government is a corporation; the book also contains a story that continues Gilda's adventures.

Fans of verse should check out Gomez's three volumes of poetry: *The Lipstick Papers* (Grace Publications, 1980), *Flamingoes and Bears* (Grace Publications, 1986), and *Oral Tradition* (Firebrand Books, 1995).

Theater fans may be interested to know that Gomez, with Harry Waters Jr., wrote *Waiting for Giovanni*, a play that examines a brief moment in the life of author James Baldwin. Literary figures like Lorraine Hansberry and Richard Wright are characters in the play, which is set in 1957 in New York and Paris. *Waiting for Giovanni* debuted in 2011 in San Francisco.

Related work: Readers of *The Gilda Stories* will see similarities to Octavia Butler's *Fledgling* (Seven Stories Press, 2005), about another unusual vampire who looks like an African American girl, though she is, of course, much older. Butler's book *Kindred* (Doubleday, 1979) is a time travel story featuring a young African American woman who journeys from the present day to a nineteenth-century Southern slave plantation. Her short story "Bloodchild," originally published in *Isaac Asimov's Science Fiction* magazine in 1984 and later collected in *Bloodchild and Other Stories* (Four Walls Eight Windows, 1995) is about pregnant men on an alien planet; it won numerous awards.

Another author who draws comparisons to Gomez is Nalo Hopkinson. Her novel *The Salt Roads* (Grand Central Publishing, 2003) tells of a goddess who possesses various female main characters in the course of freeing an enslaved African nation. Her earlier novel *Brown Girl in the Ring* (Warner Aspect, 1998) is a dystopian postapocalyptic story set in Toronto that follows the struggles of a young mother named Ti-Jeanne. She lives with her grandmother and must come to terms with this powerful woman who holds the family's past and continues to practice cultural healing knowledge in their community.

Nnedi Okorafor's novella *Binti* (Tor, 2015) and its sequels, *Home* (Tor, 2017) and *The Night Masquerade* (Tor, 2018), are wonderful examples of what science fiction can be when it includes the African diasporic experience. The heroine of this Nigerian American author's trilogy is a young African woman who has been accepted to an elite interstellar university and must discover her potential without forgetting her family and home. Okorafor's *Akata Witch* (Viking, 2011) tackles the same kind of African diasporic material, but this time imagines it for a young adult audience. The fantasy involves a group of magical teens of the "Leopard people" in Nigeria. The series continues with the prequel *Akata Warrior* (Viking, 2017), which won a 2018 Locus Award. It would seem that fantasy stories with Afrofuturist twists are Okorafor's sweet spot; in 2018 she wrote *Shuri*, the Marvel comic that tells the story of Black Panther's genius sister.

"Murder was as much a part of their hunger as the blood.

—"Chicago 1927"

PART EIGHT

The Future of Horror and Speculative Fiction

As the previous chapters have proven, women authors have been writing horror fiction since the birth of the genre. And they've kept the category moving, contributing to the various offshoots and subcategories and innovating along the way.

And is it ever moving! In 2018, the *Washington Post* proclaimed that horror was "having a renaissance." Readers are reaching for horror and speculative fiction more and more, and books by women are lining their bookshelves. Also in 2018, Kelly Link, a writer of speculative and science fiction (among other things), was named a recipient of the MacArthur Fellowship. This was two years after her collection of sometimes dark and always magical short stories *Get in Trouble* (Random House) was a finalist for the Pulitzer Prize for fiction.

Let us repeat: a MacArthur Fellowship and a Pulitzer finalist. Fiction, let alone the speculative, horror, and weird varieties, doesn't get much more acclaim than that.

Yet there's still an attitude that these kinds of stories are the territory of male writers. In October 2018, the horror film producer Jason Blum, whose production company, Blumhouse, is responsible for *Paranormal Activity*, *The Purge*, and *Get Out*, nearly started a Twitter war when he told the gaming website Polygon.com that "there are not a lot of female directors period, and even less who are inclined to do horror." To be fair, Blum also said that he wanted to hire a female director—which the Twitterverse answered with name after name to contact. The debate was so heated that *Variety* responded with an article by Rachel Yang titled "15 Horror Directors Jason Blum Can Add to His List." *Harper's Bazaar*, the *Atlantic*, *Vulture*, and the *Washington Post*, among other outlets, also published responses expressing support for female horror writers and directors. Blum apologized on Twitter, and in December 2018, Blumhouse announced the hire of director Sophia Takal.

This online debate is indicative of the paradox facing women writers and other creatives. There seems to be an unspoken assumption that women aren't interested in horror and speculative fiction, despite ample evidence to the contrary.

An example of both the renewed interest in the genre and the influx of women writers drawn to it is Carmen Maria Machado. Her breathtaking, and heartbreaking, collection *Her Body and Other Parties* (Serpent's Tail, 2017) was critically well received and is reportedly being adapted for a television series by FX. The story "The Husband Stitch" begins with a parenthetical instruction for the voices one should use if reading the text aloud. Her direction for enunciating the character "me" reads: "as a child, high-pitched, forgettable; as a woman, the same."

These lines make the reader immediately aware of gender, which Machado deals with quite a bit in her work, particularly in representing how women are perceived in a misogynistic culture. In an interview with the *Paris Review* (October 3, 2017), Machado said, "Horror is one of my favorite genres because it's so limber . . . horror can be a very transgressive space."

Machado uses the genre, much in the same way Angela Carter did, to push traditional stories in new directions. In "The Husband Stitch" she plays with the form of urban legends and tales told aloud around a campfire. The story deals with a young woman's first sexual experience, as well as men's desire to control women and women's desire to withhold parts of their experience from men—if only to maintain some power and autonomy. "Eight Bites" touches upon body image; "Inventory" takes a look at one woman's sexual history. Mere ghost stories these are not.

As we've seen throughout this book, women have long dealt with these themes in genre fiction, and Machado is not alone in picking up the torch. *Body* (Vertical, 2012) by Japanese horror writer Asa Nonami (translated into English by Takami Nieda) is a collection of stories that each involves some part of the human corpus (and people's perceptions of their own bodies), with twists worthy of *The Twilight Zone*. The stories are less supernatural than others discussed in this book—expect more *Black Mirror*–style horror. However you classify it, this collection marks Nonami as a writer to watch.

Helen Marshall's *The Migration* (Titan Books, 2019) is another noteworthy example of horror and speculative fiction written by a woman. Drawing comparisons to Stephen King's *Pet Sematary* (Doubleday, 1983), Marshall's novel begins with a group of people studying the Black Death. If history has taught us anything, that's not going to end well.

Need further proof that women are writing some of the best new horror and dark fiction? We challenge you to read Kea Wilson's 2016 novel *We Eat Our Own* (Simon and Schuster), a book in the tradition of Ruggero Deodato's 1980 gorefest film *Cannibal Holocaust*, or a harrowing novel like Alma Katsu's *The Hunger* (G.P. Putnam's Sons, 2018).

Other favorite new authors include Sarah Langan, Megan Abbott, Marisha Pessl, Sarah Pinborough, Tana French, and Livia Llewellyn. We also can't get enough of the short stories from Damien Angelica Walters and Kelly Link.

We are living in a kind of renaissance for horror fiction, which is widely available, maybe more than ever. And so much of it is being written by women. In this final chapter, we look at current trends in horror and weird fiction and discuss our favorite women writers who refuse to stop haunting and terrifying readers.

Lovecraft Revisited and Revised
The New Weird

Weird fiction has been a subgenre of horror since the early 1900s. Like the word *Gothic*, the term *weird* has a particular meaning in literature. In his 1927 essay "Supernatural Horror in Literature," H. P. Lovecraft insisted that weird fiction is disturbing in a way that goes beyond the tropes of ghost stories and Gothic horror. For Lovecraft, a weird story has an ethereal quality because it deals with things beyond the physical world. It incorporates cosmic fear, or a fear of the unknown and unknowable. Events in weird fiction are truly unmoored from rational or scientific understanding; the weird is alien to humanity, whether from outer space, beneath the ocean, or another universe that is just a hair's breadth away at any moment. Ann and Jeff VanderMeer define weird fiction like this: "Although dark like horror, it is generally about encounters with the inexplicable where there may never be a full explanation for strangeness."

Authors like Margaret St. Clair and Daphne du Maurier, and their successors in the era of the pulps, used the weird as a door into commercial fiction, a world that seemed to be mostly male. In fact, women who write have always used uncanny and supernatural storytelling for sharing tales about their lives and for illustrating the deep traumas of life. They continue to do so today in greater numbers and more diverse forms, maybe because women's experiences are discredited and considered . . . well . . . weird in a patriarchal society. When fiction embraces the strange, the odd, the otherness, women can relate. Women know what it means not only to exist on the margins of society but also to revel in that existence. And so women flock to writing the weird because they can write the nastiest of it, the strangest of it, the most magical of it. Women can see what exists beyond the "normal" society—and we are glad they can.

Although the term *weird fiction* most likely calls to mind Lovecraft and his early twentieth-century contemporaries, a more recent iteration of this subgenre has emerged. The so-called new weird began in the 1990s and continued into the millennium with works like China Miéville's *Perdido Street Station* (Macmillian, 2001), which features a grimy dystopian cityscape and opens with a sex scene between a human character and a half-beast cockroach-like character. New weird fiction may incorporate some themes and tropes of the old (cosmic horror is still a favorite), but authors are moving past Lovecraftian-type mythos and exploring social and political inequalities, race, and gender. More writers of color and women are engaging with the weird than ever before.

One of the first women to write the new weird is the Australian **K. J. Bishop**. *The Etched City*, her first novel (Prime Books, 2003), seems to transcend genre, although it's usually classified as science fiction. The book is influenced by the Decadents of the late nineteenth century, such as Charles Baudelaire and Arthur Rimbaud, with its excesses, weird imagery, and the coexistence of art and corruption. We meet the story's main characters after they've lost a civil war. In the titular city, Ashamoil, the two men find various cultures, warlords, strange creatures, shamans, occultists, mediums, and medical doctors. The lines between living and dead, and between dreams and reality, are razor thin, and the very existence of the city is called into question. A review in *Publishers Weekly* described the novel as "equal parts of Stephen King's Dark Tower series and China Miéville's *Perdido Street Station*," with "a dash of Aubrey Beardsley and J. K. Huysmans." *Locus* magazine compared it to the work of Jorge Luis Borges and Italo Calvino, both writers of postmodern works that defy labels.

The Canadian horror writer **Gemma Files** described weird fiction this way: "For me, the appeal is the idea of creating something that will make the person reading it look over their own shoulder uneasily, but also feel as though they recognize it on some inmost level . . .

to create an unnatural concept which nevertheless seems part of the natural order."

She achieves this level of uncanny weirdness in her 2015 Shirley Jackson Award winning novel *Experimental Film* (ChiZine Publications, 2013). In it, a film critic named Lois who is struggling to come to terms with her son's autism diagnosis attends a film festival for an article she's writing. While there, she sees a rare piece of silver-nitrate silent-film footage that is part of a larger project called *Untitled 13*. This scrap of footage shows a woman wrapped in a white veil and holding a scythe, and Lois becomes obsessed with learning all about it and its creator. Weird events ensue as she attracts the attention of the woman in the footage . . . who might not be mortal and who might have some thoughts on Lois's fascination. In true forbidden text fashion, Lois is haunted by the film she shouldn't have seen. The *Los Angeles Review of Books* compared Files's writing to that of Algernon Blackwood and Arthur Machen, as well as contemporary authors Thomas Ligotti and Jeff VanderMeer.

Another writer who's been affiliated with the new weird since the appearance of her first work is Ireland-born, Alabama-raised **Caitlín R. Kiernan**. Kiernan studied vertebrate paleontology and has written papers in the fields of herpetology and paleontology, and these scientific interests are clearly visible in her fiction. She is a prolific and award-winning writer who so far has penned ten novels, several comic books, and more than two hundred stories and novellas. In the introduction to their 2012 anthology of weird fiction, Ann and Jeff VanderMeer call Kiernan "perhaps the best weird writer of her generation."

Kiernan's well-received 2009 novel *The Red Tree* (Ace) won the best novel category of the Shirley Jackson Awards, the Locus Awards, and the World Fantasy Awards. It follows Sarah Crowe as she moves to Rhode Island, in an attempt to run from her problems, and discovers an old manuscript in her new home. The novel stands out for many reasons, among them the central queer relationship and the use of an unreliable narrator through the postmodern technique of reading a so-called edited journal. In the course of telling a supernatural story, Kiernan also addresses themes of mental illness and the ambiguity of reality.

Recently, Kiernan added to her weird oeuvre with her novellas *Agents of Dreamland* (Tor, 2017) and *Black Helicopters* (Tor, 2018). Both include dark Lovecraftian forces stalking the Earth, black-ops secret agents for unknown agencies, and characters damaged by science experiments gone wrong.

Kiernan's writing demonstrates the fluidity of the new weird genre, moving freely between the boundaries of science fiction and dark fantasy and speculative fiction. Other writers have a more direct connection to the weird fiction of the early twentieth century. For women re-visioning H. P. Lovecraft, check out **Cassandra Khaw** and **Kij Johnson**. Johnson's novella *The Dream-Quest of Vellitt Boe* (Tor, 2016), which won a World Fantasy Award, is a woman-centered revisitation of, and commentary on, Lovecraft's 1943 novella *The Dream-Quest of Unknown Kadath* (Arkham House). In it, Johnson weaves a brand-new tale set in a world inspired by Lovecraft's Dream Cycle series. Mathematics professor Vellitt Boe, who teaches at an elite and otherworldly women's college, must go on a fantastical journey to rescue a student who has ticked off her grandfather (who is a god, by the way) by running away with a dreamer from the waking world.

Malaysian writer Cassandra Khaw has married the Lovecraftian weird with noir detective fiction in her novellas *Hammers on Bone* (Tor, 2016) and *A Song for Quiet* (Tor, 2017). In the former, a child hires a private eye, who just happens to be a monster, to kill his abusive stepdad, who is also a monster. Khaw carefully inserts an underlying Lovecraftian monstrous horror beneath the terrifying experience of domestic abuse. All of her writing is weird, from her female werebears rooming with vampires in *Bearly a Lady* (Book Smugglers Publishing, 2017) to *Food of the Gods* (Abaddon, 2017), part of her Rupert Wong series that includes various gods from all over the world and a cannibal girlfriend.

Kelly Link, **Karen Russell**, and **Nadia Bulkin** also deserve mention. Link's three short story collections, *Stranger Things Happen* (Small Beer Press, 2001), *Magic for Beginners* (Small Beer Press, 2005), and *Get in Trouble* (Random House, 2015), have garnered comparisons to Neil Gaiman, George Saunders, Aimee Bender, Jorge Luis Borges, and . . . Karen Russell. Link's fellow Pulitzer finalist, Russell has written fine and unnervingly weird tales such as *Swamplandia!* (Knopf, 2011), about a family of alligator wrestlers who live in a Florida theme park; *St. Lucy's Home for Girls Raised by Wolves: Stories* (Knopf, 2006); and the novella *Sleep Donation* (Atavist Books, 2014), about an insomnia pandemic that corporate America tries to solve by monetizing sleep that has been donated to insomniacs from healthy sleepers. Bulkin's 2017 short story collection *She Said Destroy* (Word Horde) is hard to classify. She uses plenty of cosmic horror that Lovecraft fans will recognize, but her work doesn't fit neatly into any category.

"Everyone who is alive has a ghost inside them, don't they?"

—"The New Boyfriend" by Kelly Link

Polishing the Fangs •
The New Vampire

Vampires mean glamour. They are sexy. They are wealthy. They live life without regrets. Ever since Bram Stoker's aristocratic ghoul from Europe landed on book pages, readers have flocked to vampire stories to find an escape from the mundane realities of everyday life. Contemporary vampires are just as alluring and seductive as their predecessors, but their plots are more in step with lives of modern readers. For example, in Anne Rice's *Interview with the Vampire*, Lestat, Armand, and the cherubic little Claudia make a family with two dads. What makes vampires so enduring is that they don't worry about the consequences of their actions, not when they know they will outlast whatever problems currently plague them. Perhaps this is what most appeals to us humble mortals. Thanks to that appeal, vampires have remained a mainstay of horror fiction for decades, and they show no intentions of dying out anytime soon.

The first decade of the twenty-first century saw a spike in fanged stories, and the trend reached its fevered frenzy with three mega-hits, all written by women: **Stephenie Meyer**'s novel *Twilight* (Little, Brown, 2005) and its numerous sequels, movies, and graphic novels; **L. J. Smith**'s *The Vampire Diaries* (Harper, 1991), which spawned a series and a hit television show on the CW network; and **Charlaine Harris**'s Sookie Stackhouse novels, the thirteen-book series from Ace Books published from 2001 to 2013, which were adapted for television as the series *True Blood*. Each of these offers a rich tapestry for a vampire story, but they also illustrate a truth: Where there's a vampire, there's frequently a werewolf or two not far behind. And sometimes even a fairy.

Vampires are the gateway to other supernatural beings in the work of **Laurell K. Hamilton** as well. Her heroine Anita Blake is a vampire hunter—though less a fighter like Buffy and more a necromancer detective. The series begins with *Guilty Pleasures* (Ace Books, 2002) and posits a world where equal rights have been granted to the living and the undead. Of course, supernatural trouble is always brewing, and Anita ends up contending with not only vampires but also shapeshifters, fey, and various undead creatures.

One reason the vampire narrative is a perennial feature of horror, science fiction, and fantasy is that the concept is strong enough to evolve in all sorts of ways. **Octavia Butler** merged science fiction and horror with her 2005 novel *Fledgling* (Seven Stories Press), which tells the story of an ancient vampire lineage. The main character is fifty-three years old, still young for her race of beings, but she looks like a child, specifically an African American girl. Butler's novel is more science fiction than pure horror, but it revitalizes the vampire trope and is a welcome addition to the canon. Another fresh take comes from **Karen Russell**. The title story of her collection *Vampires in the Lemon Grove* (Knopf, 2013) is a blend of fantasy and magical realism that demonstrates the potential of the vampire as a metaphor for the struggle of the human condition and, especially, folks who exist on the margins of society. The book was a finalist for the Pulitzer Prize for fiction.

Elizabeth Kostova rewrote the idea of the historical vampire with her book *The Historian*, published in 2005 by Little, Brown. The novel is a retelling of Bram Stoker's *Dracula* ... sort of. Kostova bypasses what could be an overwrought homage and instead writes a book that is more about the romance of historians who become enamored with a subject than it is about vampire lore. The story of a professor turned hunter and his daughter is compelling and rich with detail.

Though Kostova's vampires are the only monsters in *The Historian*, vampires in fiction are often accompanied by a variety of other supernatural beings. **Deborah Harkness**, in her *All Souls* trilogy, explores her own world where the supernatural exists in the same realm as humankind. *A Discovery of Witches*, published in 2011 by Penguin, introduced readers to Diana Bishop, a professor who finds a long-lost manuscript that awakens magic within her. The book was a *New York Times* best seller, and the media rights were quickly snapped up. A British television program based on Harkness's book was filmed for Sky One. Bishop's adventures meeting witches, vampires, and other magical creatures were continued in the subsequent novels *Shadow of Night* (Penguin, 2012) and *The Book of Life* (Penguin, 2014).

But not all vampires are comfortable in the supernatural world. Some, like **Tananarive Due**'s African Immortals, are vampires who never claim that title. The first book of Due's series, *My Soul to Keep* (HarperCollins, 1997), starts as a family drama, focused on a young couple, David and Jessica, just settling into marriage. Life changes when David confesses to his new wife that he is centuries old, having obtained immortality in Ethiopia. Soon Jessica is fighting for her family and her soul. Due's story presents an interesting reversal, with humans preying on the immortals for their life-saving blood. The series comprises four novels.

Another example of vampires' endless versatility is *The Vampire Tapestry* (Orb Books, 1980) by **Suzy McKee Charnas**, in which vampirism is more akin to a virus than a supernatural curse. It was a finalist for both the Locus and Nebula Awards.

On the other end of the spectrum from the horror/science-fiction hybrid are more lighthearted vampire novels, such as **MaryJanice**

Davidson's *Undead and Unwed* (Berkley Sensation, 2004), a paranormal romance that follows the (mis)adventures of a young single woman who wakes up one day in a coffin. Davidson proves that even vampires need love in their eternal lives. *Undead and Unwed* was a best seller, and Davidson continues to write the series for her fans. The books' fun tone makes them perfect for teenage readers. Also recommended for a younger audience is *Sucks to Be Me: The All-True Confessions of Mina Hamilton, Teen Vampire (Maybe)* by **Kimberly Pauley** (Mirrorstone, 2009). We love the main character's name, which is an homage to the first female vampire hunter, Bram Stoker's Mina Harker.

As this long history of the vampire story shows, these creatures may take various forms, but they'll be with us for some time, lurking in the shadows of our stories for as long as we tell them. Fiction is what makes them truly immortal.

"When your rage is choking you, it is best to say nothing."

—Fledgling by Octavia Butler

Home, Deadly Home
The New Haunted House

In Part Five, we saw how writers like Daphne du Maurier and Elizabeth Engstrom made perfect use of the haunted house as a setting for domestic and psychological horror. Homeownership is the core of the American dream, and the home continues to hold potential for both comfort and horror, especially in times of economic turbulence. Contemporary writers continue this long-established trope and evolve it, setting stories in spirit-plagued apartments, residence halls, boarding schools, salvage properties, and other living spaces.

In Japanese writer **Mariko Koike**'s 1986 book *The Graveyard Apartment*, which was translated into English in 2016 and published by St. Martin's Press, a young couple and their child move into a fantastic, newly constructed residence that's surprisingly affordable and allows an easy commute for the husband. That low price might be due to the graveyard on one side of the apartment building . . . and the crematorium on another . . . and the Buddhist temple on a third side. The family's pet bird dies on their first night in the house. Then the daughter announces that the bird has returned to deliver warnings about their new home. Almost immediately, the other tenants begin moving out. Soon the family is living alone at the top of the complex. And something evil is in the basement.

Rachel Klein's debut novel *The Moth Diaries* (Counterpoint, 2002) straddles a few horror themes. There is a hint of the new vampire; one of the mysteries that obsesses the unnamed narrator is whether or not her fellow student Ernessa is undead. All the weird happenings at the girls' boarding school where the narrator lives place this book in haunted house territory. The storyteller is at Brangwyn Hall because of her father's suicide, and the school is haunted by the pain of the girls who live there. They grieve the loss of their parents; they self-medicate with drugs; they struggle with mental illnesses and eating disorders. And given that the narrator has been diagnosed with psychosis, as well as borderline personality disorder and depression, she is unreliable, to say the least. The story vacillates between real and unreal: could the book's events be evidence of the supernatural or rather, the very real attempts of young women to cope with trauma? The novel was adapted to film in 2011, directed by Mary Harron and starring Lily Cole as Ernessa.

Want more dormitory horror? "*Poltergeist* meets *The Breakfast Club*" was the *Kirkus* review blurb for **Alexandra Sokoloff's** *The Harrowing* (St. Martin's Press, 2006). Celebrated horror writers Ira Levin and Ramsey Campbell also had nothing but praise for this first novel. It's Thanksgiving, and all the pupils at Baird College have left for home except for Robin Stone and four other students she just met. They are staying in a hundred-year-old dormitory, and a massive storm is approaching. This doesn't sound bad at all, does it? It turns out there's an "entity" at the residence hall that also decided to stay at the school during break, proving that you don't have to go home to be haunted.

For something a little different, check out *The Apartment* (Blumhouse Books, 2016) by **S. L. Grey**, the writing team of Sarah Lotz and Louis Greenberg, which explores what can go wrong with a housesharing service like Airbnb. Mark and Steph and their daughter are happy living in Cape Town, South Africa, until armed and masked men break into their home. Although no one is physically injured, the terrifying episode leaves the family wanting a change of scenery. They decide to swap homes with someone in Paris—who, it turns out, never shows up to stay at their place in Cape Town.

The family's France vacation is filled with mysterious and uncanny happenings—the authors' descriptions of shadows jumping across walls induce goosebumps—and their accommodations come with a creepy neighbor who warns them of vague danger and isn't long for this world. When they return home seeking normalcy, parents and child sink further into darkness, which may be an effect of the Paris apartment or of their own making. For another example of the Grey writing team's excellence at conjuring haunted spaces, see *The Mall* (Atlantic, 2011), in particular their description of a dark room full of clothing-store mannequins, discarded in a motionless pile . . . until one of them starts to move.

Over the years, the novelist **Cherie Priest** has written everything from Gothic and zombie fiction to Lovecraftian themes, but *The Family Plot* (Tor, 2016) is a haunted house novel set in Chattanooga, Tennessee. Chuck Dutton owns a salvage operation that specializes in historic properties, and he has fallen on hard times. Desperate for a job, Dutton jumps at the chance to purchase the Withrow estate for stripping and resale. Unfortunately, the owner, Augusta Withrow, failed to mention that spirits dwell in the house. And the creepy cemetery on the property. And the fact that those spirits are irritated by something that happened in the past. The four people who arrive to salvage the property's contents will face a dangerous presence that doesn't like houseguests.

In **Jac Jemc**'s *The Grip of It* (FSG Originals, 2017), a young couple buys their first house and, rather than a leaky roof or appliances that need updating, the issues involve moving wallpaper and strange stains and writing on the walls. The townspeople have many secrets, and the house has a history. Jemc moves beyond typical haunted house tropes by playing the two main characters' perspectives off each other in an alternating narrative. She shows the reader that the lines between exterior and interior, and real and not real, are thinner than we think. The book has been compared to Henry James's *The Turn of the Screw* (Macmillan Publishers, 1898), Shirley Jackson's *The Haunting of Hill House* (Viking, 1959), and Mark Z. Danielewski's *House of Leaves* (Pantheon, 2000).

> ## "The inability to trust ourselves is the most menacing danger."
>
> —The Grip of It by Jac Jemc

This Is the End (Again)
The New Apocalypse

Since the writing of the book of Revelation, the concept of the apocalypse has been part of human consciousness—and the subject of human fear. Though *apocalypse* originally meant a disclosure of secret knowledge, often with religious connotations, the term is now commonly understood as the end of everything, or at least the end of the world as we know it. The end of everything is scary enough, but even scarier is the question: what will follow the end?

Spikes in apocalyptic fiction track with major national and world events. An uptick in apocalypse stories accompanied and followed the advent of atomic and nuclear weapons and the concurrent, very real chance of worldwide destruction. Children of the 1950s and 1960s can recall "duck and cover" drills; children of the 1970s and 1980s have traumatic memories of the 1983 TV movie *The Day After*. Although the threat of nuclear catastrophe remains, fiction from the 1990s and 2000s through today seems to favor a world-ending disease pandemic. Sometimes these global plagues kill most of the world's population, and terrible things follow; sometimes zombies are the pandemic that kills most of the world's population, and terrible things follow.

The apocalyptic novel (and the related postapocalyptic and dystopian novel) presents a story that emerges from contemporary social issues. It allows for discussion of difficult topics such as poverty, social inequality, and racial injustice. **Margaret Atwood**'s 1985 novel *The Handmaid's Tale* (McClelland and Stewart) has moved into the pop-culture zeitgeist thanks to the adaptation that began streaming on Hulu in April 2017, and the iconic red dresses and white hoods worn by her characters have become garb for political protesters advocating for women's equality.

Atwood didn't leave the apocalypse alone with that book, either. Her MaddAddam trilogy (McClelland and Stewart), which debuted in 2003, follows the survivors of a genetically engineered virus as they deal with the transformations of sentient life in the wake of death, illness, and environmental damage.

Christina Dalcher's *Vox* (Berkley, 2018) is, in many ways, a successor to Atwood's *Handmaid's Tale*; it imagines a world in which women are permitted to speak only one hundred words a day. **Naomi Alderman**'s *The Power* (Little, Brown, 2017) tells of a different sort of world turned upside down, in which special powers are bestowed upon the most unlikely of beneficiaries—teenage girls. The results are dramatic, though no one who has watched anything made by Joss Whedon will be surprised at what ensues. The question at the heart of the book is whether strength, when unevenly distributed, is a sweet or sinister gift.

Young adult fiction has been overwhelmed by **Suzanne Collins**'s Hunger Games trilogy (Scholastic, 2008–10), whose popularity was amplified by the movie adaptations starring Jennifer Lawrence as the protagonist, Katniss Everdeen. The stories are set in a post-apocalyptic North American dystopia in which a strong authoritarian government punishes citizens for a failed rebellion by holding an annual lottery that selects children to fight to the death in a televised competition. Echoes of Shirley Jackson, George Orwell's *1984*, and the phenomenon of TV reality show abound. On the heels of Collins's books came **Veronica Roth**'s Divergent series (HarperCollins, 2011–13). This franchise takes place in a post-apocalyptic Chicago where people are categorized based on personality and social position.

The popular science-fiction post-apocalypse novel *Station Eleven* (Knopf, 2014) by **Emily St. John Mandel** follows several loosely connected characters as they try to survive in a world devastated by swine flu. Mandel explores how human culture, not just human lives, might outlast disaster. Among the surviving population is a group of musicians, actors, and artists who travel among the sparse settlements to provide entertainment and fellowship. *Station Eleven* won the Arthur C. Clarke Award in 2015 and was nominated for a National Book Award.

Tananarive Due, whom we discuss in the Toni Morrison profile (see page 176), has also ventured into apocalyptic territory. Her collection *Ghost Summer* (Prime Books, 2015) includes an entire section of stories, titled "Carriers," devoted to the end of the world and what may or may not follow. One of those stories, "Patient Zero," is a painfully poignant account of a young boy who lives in quarantine and doesn't fully understand what is happening or why. The story is told from the boy's point of view, and he describes his interactions with the doctor, nurse, and tutor who make up his tiny community. The way that Due unfolds the narrative, so the reader realizes what's happened before the boy does—if he even can—is devastating. Her story "Danger Word," written with her husband, Steven Barnes, is an exploration of family relationships: a grandfather who has prepared for the end of the world faces a post-pandemic zombie apocalypse with his grandchild. It was adapted in 2013 as a nineteen-minute short film.

Urban fantasy writer **Seanan McGuire** has ventured into zombie territory with her Newsflesh trilogy (Orbit Books, 2010–12), written under her pen name Mira Grant. The series, which includes *Feed*, *Deadline*, and *Blackout*, follows blogger journalists and social media savants as they report on a much-changed world following a drug-induced zombie apocalypse. The first book takes place once things have calmed down

and humanity is trying to figure out the new normal. But the intrepid journalists find evidence of a vast conspiracy underneath the events that precipitated the catastrophe, and it turns out that the zombies may not be as easily controlled and vanquished as people thought. Newsflesh is planted solidly in our contemporary moment, with scare-tactic politics and a postmodern text full of blog and social media posts.

The prolific Nigerian American author **Nnedi Okorafor** writes science fiction and fantasy for adults and children and is known for her two series, Binti (Tor, 2015–18) and Akata Witch (Viking/Penguin, 2011–17). Her book *Who Fears Death* (DAW/Penguin, 2010) is set in a future Sudan rent by racial and genocidal conflict and focuses on women's experiences. The main character is an Ewu, the child of a rape, seeking revenge on behalf of her mother. The novel won World Fantasy and Carl Brandon Kindred Awards, and in 2017, Okorafor announced that it had been optioned by HBO, with George R. R. Martin attached as an executive producer.

N. K. Jemisin's three-peat Hugo-winning Broken Earth trilogy, *The Fifth Season*, *The Obelisk Gate*, and *The Stone Sky* (Orbit, 2015–17), may take place on a fantasy world, but the premise, of an apocalypse created by climate change disasters, hits close to home. Jemisin's characters face systems of power and oppression represented by various forces that, although fictitious, feel familiar to contemporary readers. Jemisin creates a society based on a caste system in which a powerful leading class exploits the strengths and talents of the workers. In a review of *The Fifth Season* for the *New York Times*, Naomi Novik wrote: "The end of the world becomes a triumph when the world is monstrous, even if what lies beyond is difficult to conceive for those who are trapped inside it."

Two more post-apocalyptic tales worth praising are **Louise Erdrich**'s *Future Home of the Living God* (HarperLuxe, 2017) and **Rebecca Roanhorse**'s *Trail of Lightning* (Saga Press, 2018). Erdrich, a literary fiction powerhouse, is best known for her Native American saga beginning with *Love Medicine* (HarperCollins, 1984). In *Future Home*, she turns her attention to speculative fiction in the vein of Atwood's handmaids. Something is wrong with the babies that are being born; they appear to be devolving into something... not human. But the protagonist Cedar Hawk Songmaker has a "normal" child in her womb, and she must run from kidnappers who, for unknown reasons, are capturing women like her whose babies who haven't changed. This dystopian world is spinning out of control astonishingly quickly.

Roanhorse won 2018 Hugo and Nebula Awards for her story "Welcome to Your Authentic Indian Experience™." She also won the 2018 John W. Campbell Award for best new writer. *Trail of Lightning* takes place in a world where rising waters from climate change have taken over much of the land. Because of its location, the former Navajo reservation now called Dinétah is in a place of power. The protagonist Maggie Hoskie is a monster hunter, and her knowledge and skills are in high demand.

"Hell is the absence of the people you long for."

—Station Eleven by Emily St. John Mandel

Sharper Weapons, Sharper Victims
The New Serial Killer

If the horror genre had a mascot, it would be the serial killer. Horror films are synonymous with slasher flicks, at least to the uninitiated. After all, what is more ubiquitous in horror than a group of scantily clad teenage girls being pursued first by horny teenage boys and then by machete-wielding, mask-wearing maniacs? Crime and thriller authors who've portrayed serial killers include Tami Hoag, Lisa Gardner, and Karin Slaughter. The women writing horror today are taking the familiar plots and character tropes to new and unusual places.

Joyce Carol Oates is not tied to any specific genre. She's a superstar in the literary world who has written everything from family drama to a fictional novel about Marilyn Monroe based on facts from the actress's life. Her writing is proof that serial killer stories can have more depth and craft than just a dull-eyed maniac holding the first sharp object he can find. Her novel *Zombie* (Ecco, 1995) is about a young man, Quentin P., who wants to make a real-life zombie. That is, Quentin wants a handsome, and compliant, sexual partner. It should be easy—Quentin only needs an ice pick and swift hammer to the brain to lobotomize his perfect man. When Oates wrote it, she once again turned to a historical figure for inspiration, extensively researching the real-life cannibal killer Jeffrey Dahmer. Though the book is horrific, it is also an interesting look into a depraved mind.

Modern authors seem to spend more time crafting their serial killers, and as much as we love a charismatic villain, we also love an equally well-realized heroine. South African writer **Lauren Beukes** has earned critical attention for her socially conscious horror, as well as numerous awards, including the Arthur C. Clarke Award and the *Romantic Times*

RT thriller of the year. Her novel *The Shining Girls* (Penguin Random House, 2013) adds time travel to the serial killer story, and in this case the hunter becomes the hunted. Beukes is one of a group of modern writers updating the "final girl" trope. These girls are not shrinking violets. They aren't the virginal survivors who summon the will to live at the

last minute of the story. Rather, they are strong and smart and daring from the beginning.

Beukes writes of a killer on a spree in her novel *Broken Monsters* (Mulholland Books, 2014), which explores the underground art scene that exists in the abandoned neighborhoods of Detroit. The killer is notable for his attempts to re-create the world through macabre art; the dead bodies are, let's say, *rearranged* and left on display. But even more notable is the relationship between the detective on the case, a single mother, and her daughter. Beukes also wrote *Survivors' Club*, a horror comic series, with Dale Halvorsen and Ryan Kelly; Vertigo published the complete series in 2016.

Lauren Beukes is often compared with the American writer **Gillian Flynn**, whose novel *Gone Girl* (Crown Publishing Group, 2012) became a hit and was adapted by Reese Witherspoon's production company into a successful film, starring Rosamund Pike and Ben Affleck. In the book, Flynn upends the familiar plot of a victimized woman and masterfully hides details from both her readers and her main characters so that no one is who they seem to be. She tackled killers, and the trauma that their surviving victims must endure for years to come, in her previous novels *Sharp Objects* (Shaye Areheart Books, 2006) and *Dark Places* (Shaye Areheart Books, 2009). These were adapted, for television and film, respectively; the HBO miniseries adaptation of *Sharp Objects*, starring Amy Adams and Patricia Clarkson, is a masterpiece of Southern Gothic and family horror.

Another honorable mention in Flynn's oeuvre is the Edgar Award winning novella *The Grownup* (Crown Publishing Group, 2015), which is her take on a ghost story with a Gothic flair. Fans of the Victorian ghost story will recognize familiar elements such as an old manor house, characters with secrets, and psychics reading auras. But as in her other work, Flynn pushes the boundaries of identity, exploring who we are on the inside versus who we present to the world.

Caroline Kepnes, like Joyce Carol Oates, defies the confines of genre, and she's one of our favorite authors on this list. Her debut novel *You* (Atria, 2014) is a thriller that is equal parts charming, terrifying, and compelling. Joe Goldberg is a seemingly average bookstore clerk who just can't help but fall in love with a woman who comes into his shop one day. He's a romantic, but the kind that stalks and sometimes kills, too. Stephen King called the novel "totally original," saying that Kepnes is "a little Ira Levin, a little Patricia Highsmith" with "plenty of serious snark." King even named one of his characters Olive Kepnes in *Gwendy's Button Box* (Cemetery Dance Publications, 2017), a novella that he wrote with Richard Chizmar. Joe Goldberg's story was continued in the sequel *Hidden Bodies* (Atria, 2016) and was recently adapted for television on the Lifetime network and later picked up by Netflix.

Other standouts in the killer subgenre are **Stephanie Perkins's** *There's Someone Inside Your House* (Dutton Penguin, 2017) and **Jessica Knoll's** *Luckiest Girl Alive* (Simon and Schuster, 2015). Both books involve characters hiding dark pasts and even darker secrets. A recent favorite is newcomer **Dot Hutchison**, who writes in the tradition of Thomas Harris and his infamous serial killer Hannibal Lecter. In *The*

"'Don't worry,'
he tells the
puce-faced corpse,
'you'll have
company soon.'"

—*The Shining Girls by Lauren Beukes*

Butterfly Garden (Thomas and Mercer, 2016), the first book in her Collector series, Hutchison creates a unique killer, named the Gardener, who collects beautiful young women, tattoos butterfly wings on them, and keeps them in his enclosed garden until they turn eighteen. Then he "preserves" them in glass cases. The story's plot is unique, but what makes Hutchison an author to watch is the care she gives to the Gardener's victims. The women have rich lives, told in achingly beautiful detail, and Hutchison writes about their relationships with each other with impressive empathy. The novel introduces readers to FBI agents Brandon Eddison and Victor Hanoverian, whose stories continue in later installments in the Collector series. *Roses of May* (Thomas and Mercer, 2017) sees the agents tracking a new killer who leaves dead women in cemeteries surrounded by beautiful flowers. The third book, *The Summer Children* (Thomas and Mercer, 2018), offers another heart-pounding FBI chase. This time a child shows up at an agent's apartment and claims that an angel killed his parents.

In Nigerian author **Oyinkan Braithwaite**'s debut novel, *My Sister, the Serial Killer* (Doubleday, 2018), Korede is a great older sibling, always there to help her baby sister Ayoola dispose of dead bodies. And there seem to be a lot of them. Ayoola apparently has horrible luck; all of her boyfriends end up dying. The plot tightens, however, when Ayoola sets her sights on a man that Korede secretly loves. The book is fun and irreverent but still gut-punches readers with emotion.

Another recent entry to the subgenre is *Jane Steele* (Penguin Random House, 2017) by **Lyndsay Faye**, about a Victorian-era orphan who finds a home in an English manor house. It sounds like a Gothic novel, but the title character is no one's victim; in fact, Jane is the one with a murderous secret in her past. *Cosmopolitan* magazine described the book as "Jane Eyre gets a dose of Dexter," and Faye even includes a riff on Charlotte Brontë's famous line: "Reader, I murdered him." Trust us, this one is a fun read.

Conclusion

In profiling the authors in this book, we have described, discussed, and admired women who, as Carmen Maria Machado described it, used horror and the weird to be transgressive, to push against the status quo. These genres of fiction are instruments with which women writers can shake up society and prod readers in an uncomfortable direction, to an unfamiliar space where our anxieties and fears run free. But this is also a space where strength emerges. Women experience horrors in everyday life; the eerie and the terrifying become tools for these writers to call attention to the dangers: frayed family relationships, domestic abuse, body image issues, mental health concerns, bigotry, oppression.

It's no surprise that women's fiction focuses on voice and visibility. Women might be told to be quiet, but they still speak up. They might be made invisible, but they still are present. They might be hunted, but they can also be the hunter. Horror fiction shows us that sometimes the things that break us really can make us stronger.

The future of horror and other dark fiction is bright. And as women continue to persist and innovate in the telling of these stories, it's clear that the future is female.

Glossary

What We Mean When We Talk About Horror

Horror as genre is notoriously difficult to define; it bleeds into other kinds of stories. It's the rebel genre. For one person, *horror* may refer to a page-turner about a serial killer. Someone else may envision a supernatural story full of dread and terror. And a third person may use the term interchangeably with *thriller* or *dark fantasy*. To avoid confusion, here are our definitions for key terms used throughout this book.

Cosmic horror: Tales in which ordinary people are faced with a force so big, so otherworldly, that they must accept that they are insignificant in the greater universe. If you've read anything by H. P. Lovecraft, you've read cosmic horror.

Gothic: Gothic literature has several subgenres; Southern Gothic and Gothic romance are two examples. Unless otherwise stated, assume we refer to Gothic horror, which usually involves a young woman caught up in conflict when a troubled past comes back to haunt the present. Typically the narrative offers a crumbling manor home and a few ghosts.

Horror: We use this term broadly. If it scares, if it horrifies, if it causes the creepy-crawlies, then to us it is horror. Horror fiction can involve supernatural elements, but it doesn't always.

Penny dreadful: Also called a *sixpenny* or *penny blood*, the penny dreadful was a book printed on cheap paper meant for mass distribution in the eighteenth and nineteenth centuries. Often they contained Gothic and horror tales.

Pulps: These were cheaply printed magazines that introduced readers to a range of stories, usually science fiction or horror. Think of them as the twentieth-century version of penny dreadfuls. The term *pulps* also refers to the cheaply printed paperback books of the 1970s and '80s.

Speculative fiction: This type of literature imagines a world that could be. It is closely related to science fiction but is a broader category that includes fiction with fantastic elements not drawn from a science-based premise. The term is often applied to the work of writers who incorporate several different genres into one tale.

Terror: We rely on Ann Radcliffe's definition (see her profile in Part One): Horror has the effect of a bomb; it completely destroys the reader, or tries to. Terror, on the other hand, makes readers feel more alive, by bringing them to the edge of a cliff without pushing them over.

Thriller: In our experience, authors use this term when they don't want to be pigeonholed by the term *horror*. There is a difference, however. Horror is about the emotions readers feel as they experience a story, usually through empathy with the protagonist. A thriller relies on plot devices, like a metaphorical ticking clock, to elicit a response.

Weird fiction: This is a notoriously tricky genre to define. Stories in this category often contain elements of the supernatural, but not always. The weird tale goes beyond just a "ghost haunting a home" story and turns the supernatural into something unexplainable. The tension in the weird tale, like cosmic horror, is the sense of dread that results when an ordinary protagonist confronts the unknowable.

Notes

18   *Known among the upper-class circles as "Mad Madge"*: Scholars debate when Cavendish was bestowed this nickname. We could not find evidence that the name was used during her lifetime; by the nineteenth century, however, the name was frequently used. See Katie Whitaker, *Mad Madge: The Life of Margaret, Duchess of Newcastle* (New York: Basic Books, 2002).

18   *Her nipples, which she had thoughtfully painted red*: This incident occurred on April 11, 1667, at a performance of *The Humorous Lovers*. See Mona Narain, "Notorious Celebrity: Margaret Cavendish and the Spectacle of Fame," *Journal of the Midwest Modern Language Association* 42, no. 2 (2009), 69–95.

18   *Samuel Pepys, the famous diarist, called her "mad, conceited and ridiculous"*: See *Diary and Correspondence of Samuel Pepys* volume 8, October 1, 1667–August 15, 1668 (New York: Dodd, Mead, 1901).

23   *It earned Radcliffe three shillings*: Radcliffe's first book sale probably earned her the equivalent of one day's wages for a "skilled tradesman," according to the British National Archives online currency converter (nationalarchives.gov.uk/currency-converter). She sold her fourth book for nearly 333 times that much, or what would have been a decent yearly salary at the time.

25   *Sir Walter Scott, the Marquis de Sade, and even Edgar Allan Poe have cited her influence*: Scott called Radcliffe a "mighty enchantress." See Rictor Norton, *Mistress of Udolpho: The Life of Ann Radcliffe* (New York: Bloomsbury, 1999).

25   *"Terror and horror are so far opposite"*: Radcliffe published her ideas on horror and terror in "On the Supernatural in Poetry," *New Monthly Magazine and Literary Journal* 16, no. 1 (February 1826), 145–152.

32   *She was still considered "the daughter of William Godwin" or "the wife of Percy Bysshe Shelley"*: An 1851 obituary of Mary Shelley describes her as daughter and wife twice before mentioning any of her literary works. "Mary Wollstonecraft Shelley," *International Monthly Magazine of Literature, Science, and Art* 3, no. 1 (April–July 1851), 16–18.

33   *Mary Shelley kept her husband Percy's heart*: Although this story is well documented, as far back as 1885, critics suggested it may not be true and that Mary may have held on to Percy's calcified liver, which would have been more likely than the heart to survive cremation. "Possibly Not Shelley's Heart," *New York Times*, June 28, 1885.

36   *Best-selling hit for Minerva Press*: Prior to the 1790s, it was socially unacceptable for a woman to pursue a career of any kind, particularly one in writing or the arts. Few women even received an education. Mary Wollstonecraft (mother of Mary Shelley) advocated for girls to be afforded the same education as boys, and her efforts changed popular opinion ever so slightly—at least enough to make it possible for later women like Regina Maria Roche to pursue writing professionally, rather than as a recreational dalliance. Minerva Press, named for the Greek goddess of wisdom, was one of the largest publishers of fiction between 1790 and 1820, with a large catalogue of women writers. Though it wasn't launched specifically to publish work by women, simply by serving the market Minerva Press became the largest purveyor of both Gothic fiction and fiction written by women. London bookseller William Lane founded the press in 1780, and when Lane retired, the publishing company was overseen by Anthony King Newman, who eventually changed the name to A. K. Newman and Co.

41   *Born Mary Clayton around 1746*: See Dale Townsend, ed., *Man-*

froné: Or, The One-Handed Monk (Richmond, VA: Valancourt Books, 2007). In his afterword, Townshend explores who the real Mary Anne Radcliffe might have been.

44 *Her father, John King, was a Jewish money broker*: For more on Dacre's fascinating father, see Todd M. Endelman's article in the journal of the Association for Jewish Studies. "The Checkered Career of 'Jew' King: A Study in Anglo-Jewish Social History," *AJS Review* 7–8 (1983), 69–100.

Part Two: Haunting Tales

51 *Sir Arthur Conan Doyle was one devotee*: Doyle was a vocal supporter of spiritualism while other celebrities—including, famously, Doyle's friend, the magician Harry Houdini—were outspoken skeptics. For more on Doyle, see Daniel Stashower, *Teller of Tales: The Life of Arthur Conan Doyle* (Henry Holt and Co., 1999).

56 *And in 1865 bought a house*: Gaskell had intended to keep the Hampton home, called the Lawn, as a retirement surprise for her husband, but she died that same year before she could tell him. See Mrs. Ellis H. Chadwick, *Mrs. Gaskell: Haunts, Homes and Stories* (London: Sir Isaac Pitman & Sons, 1913), 302.

67 *Fierce defender of women's rights*: Among other things, Amelia Edwards signed the 1866 Women's Suffrage Petition, which can be viewed online on the United Kingdom parliamentary archives (parliament.uk).

68 *A place of pilgrimage for the LGBTQ community*: See Paddy Dinham, "Grave of Victorian author who was buried alongside her female partner is given listed status in new campaign to recognize gay history," *Daily Mail*, September 27, 2016.

76 *Author Henry James*: See Carl J. Weber, "Henry James and his Tiger-Cat," *PMLA* 68, no. 4 (September 1953), 683. Weber includes in his article the majority of a letter by Henry James to his brother William, in which he says about Lee, "There is a great second-rate element in her first-rateness."

85 *Edith Newbold Jones*: The saying "keeping up with the Joneses" was coined about Wharton's family. Her father, George Frederic Jones, was an affluent real-estate mogul in New York City, and everyone who was anyone aspired to be like their family.

86 *Anxiety and hallucinations that plagued her into early adulthood*: In a biographical fragment she called "My Life and I," Wharton wrote: "When I came to myself, it was to enter a world haunted by formless fears. I had been a naturally fearless child; now I lived in a state of chronic fear." Cynthia Wolff, ed., *Edith Wharton: Novellas and Other Writings* (New York: Library of America, 1990).

Part Three: Cult of the Occult

93 *Belief system called Thelema*: Many books have been written on this complex philosophy begun by Aleister Crowley. Crowley's own *The Law Is for All: An Extended Commentary on the Book of the Law* (Phoenix: Falcon Press, 1983) explores the text on which Thelema is based. The website Thelema.org lists many free resources on the belief system.

95 *Moved to a new home*: Some time before Bowen's marriage in 1912—the exact year isn't known—she and her family moved to a house near "the cricket grounds at Lord's" in London; see Bowen's autobiography, *The Debate Continues: Being the Autobiography of*

Marjorie Bowen (London: William Heinemann, 1939), 155. Bowen's sister, her Nana, and the men who worked in and around the house all firmly believed that the unusual events were spectral in nature; Bowen's mother was initially skeptical, but soon both she and Bowen were experiencing unexplained phenomena, like disembodied moans and lights flashing on the stairs.

100 *The J. K. Rowling of her day*: Beth Rodgers makes this comparison in "LT Meade, the JK Rowling of her day, remembered 100 years on," *Irish Times*, October 26, 2014. This article provided much of the biographical information on Meade.

105 *Adapted for six silent films*: The Internet Movie Database (imdb.com) lists entries for the films adapted from the Askews' work: *The Folly of Desire* (1915), *The Pleydell Mystery* (1916), *God's Clay* (1919), *Testimony* (1920), *John Heriot's Wife* (1920), and *Under the Lash* (1921).

107 *Brought us a number of modern characters and stories*: Two great occult detectives of modern fiction are John Constantine and Carl Kolchak. Constantine was a damaged magician in DC Comics stories created by Alan Moore; Keanu Reeves portrayed him on the silver screen in 2005, and Matt Ryan has portrayed him in television series on NBC and the CW. Kolchak was a reporter who investigated the supernatural in *Kolchak: The Night Stalker*, a television series launched in 1974, starring Darren McGavin. Spin-off television movies and comics followed; the TV series was revived, as *Night Stalker*, in 2005 starring Stuart Townsend.

111 *published a disclaimer*: See Daniel Delis Hill, *Advertising to the American Woman, 1900–1999* (Columbus: Ohio State University Press, 2002), 78.

112 *"The malice of inanimate objects"*: M. R. James detailed this theory, that seemingly inanimate objects sometimes choose to cause people harm, in a story of the same name, which was republished in the collection *The Haunted Doll's House and Other Ghost Stories* (New York: Penguin, 2006), 201–5.

113 *the Ghost Club*: More information on this still-active group is available on their website (ghostclub.org.uk); see also Peter Hoskin, "Ghost Club: Yeats's and Dickens's Secret Society of Spirits," *Paris Review*, October 31, 2017.

Part Four: The Women Who Wrote the Pulps

122 *Some pulps survive today*: Though much early-twentieth-century pulp fiction has been lost, digital technology has helped collectors preserve some stories and covers and share them with a modern audience. Good online sources include the Pulp Magazines Project (pulpmags.org), the Pulp Magazine Archive (archive.org/details/pulpmagazinearchive), ThePulp.net, and the blog *Tellers of Weird Tales* (tellersofweirdtales.blogspot.com). In addition, thanks to the expiration of early copyright laws, some pulp stories are in the public domain.

125 *Connie Willis has cited St. Clair*: Willis is an award-winning science fiction writer, whose numerous works include *To Say Nothing of the Dog* (Bantam Spectra, 1997) and the Oxford Time Travel series. According to the Science Fiction & Fantasy Writers of America website (sfwa.org), she has won more major awards than any other science fiction writer, including eleven Hugo Awards and seven Nebula Awards.

126 *Margaret Brundage*: For more about this popular 1930s *Weird*

Tales cover illustrator, see Antoinette Rahn, "Ten Things You Didn't Know About: Margaret Brundage," *Antique Trader*, October 3, 2017; and Stephen D. Korshak and J. David Spurlock, *The Alluring Art of Margaret Brundage: Queen of Pulp Pin-Up Art* (Coral Gables, FL: Vanguard, 2013).

126 *The back cover copy on a 1963 edition*: Snapshots of the back cover of *Sign of the Labrys* can be found online accompanying Gideon Marcus's review of the novel, "The Old School," at *Galactic Journey* (galacticjourney.org), posted September 25, 2018.

134 *"The Stephen King of Alabama"*: See Kelly Kazek, "Horror author Mary Counselman was the Stephen King of Alabama," Al.com, October 22, 2015. Kazek's article provided biographical information, as did Counselman's obituary on findagrave.com.

139 *He now believes Gertrude Barrows Bennett deserves credit*: See Gary Hoppenstand, ed., *The Nightmare and Other Tales of Dark Fantasy* (Lincoln: University of Nebraska Press, 2004), x.

140 *Lovecraft and Merritt were influenced by her work*: Hoppenstand, xxiv.

140 *Published serially in* Argosy Weekly: This magazine changed its name many times, from the original *The Golden Argosy* to *Argosy Weekly*, as a result of merging with different publications. For more on the history of pulp magazine publishing, see Tim DeForest, *Storytelling in the Pulps, Comics, and Radio: How Technology Changed Popular Fiction in America* (Jefferson, NC: McFarland, 2004).

141 *Earlier, and perhaps the earliest, examples of parallel universes*: Some critics assert that Margaret Cavendish, discussed in Part One, was the first author to write about alternate realities.

149 *One of the most popular stories of the April issue*: Every issue of *Weird Tales* invited readers to write in and name their favorite story. The results were then tallied and published in a later issue. Counter was frequently among the favorite authors listed. Her fourth install-ment of "On the Dead Man's Chest" nearly beat H. P. Lovecraft for top story in the April 1926 issue, as reported in the June 1926 issue. Her January 1927 *Weird Tales* story "The Last Horror" came in second for reader favorite, again behind a Lovecraft story, and was reprinted in the February 1939 issue.

Part Five: Haunting the Home

161 *The 1944 film* The Ininvited: This movie was a favorite of director Martin Scorsese. See Rodrigo Perez, "Martin Scorsese Names His 11 Scariest Horror Movies of All Time," IndieWire.com, October 31, 2010.

163 *More negative mail than ever before*: For readers' intense reactions to Jackson's story, see Ruth Franklin, "'The Lottery' Letters," *New Yorker*, June 25, 2013.

166 *Modeled his famous haunted Overlook Hotel*: In a footnote in *Danse Macabre* (Gallery Books, 2010; see page 297) King noted that *The Shining* "was written with *The Sundial* very much in mind." Both King's grand hotel and Jackson's Hill House are isolated spaces that seem alive as they prey on their vulnerable inhabitants.

167 *Recognize similarities to her in Tremblay's protagonist Merry*: It's easy to see the resemblance between Tremblay's Merry and Jack-son's Merricat Blackwood; it's right there in the name. Tremblay wrote in an August 2012 post on his blog, *The Little Sleep* (thelit-tlesleep.wordpress.com), that "Merricat is the ultimate unreliable

narrator of Jackson's masterpiece, *We Have Always Lived in the Castle*. And, all right, I'm kind of in love with Merricat, too."

173 *The 1973 Nicolas Roeg–directed film*: So convincing was the sex scene in Roeg's adaptation of *Don't Look Now* that some forty-five years later, in 2018, star Donald Sutherland was still answering questions about the on-screen action. "Donald Sutherland says sex scene in 'Don't Look Now' wasn't real despite rumors," *New York Daily News*, January 14, 2018.

Part Six: Paperback Horror

191 *Michael McDowell, a great and underappreciated horror writer of the late twentieth century*: In addition to his Blackwater series, six volumes of Gothic horror set in the American South, McDowell also wrote the screenplay to Tim Burton's 1988 film *Beetlejuice*.

188 *Every paperback needed disturbing cover art*: For more on the insane cover art of paperback horror, see Grady Hendrix, *Paperbacks from Hell: The Twisted History of '70s and '80s Horror Fiction* (Quirk Books, 2017).

196 *Little is known about her life*: Biographical details for Jensen are difficult to find. We relied on obituaries for some information, like the one found at findagrave.com/memorial/61904674.

196 *"the skeleton farm," as Zebra was sometimes called*: Although the genesis of Zebra Books' nickname is unknown, the name was widely used in the publishing industry. See Hendrix, 185.

201 *no mention of "dirty pillows" in this book*: Stephen King, in our opinion, wrote the best evil mother of all in his novel *Carrie* (Doubleday, 1973).

202 *The Audrina series*: The Audrina series includes *My Sweet Audrina* (New York: Pocket Books, 1982), written by Andrews, and *Whitefern* (New York: Pocket Books, 2016), penned by Andrews ghostwriter Andrew Neiderman.

203 *Kept her literary legacy alive through a ghostwriter*: The Complete V. C. Andrews website (completevca.com) is a great source of information about the author, her career, and the ghostwriters who've written under her name since her death.

Part Seven: The New Goths

222 *This term's meaning is slippery*: Just as the Gothic has always embraced the blending of genres, for example Gothic romance, the Gothic surge of recent years isn't limited to horror fiction. See Kate Morton, *The Distant Hours* (New York: Atria, 2010) and Audrey Niffenegger, *Her Fearful Symmetry* (New York: Scribner, 2009). These authors follow the Southern Gothic literary tradition of writers like Carson McCullers and Flannery O'Connor.

227 *Rice was skeptical of the decision to cast Cruise as the lead character*: See Judy Brenna, "Rice's About-Face: Cruise Is Lestat : After Screening 'Interview With the Vampire,' Author Lauds His Work," *Los Angeles Times*, September 21, 1994.

237 *caused the gossip mills to turn*: See Richard Eden, "Husband of The Woman in Black author Susan Hill exits, stage left," *Telegraph*, December 8, 2013.

241 *representing lesbians in fiction*: See "Author Sarah Waters on being that 'lesbian writer,'" *Wales Online*, October 1, 2011; and "'It was an electric time to be gay': Sarah Waters on 20 years of Tipping the Velvet," *Guardian*, January 20, 2018.

248 *the white-haired fairy godmother you always wished you had*: See "Margaret Atwood: By the Book," *New York Times*, November 25, 2015.

251 *raised by a great-grandmother*: See Gomez's interview with Rochelle Spencer, "Of Afrofuturism and Social Change," *Gay and Lesbian Review*, June 21, 2016.

Part Eight: The Future of Horror and Speculative Fiction

260 *Horror was "having a renaissance"*: See Bill Sheehan, "Horror novels are having a renaissance. Here's what to read," *Washington Post*, October 6, 2018.

269 *Their plots are more in step with lives of modern readers*: This trend is not limited to books. A notable addition to the vampire canon is the award-winning 2014 Iranian vampire film *A Girl Walks Home Alone at Night* by writer and director Ana Lily Amirpour. *Variety* described Amirpour's film as a "Middle Eastern feminist vampire romance," proving that the vampire is well equipped to cross—in this case, by skateboarding in a hijab—genres and refuses to be limited to any mold. Guy Lodge, "Sundance Film Review: 'A Girl Walks Home Alone at Night,'" *Variety*, January 24, 2014.

286 *"plenty of serious snark"*: Stephen King's shared his thoughts on Kepnes's debut novel on his Twitter feed on December 15, 2014. In a follow-up to her reply, he added "Hope you're working on a new one."

Suggested Reading

It quickly became clear to us when writing this book is that there are too many women writers of horror fiction to include in a single volume, and we had to sacrifice many of our favorites simply for the sake of space. If you're wondering what to read next, we can help.

General Reading

A good starting resource is the Ladies of Horror Fiction online directory (ladiesofhorrorfiction.com), which features an extensive list of women authors. We also recommend the Graveyard Shift Sisters website, which is dedicated to women of color who write horror and science fiction (graveyardshiftsisters.com).

To find your new favorite author, anthologies are a good bet, especially those devoted to, or including, female writers. If speculative fiction interests you, try the anthology *Sisters of the Revolution: A Feminist Speculative Fiction Anthology*, edited by Ann VanderMeer and Jeff VanderMeer (PM Press, 2015); this includes writing by Octavia Butler and Joanna Russ. Lisa Yaszek edited *The Future Is Female!: 25 Classic Science Fiction Stories by Women, from Pulp Pioneers to Ursula K. Le Guin* (Library of America, 2018). Although not exclusively female-focused, Jeff and Ann VanderMeer have edited two anthologies on weird fiction that include great stories by women writers: *The Weird* (Tor Books 2012) and *The New Weird* (Tachyon, 2008).

Sycorax's Daughters (Cedar Grove Publishing, 2017) is a Stoker Award–nominated anthology showcasing African American writers, edited by Kinitra Brooks, Linda D. Addison, and Susana Morris. We also enjoyed *Dark Matter: A Century of Speculative Fiction from the African Diaspora* edited by Sheree Renée Thomas (Warner Books, 2000) which includes stories from Nalo Hopkinson, Tananarive Due, Linda Addison, and many more. In June 2015, Lightspeed Magazine released a special issue, titled Queers Destroy Science Fiction! and guest edited by Seanan McGuire, that featured some great authors.

We relied on Eric Leif Davin's *Partners in Wonder: Women and the Birth of Science Fiction, 1926–1965* (Lexington Books, 2005), a non-fiction book about women who created many of the stories in the pulp magazines of the mid-twentieth century. If pulp horror is more your speed, we highly recommend *Paperbacks from Hell: The Twisted History of '70s and '80s Horror Fiction* (Quirk Books, 2017).

Specific Authors and Topics

Much of the biographical information for the British authors profiled in this book came from the Orlando Project (orlando.cambridge.org), an online resource available by subscription from Cambridge University focused on women's writing in the British Isles.

Margaret Cavendish: *Forgotten Women: The Writers* by Zing Tsjeng (Cassell Illustrated, 2018). An explanation of Cavendish's philosophies can be found in *The Well-Ordered Universe* by Deborah Boyle (Oxford University Press, 2017).

Ann Radcliffe: *Mistress of Udolpho: The Life of Ann Radcliffe* by Rictor Norton (Leicester University Press, 1999).

The Year Without a Summer: For more on the bizarre weather events of 1816, see William K. Klingaman and Nicholas P. Klingaman's book *The Year Without Summer: 1816 and the Volcano That Darkened the World and Changed History* (St. Martin's Press, 2013).

Frankenstein: Charles E. Robinson edited *The Frankenstein Notebooks: A Facsimile Edition of Mary Shelley's Novel, 1816–17 (Parts One and*

Two) (Garland, 1996), which shows the drafts of the novel, along with notes written by both Mary Shelley and Percy Bysshe Shelley that reveal the changes and edits suggested by each.

Christmas Ghost Stories: Find the spirit of the season in *The Valancourt Book of Victorian Christmas Ghost Stories*, vols. 1–3 (Valancourt Books, 2016–18).

Elizabeth Gaskell: *Mrs. Gaskell: Haunts, Homes and Stories* by Mrs. Ellis H. Chadwick (Sir Isaac Pitman & Sons, 1913).

Charlotte Riddle: *The Collected Ghost Stories of Mrs. J. H. Riddell* (Dover, 1977). Riddell's magazine career is detailed in the book *Riddell's City Novels and Victorian Business· Narrating Capitalism* by Silvana Colella (Routledge, 2016).

Pauline E. Hopkins: See the Biography section at the Pauline Elizabeth Hopkins Society website (paulinehopkinssociety.org).

Vernon Lee: *Vernon Lee: A Literary Biography* by Vineta Cole (University of Virginia Press, 2003). We also appreciated the *Stuff You Missed in History Class* podcast episode titled "Vernon Lee" from October 8, 2018, which can be found online at https://www.missedinhistory.com/podcasts/vernon-lee.htm.

Edith Wharton: The biography *Edith Wharton* by Hermione Lee (Knopf Doubleday, 2008).

Alice Aksew: Biographical info for the Askews can be found in *The Oxford Companion to Edwardian Fiction* edited by Sandra Kemp, Charlotte Mitchell, and David Trotter (Oxford University Press, 2002).

Dion Fortune: See Gareth Knight's edition of her letters *The Magical Battle of Britain* (Skylight Press, 2012).

Margaret Brundage: Stephen D. Korshak and J. David Spurlock's *The Alluring Art of Margaret Brundage: Queen of Pulp Pin-Up Art* (Vanguard, 2013). Also Steven Heller's "The Revenge of Margaret Brundage" in the *Atlantic* (January 31, 2013), and Susan Karlin's "Weird Tales: Meet Margaret Brundage, The First Lady of Pulp Pinup Art" in *Fast Company* (May 7, 2013).

Catherine Lucille Moore: Biographical information can be found on the blog *Tellers of Weird Tales* (tellersofweirdtales.blogspot.com) and in "The Many Names of Catherine Lucille Moore" by Andrew Liptak in *Kirkus Reviews* (February 7, 2013).

Toni Morrison: *Conversations with Toni Morrison*, edited by Danille K. Taylor-Guthrie (University Press of Mississippi, 1994).

Elizabeth Engstrom: Much of the biographical information came from Engstrom's website (elizabethengstrom.com). Some also came from "Evil Eighties: The Creepy Nursery Rhymes of Elizabeth Engstrom" by Grady Hendrix (Tor.com, March 6, 2015).

Jewelle Gomez: You'll find a great entry on Gomez written by Josie A. Brown-Rose in *Encyclopedia of African American Women Writers*, edited by Yolanda Williams Page (Greenwood Press, 2007). Also see Ezra Kronfeld's article "Jewelle Gomez on Queer Activism, Feminism, and Founding GLAAD" in *Out Front* (January 12, 2018).

Index

Index of Works

Subject Index

Acknowledgments

This book was our passion project, but it doesn't belong to us. It belongs to the women who have written the tales that we love, to those who helped shape the genre, and to those who right now have pen in hand, crafting the stories we will devour in the future. So to all the women writers—past, present, and future—we thank you.

The idea for this book came from years of reading and many discussions over coffee, beginning with our time at the University of Mississippi and later on our podcast, the *Know Fear Cast* (a special thanks goes to Matt Saye, our cohost). *Monster, She Wrote* truly began to take shape at Stoker Con, where, thanks to the Horror Writers Association, we were able to pitch this book to Quirk Books. The entire team at Quirk has been phenomenal, especially super editor Rick Chillot, who helped guide us our entire way. We offer up our sincere gratitude, Rick. Special thanks, too, to our illustrator, Natalya Balnova, who exceeded our expectations. This book is truly a work of art. It takes our breath away every time we look at it.

Lisa would like to offer special thanks to her boys at home, Robbie, Leo, and Eli. Robbie, you are forever my rock and my source of inspiration. Leo and Eli, my little monsters, I love you more than you will ever know. I write for you. Never forget that. Thank you to my father, for giving me my love of horror, and thank you to my mother, for encouraging me.

Melanie would like to thank her family, particularly her parents, Paul and Deborah Anderson, for their support up to this point, and beyond. Bobbie, one of the best of man's best friends, also deserves an honorable mention of gratitude. When I came home from the day job to sit down and write, she was always patient and pleasant company.

And finally, thank you to the readers. This book is for you.

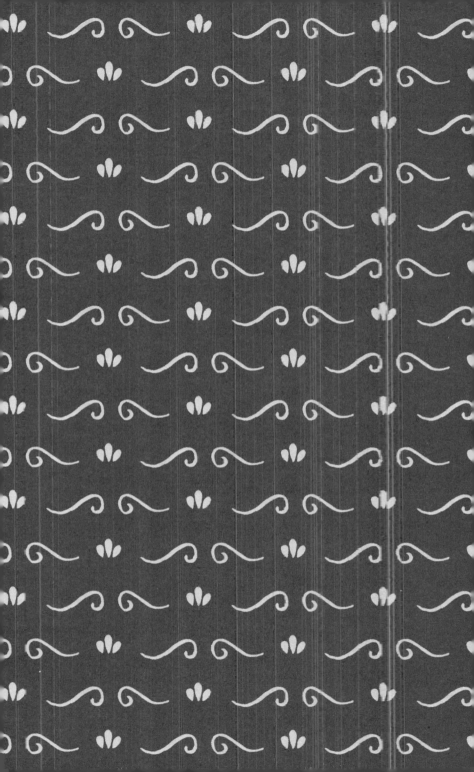

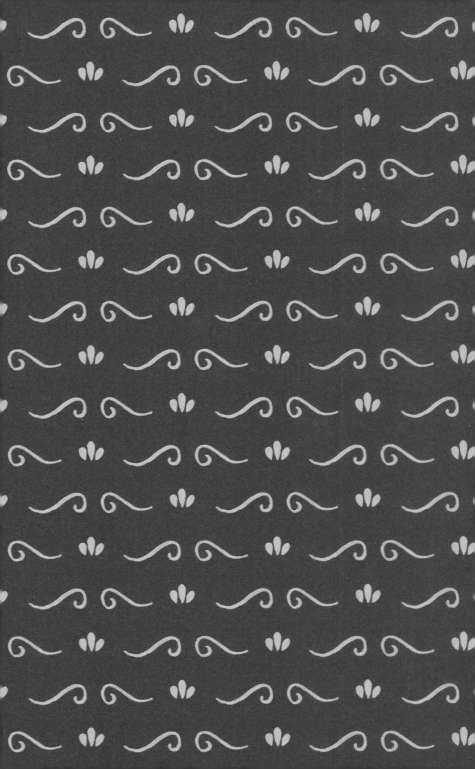